Studying Classical Judaism

Studying Classical Judaism

A Primer

Jacob Neusner

Westminster/John Knox Press
Louisville, Kentucky

Book design by Gene Harris

First edition

Published by Westminster/John Knox Press
Louisville, Kentucky

PRINTED IN THE UNITED STATES OF AMERICA

9   8   7   6   5   4   3   2   1

Library of Congress Cataloging-in-Publication Data

Neusner, Jacob, 1932–
    Studying classical Judaism : a primer / Jacob Neusner. — 1st ed.
        p.   cm.
    Includes bibliographical references and index.
    ISBN 0-664-25136-6

    1. Judaism—History—Talmudic period, 10–425—Historiography.
    2. Rabbinical literature—History and criticism.   I. Title.
BM177.N4795   1991
296′.09′015—dc20   90-13032

For

my new colleagues
in the
Department of Religious Studies
at the
University of South Florida
Tampa

a token of thanks
for their cordial welcome

Contents

Preface   11

Prologue   17

I. From Judaism to Judaisms   27

   Learning a Half-Century Ago: What Did We Know
   and How Did We Know It?   27

   Archaeology and the Demise of
   "Normative Judaism"   30

   From "Normative Judaism" to Judaisms:
   The Beginning of the New Learning   32

II. From Yeshiva and Seminary to University   37

   Learning in Movement: Arrival at the Academy   37

   Generation of Transition: The End of the Old
   or the Beginning of the New   39

   Modes of Thought, Old and New   43

   History or Gibberish: Lieberman's Case   46

   The Intellectual Failure of Critical Exegesis   50

   The End of the Old, the Beginning of the New   52

III. What Do We Now Want to Know About Judaism
    in the First Six Centuries A.D.?   53

The Beginnings of the Critical Enterprise:
The Recognition of the Religious Dimension   53

From History to History of Religion and Society:
The New Paradigm and Its Formation   54

Autonomy, Connection, Continuity   56

Reframing the Paradigm   58

Viewing Religions as Systems, Illustrated
by Cases Drawn from Judaism   60

Explaining an *Oeuvre*   62

What We Want to Know About Judaism:
What Is Worth Knowing?   63

IV. Historical-Critical Method in the Study
of Formative Judaism   66

The Move from Gullibility to Criticism   66

He Really Said It   71

New Testament Scholarship on History
and Biography   74

When the Question You Ask Shows Credulity
About the Answers You Expect to Find   76

From Honest Gullibility to Pseudo-Criticism:
The Younger Generation   85

The Bankruptcy of Historical-Critical Method   91

V. From History to Religion   93

Why History and Biography Are Irrelevant
to Judaism: (1) Biography   93

Why History and Biography Are Irrelevant
to Judaism: (2) Events in Judaism   95

History as a Cultural Indicator   97

An Event as a Contingent Realization
of the Cultural Pattern   99

History in the Cultural Heritage of a Judaism   99

The Religious Uses of Historical Events   101

The Theological Uses of History   107

VI. Philosophy and Religion: The First Two Stages
in the Formation of Judaism 113

Outlining a Constructive Program 113

The Canonical Writings in Sequence 114

The Analytical Program of Systemic Analysis:
Description 115

The Analytical Program of Systemic Analysis:
Comparison of Systems 116

VII. The Formation of Judaism:
The Mishnah and Philosophy 120

The Philosophical Character of the Mishnah's
Method and Paramount Proposition 120

The Mishnah's Generative Proposition 121

How the Mishnah Demonstrates
the Hierarchical Unity of Being 121

The God of a Philosophical Judaism 129

A Philosophical Judaism in Philosophical Context:
The Mishnah's System, Aristotle, and Neoplatonism 130

VIII. The Formation of Judaism:
The First Talmud and Religion 139

The Reception of the Philosophical System:
Categorical Reformation and the New Structure 139

From Philosophy to Religion 141

Differentiating a Later Religious,
from an Earlier Philosophical, System 143

Systemic Integration and Theology:
The Concept of *Zekhut* 146

The Paramount Systemic Position of *Zekhut* 149

Religion and the Social Order 156

IX. Judaism's City of God 161

The Place of God in the Social Order 161

Why Did Philosophy Give Way to Religion
in the Formation of a Judaism? 163

The Social Foundations
of a Judaic Religious System   169

Epilogue   175

Notes   179

General Index   203

Index of Biblical and Talmudic References   207

Preface

During the past half-century what we know about the history, literature, and religion of the paramount Judaism in its formative age and how we know it have been completely redefined. In the pages of this book I explain where we now stand and why. In the Epilogue, I spell out what I think is at stake for our understanding of the importance of religion in the revolution that has taken place in our understanding of the formative age of Judaism.

That particular Judaism, variously called "classical," "talmudic," "rabbinic," "normative," or simply "Judaism," is no longer defined in the way that it was; the canon of that Judaism is no longer read in the received manner. Then how is that Judaism defined, how is its holy writing supposed to be read? Here I spell out what has happened and why in consequence our entire program of study about the formative age of both Judaism and—consequently also—Christianity as a matter of fact has changed.

The issues of this book concern scholarship, but I do not write for specialists in the study of Judaisms or of this particular Judaism. I mean to speak not so much to specialists and scholars as to religious women and men in synagogues and churches alike. Most Jews and a great many Christian believers are college educated. I aim to speak to that enormous audience of literate Jews and Christians who read and follow current scholarship with genuine interest—if scholarship makes itself accessible to more than technicians. Anyone who writes down to the Judaic and Christian faithful will miss a vast and important audience of religious intellectuals, the largest single body, I suspect, of serious readers about religion in any country in the world.

Admittedly, I want especially to write to their pastors, rabbis, and ministers. I want to tell Father Murray, Rabbi Murray, and the Reverend Mr. Murray—in America our names have begun to converge, and pastors, rabbis, and ministers can all have the same family name!—how, in their own study and in the intellectual life of believing Jews and Christians, we may address the holy books of Judaism in the age in which the canonical classics most matter to both Judaism and Christianity. The reason is that I believe scholarship has important things to contribute to the life of faithful Judaism and believing Christianity, and as a believing and practicing Jew (with affinities in one way or another to Reform, Orthodox, Conservative, and Reconstructionist Judaisms alike), I have given my life and career to learning in Judaism because it has been the way in which I have wanted to serve God, to use such gifts as I may have been given for the One who gave them.

But how to do so? In this book I hope to help the intellectual life of the faithful draw abreast of the scholarly results of a half-century of sustained and, I think, even holy labor. That work has meant to form a religious understanding of religion in this world, its power to shape human society. I begin with the convictions, first, that religion is social and public, something a "we" does together, and, second, that religion is the single most powerful force in the shaping of humanity, its history and civilization. And, among religions, my own not only has exercised remarkable influence outside its own circles but has in its own terms set forth a stunningly apt example of the power of religion to shape society and the compelling force of religion as a public and social fact. That is what I mean by a religious understanding of religion: not reducing religion to private belief, on the one side, or explaining religion away by appeal to other forces, on the other. Religion is what in social science is called an independent variable, that which explains, but is not explained by, other factors. Reducing religion to less than its world-defining dimensions, failing to see the world that humanity has made as the work of religion more than any other single human drive or aspiration—these deprive us of the possibility of making sense of the world as it is. It is only when, as a religious Jew, a Judaist, I add, "that is, the world as God made it," that I introduce my own fierce faith in the Torah.

I believe that a religious understanding of the holy books of this Judaism illuminates today's world of Judaism, because these are holy books and mean to set forth a religious message of ultimate weight. I want to say what I think that message was, because I maintain that the same message, properly recast into the idiom of our time and place, is Torah: God's revelation to our rabbi, Moses, at Sinai. The Judaism of which I write in these pages calls me to the vocation to the service of God through the study of those holy books which, for this Judaism in the case of the writings from the Mishnah through the Bavli, we deem integral components of the oral part of the one whole Torah that God gave to our rabbi, Moses, at Sinai. Having written or edited three hundred books, all but one of them devoted to Judaism and most of them bearing the word "Judaism" in some form even in the title, I may be allowed now to confess: these I have meant to place on the altar as an offering.

It is important to relate this present work to others of mine. My methods book, *Ecology of Religion: From Writing to Religion in the Study of Judaism* (Nashville: Abingdon Press, 1989), deals with the how-to of the study of formative Judaism and its sources. By contrast, I deal in this present work with the upshot of method, what I think we know about the history of the formation of Judaism in late antiquity. In this book I have not repeated any of the points made in the other. Rather, I contrast the modes of discourse and thought in other scholarship of our time and of times past, and I both spell out what is wrong with the competing results and, in considerable detail, outline my own results: if you read the canon of this Judaism correctly, then what (in my view) you learn from it. The first part of the book, chapters I through IV, explains what has changed and why. The second part, chapters V through IX, specifies what I think we now know and why I maintain that it is important to know things in my way and for my purpose.

There is yet another set of questions, besides those of method, that I do not treat: those of context and, in particular, historical persistence. I do not here explain why I think the Judaism that reached its definitive structure and system by the turn of the fifth century A.D. enjoyed such astonishing success as it has since then. For, among religions, the Judaism we consider here from that time to the present has maintained its compelling power for precisely the group of people its framers meant to address, holy Israel. A question that anyone engaged by religion in this century of religious renewal must ask is: Why does religion succeed where and when it succeeds? And why does it fail where and when it is abandoned? I have dealt with the persistence of this Judaism in other works and do not address that question here.

This Judaism took shape in a particular circumstance, but it persisted and eventually became not only normative (in its own view) but normal in an entirely descriptive sense. Before the twentieth century, all Judaisms either adopted the symbolic structure and mythic system of the Judaism of the dual Torah or defined themselves in opposition to that structure and system (the example of the former was Qabbalah; of the latter, Karaism). So the question of success demands attention. Why that Judaism succeeded as it did in winning the status of normativity and why it endured for the next millennium and a half (and, I believe, will go forward through the coming millennium as well) are distinct questions. I address them in *Judaism in the Matrix of Christianity* (Philadelphia: Fortress Press, 1986); *Judaism and Christianity in the Age of Constantine* (Chicago: University of Chicago Press, 1987); *Self-Fulfilling Prophecy: Exile and Return in the History of Judaism* (Boston: Beacon Press, 1987), and *Death and Birth of Judaism: The Impact of Christianity, Secularism, and the Holocaust on Jewish Faith* (New York: Basic Books, 1987). These works, all together, form a field theory of the entire history of Judaisms and supplement this overview of the formation of the generative Judaism of them all.

I express thanks to the Institute for Advanced Study, where I wrote this book. During my year as Member of the Institute for Advanced Study, I held a Senior Fellowship of the National Endowment for the Humanities (FA 28396-89), and I take much pride in offering to that agency in the support of humanistic learning my very hearty thanks for the recognition and material support that the Fellowship afforded to me. I found the Endowment, particularly the Division of Fellowships and Seminars, always helpful and courteous in dealing with my application and express my admiration and appreciation to that thoroughly professional staff of public servants.

Brown University complemented that Fellowship with substantial funds to make it possible for me without financial loss to spend the entire academic year 1989–1990, in full-time research. In my twenty-two years at Brown University, now concluded, I always enjoyed the university's generous support for every research initiative that I undertook, and it was a welcome challenge to be worthy of the unusual opportunities accorded to me from 1968 through 1990 as a research scholar as well as a teacher at that university.

The idea for this book came from my editor at Westminster/ John Knox Press, Dr. Davis Perkins, with whom I have worked in every phase of his career. He has been a constant source of intellectual challenge and stimulation.

I began with an inchoate idea. The plan and program for this book I owe, as I owe so much else, to my coworker, Professor William Scott Green, University of Rochester. He took an inchoate idea and helped me to shape it. I thank him for daily sharing with me his special gifts of both wit and intellect and also editorial acumen. If marriages are made in heaven, so too, if we are fortunate, are the encounters with collegiality that also make life worth living.

Department of Religious Studies   JACOB NEUSNER
University of South Florida
Tampa, Florida

July 28, 1990. My fifty-eighth birthday.

Prologue

The importance, for the study of both Judaism and Christianity, of the formative period in the history of Judaism cannot be overstated. Those six centuries marked the formation of "the oral Torah," that is to say, the other part of the canon of that Judaism, in addition to the Hebrew Scriptures, or Old Testament (in Judaism: "the written Torah"). The principal writings are these: the Mishnah, ca. A.D. 200, yielding the exegetical works addressed to the Mishnah, in sequence called the Tosefta, the Talmud of the Land of Israel (the Yerushalmi, also called the Palestinian Talmud), ca. A.D. 400, the Talmud of Babylonia (Bavli, also called the Babylonian Talmud), ca. A.D. 600, and, for Scripture exegesis, Midrash compilations of exegeses of the Pentateuch and of other liturgically important books.[1]

In the era since World War II, the entire scholarly program concerning the study of formative Judaism—what we want to know about its documents, how we shall find out what we want to know, and what is at stake in the labor of learning—has undergone complete redefinition. Nothing now is as it was. But if the very questions that we bring to the study of formative Judaism have undergone drastic revision, why does that intellectual (and religious) revolution affect also our grasp of the formative time of Christianity as well? The reason is that, as everyone knows, Christianity took shape, in all its diversity, within the framework of Judaism, in all its complexity. New learning about Judaism therefore must recast the study of Christianity as well.

If, as we now realize, there were only Judaisms but never a single normative, orthodox, everywhere established Judaism, then how shall we understand the Judaic issues that occupied

Paul and the authors of the Gospels, framed as they were in the encounter with what we must now call simply "the rest of Israel, the Jewish people"? The received exegesis of much of the New Testament and all of the Gospels and the letters of Paul, for instance, appeals to "Judaism." Whether as a principal or a merely ancillary body of facts and perspectives on what Jesus and his disciples and their continuators meant to say, that unitary and single "Judaism" defines how we read a fair portion of the New Testament and most of the Gospels. The very character of early Christian writing, with constant reference to the facts of everyday life, supplied by Judaism, and to ideas and beliefs and issues critical to all Israel, both the Christian and the Judaic sectors, leaves no choice. But if there was no one Judaism, but only Judaisms, then the exegesis of the Christian canon, as much as of the Judaic one, is going to require substantial revision.[2]

As our understanding of the history of Judaism is reshaped, therefore, our grasp of the formative history of Christianity also undergoes radical revision. And that is curiously appropriate, for the fundamental cause of the revolution in learning about ancient Judaism that has marked the last half-century is the convergence, for the first time ever, of the study of Judaism in its formative age and the study of the earliest centuries of Christianity. Scholars of Judaism and of Christianity, who had rarely undertaken dialogue, have now met in the academy and even in Protestant and Roman Catholic seminaries, as well as in Reform and Conservative Judaic rabbinical schools.

In these pages I tell the story of what happens when the academy opens its doors to new voices. It is the tale of how the newcomers find a place and are changed thereby—but also change that place in turn.

If these claims that everything has changed in the study of ancient Judaism seem extravagant at first hearing, then it is my task to make them plausible and, if anything, demonstrate that they are, if anything, an understatement: moderate and entirely reasonable. And if at stake is our fundamental understanding and interpretation of the formation of both Judaism and (therefore also) Christianity, I have to do so by reviewing the answer to two questions.

First, precisely what do I think we know, and how do I claim we know it, about the formative history of Judaism?

Second, exactly why do I think what we now are learning is more important—by which I mean, more appropriate to the character of the sources—than the results of scholarship of an earlier age?

Out of the sources, both literary and archaeological, that tell us all we know concerning the religious life of the Judaic sector of Israel, the Jewish people, in that critical time of turning, exactly what are we supposed now to learn and why does it matter? These questions require us to look at the character of the written evidence, consider the kind of history and biography that evidence can yield, assess the description, analysis, and interpretation of the religion that the same evidence means to set forth, and take up issues of harmony, system, and order that religion study must answer. The program of this book then re-presents the canon in line with how the holy books today are being read in the academy and the seminary. It is time for a broad audience outside the academy to join the new quest for the understanding of how Judaism took shape, since a fresh way of reading the canonical writings has begun to lead to new perspectives, a compelling vision—and one relevant, as I shall explain at the end, also to the religious life of Judaism and also, properly reframed, of Christianity as well.[3]

The critical question bears repeating: *What do we know and how do we know it?* It was in response to the adaptation, for the study of the Judaic canon, of the historical-critical methods of biblical studies, both in Old Testament and in New Testament scholarship, that the revolution got under way. And that is quite natural, for there is in the study of history and of the history of religion no historical a priori. We simply have no access to historical knowledge without evidence, reasoning, or argument yielding proposition. And whether the evidence is in writing and yields narrative or propositional discourse, or in iconic form, gotten through archaeology, yielding access to symbolic discourse, we have always to begin our study with clear accounts of how we think we know anything at all. The question of method—a systematic and orderly and coherent account of the methods we bring to bear upon our evidence—predominates *and should.* That means we have to explain to ourselves not only what facts we claim to have in hand but also what we mean by facts: what we wish to know and how we propose to find it out. In the study of Judaism, critical method has taken over. In consequence, we not only produce answers different from those taken at face value for many centuries. More important, we find ourselves asking questions not considered earlier, appreciating facts not noticed in the past. The entire paradigm of learning has been redefined: new answers to new questions, addressed in new methods altogether to facts formerly not deemed consequential but now found critical.

The sensational discovery, just after World War II, of new

bodies of writing at the Dead Sea, on the one side, and in Nag Hammadi, on the other, has vastly enriched learning. But what has changed in the past half-century is not only the foundations of knowledge in literary evidence. Nor do the many—also sensational—archaeological finds of the same decades complete the account of what is new. And, further, the story of the remarkable reordering of knowledge about the formative centuries of the great religions of the West, Judaism and Christianity, is not fully told when, in addition to reviewing new knowledge, we provide an account of new methods of learning. True, the methods for their part have innovated knowledge as much as the Dead Sea Scrolls and the Nag Hammadi library have renewed knowledge. Consider, for example, form criticism in literature, for example, structuralism and phenomenology in the study of religion, the whole new program of social-scientific study in both history and the history of religion, deriving from anthropology, sociology, politics, and economics. The changes in the critical sector of learning have been swift, immense, and irreversible.

But what has truly changed is not evidence or even method but paradigm: the very definition of what we wish to know and how we propose to find it out—and why we think learning matters. All of the new approaches, with their fresh agenda of questions and their reconsideration of the facts that make a difference, form part of that much greater movement, which is the shift in scholarly paradigm. And what accounts for the paradigm shift is not new knowledge, let alone new methods, but a new attitude, brought to a new setting for learning, by new participants in scholarly discourse. New people, wanting to know new things, undertaking research through new methods, into facts long known but never found consequential—that is what accounts for the paradigm shift that has reshaped studying ancient Judaism.

What marks the paradigm shift, then, is not only a new body of data and a renewed appreciation for the received canon. The recasting of the entire enterprise of learning is marked, above all, by rejection of an attitude that had been rooted for a century and a half before. It is the attitude of debunking, a basic interest in showing "it ain't necessarily so."[4] What scholars have wanted to discover is not what lies the sources tell but what truth they convey—and what kind of truth. And that shift in basic purpose marks the paradigmatic change that made the new methods welcome, the new information necessary. From the beginnings of scholarship in the Old Testament with Spinoza and the Enlightenment, and the remarkable successes of scholarship in the New

Testament in the nineteenth-century pursuit of lives of Jesus, scholarship had recognized success when it could show that what Scripture said and people believed really was not true. People had in mind a historical quest for facts. But Scriptures are not true or false, our interpretations are what are true or false. Now we have abandoned the narrowly historicistic program altogether, and what scholarship has wanted to demonstrate in the new era of learning is something else altogether. People have asked not whether a sage really said what is assigned to him or did the things the stories said he did. They have wanted to know, instead, what kind of worldview these documents convey, what religious construction of reality they propose to accomplish, how these documents bear meaning for those for whom they were written—and for those who now revere them. Two centuries of debunking have closed, and a half-century of reconstruction has begun to yield new access to documents both familiar and new.

That is why, if I had to specify one fundamental change that I think marks a shift so profound as to be classified as paradigmatic, I should identify a change in the basic attitude toward the study of these formative centuries, a change that can only be called religious, if not theological. It is the shift *from* the attitude that what matters above all is what really happened *to* the viewpoint that what matters above all is the religious structure in the social order, the religious faith brought to realization in the social system: what people then had in mind: how they saw the world and lived their lives and formed a social world that held the whole together. From the beginning of the critical study of the religious life of Christianity in the first six centuries, to be dated in the earlier ninteenth-century critical biographies of Jesus, to the end of World War II, the paramount interest of the academy—university and theological seminary alike—centered upon issues of historical fact. These were deemed to define—and settle—all interesting questions. Stated crudely, the dominant proposition was: Did Jesus really say and do the things the Gospels allege? And at stake in fact was truth: the Gospels to be preached on Sunday morning were to be defined in the scholars' seminars on Thursday afternoon. Then what did people find important? They found important the Gospels and the letters of Paul rather than the fathers of the church thereafter; the canonical Gospels, not the writings left out of the New Testament; the normative and the governing, that is, what made the applied and practiced theology of the church—for example, preaching—plausible as a matter of not faith but fact. The origins of this approach in Reformation theology, which rejected tradition in the name of Scripture and could be, and was, reshaped into historical-critical scholarship of the positivist kind, cannot be missed.

Now how to account for the program of the study of Judaism that treated as equivalent attitudes the one that proposed a critical perspective and the one that sought to disprove canonical allegations about events and persons alike? In the case of Jews' studying Judaism, as a matter of fact, critical-historical scholarship found powerful advocates within the Judaic reformation of the nineteenth century. Following the lines of the Protestant Reformation and its then contemporary continuators in nineteenth-century critical-historical scholarship, Reform Judaism appealed to history to justify the reform of Judaism, and to them, in their time, history meant historical fact in place of what was deemed historical fiction. Debunking then carried a heavy theological burden, for the justification of change always invoked precedent. People who made changes had to show that the principle that guided what they did was not new, even though the specific things they did were. The appeal to history defined the principal justification for the new Judaism: it was new because it renewed the old. Arguments on precedent drew the Reformers to the work of critical scholarship, as they settled all questions by appeal to the facts of history. Such study of the formative centuries of Judaism as took place in the nineteenth century and the first half of the twentieth therefore claimed to present matters pretty much as they had happened—*and to derive self-evidently true theological positions from that result.* So the study of Judaism as much as of Christianity rested upon a single basis. The reform of Judaism, yielding Reform Judaism and also its creation, Conservative Judaism, had to emerge from *Wissenschaft,* which means academic study. All things emerge out of time and of change. The task of theological scholarship is to describe the facts of history and then interpret those facts for contemporary belief.

The study, within such corrosive presuppositions, of the New Testament and the oral part of the Torah of Judaism naturally found little hearing among two great bodies of Western believers who were not Protestants and not reformers at all: Orthodox and other traditional Judaists, on the one side, and Roman Catholic and Orthodox Christians, on the other. To people who framed their religious lives in other ways than through appeal, initially, to the principle of *sola Scriptura* and, later on, to the conception that the facts of history could settle questions of faith, so that when we knew what Jesus "really" said, we also should know what we ought to believe and do, the academic and theological program that prevailed answered questions people were not asking. To the Roman Catholic and Orthodox Christian world, issues in the study of formative Christianity simply were other. To the Judaic faithful, questions of historical fact produced trivial information.

And it was the arrival, within the academy, of believing Jews and Roman Catholic and Greek (and other) Orthodox Christians that would reshape the reading of the canon of Judaism, on the one side, and of the New Testament and other early Christian writings, on the other. Affecting first the Christian, then the Judaic, sources, the change in the reading of these documents, moreover, signaled a more profound movement to a different set of issues altogether: the paradigm shift to which I referred.

The advent, after World War II, of new participants in the scholarly enterprise in considerable measure accounts for that shift in the scholarly paradigm, away from the critical-historical–positivistic program of the preceding century and a half, the program that, in the academic idiom, so clearly cohered with Protestant Christian theology. The received program was not rejected, it was superseded. But, along the way, its principles and its results also were taken over and recast. The newcomers were changed, as they changed the hosts, and all became something else, different from what they had been, each party, respectively.

The change came about, not because the positivist-historical program was rejected or even set aside, but because it was no longer found compelling. Other things, besides the ones people had long wished to study, seemed to new kinds of scholars to demand attention. People wanted to know more about the *religion* that texts portray and less about the *history* they may (or may not) contain. The Protestant stress on the individual conscience now competed with the Catholic view of religion as fundamental to the social order, for example.[5] The interests of Roman Catholic and Orthodox Christians marked the new age. Mircea Eliade, for example, a Rumanian Orthodox Christian (and, alas, sometime Nazi!), reshaped the study of religion in America, insisting that other than theological questions take precedence, in such works as *The Myth of the Eternal Return.*[6]

And the conception that the canonical writings presented accounts of other important matters, religious ones, in addition to the subjects long deemed consequential, principally the philological and historical ones, reached Judaic scholarship, long a bastion of articulated secularity such that rabbinical schools to date have never had professorships in the study of religion or of Judaism as a religion or even (in the case of the Conservative Judaic school) of the theology of Judaism. So alongside and somewhat after the changes attending Roman Catholic and Orthodox Christian entry into the academy, the scholarly program for the study of the Judaic canon also was recast.

Within the circle of so-called Modern Orthodox Judaism in the State of Israel, and Conservative and Orthodox Judaism in Europe and the United States, scholarship on the Jews in the first six centuries in some measure turned from the received program of exegesis of the words, phrases, and sentences of the received canon to the message of the whole, of those writings. And that message of the whole came to be understood as fundamentally religious. Whether fairly or not, the received definition of learning was deemed, as I said, essentially secular, indifferent to the matters of religious meaning, the composition, out of words and sentences, of statements that bore meaning in the formation of the social order, on the one side, and the Judaic religious worldview, on the other. So, in all, the history of the revolution in the study of Judaism cannot be told without ongoing attention to what was taking place in the study of Christianity. Every point in my account of how, these days, the history, literature, religion, and theology of Judaism are studied finds a counterpart in the ways in which these same aspects of Christianity are presented in our time.

That fact points our attention to another fact in explaining the origins of the new age in learning that is now reaching maturity. It is a shift in attitudes that is best characterized by the word "ecumenism." What has happened is that the new participants to the scholarly dialogue have changed the character of that dialogue—but they have themselves also been changed by the initial participants, the Protestant Christians who, prior to World War II, constituted the secular academy in its study of religion and, afterward, reformed it to make place for newcomers. Standing for an interest in engaging with the other—the Roman Catholic interest in dialogue with the Protestant and Orthodox Christians, the Christian interest in engagement with Judaism, the Western will to listen and also address the religions of South and East Asia—*ecumenism* in a very particular setting nourished the new age. That setting was, and is, the religious life of the United States of America, exercising profound influence also upon Canada, parts of Western Europe, the English-speaking diaspora, and, in very recent times, Latin America as well. But the movement in learning began in the United States and Canada.

What has happened, specifically, is that in the American academy—first universities, but also Roman Catholic and Protestant seminaries and even Judaic ones as well—scholars studying the holy books of Judaism and Christianity began to talk with one another and learn from one another. The received program derived from Protestant New Testament scholarship; its critical attitudes, its methods of literary study, its program of exegesis, to begin with was taken over, but then also reshaped, by Roman Catholic New Testament scholarship, on the one side, and by Jewish scholarship on Judaism in the same age, on the other. As new kinds of scholars joined the discussion and were accorded a genuine welcome by the Protestant ones who had defined the academy to that point, the newcomers were changed, even as they changed what they found. And the shared attitude, on all sides, of wanting to change and be changed, of intending to listen to the one hitherto deemed an outsider with nothing to say—that ecumenism made possible all that was to happen and that has happened.

The social history of the study of formative Judaism and Christianity should not, however, divert attention from the intellectual achievements of an entire generation of scholarship, from 1950 to the eve of the third millennium. For what people now need to know is not how we got to where we are but, rather, what we now think we know and why we now think we know it—and should know it. In the pages of this book I shall lay out where I think scholarship on the formative age of Judaism now stands: what do we know about the history, literature, and religion, and do we know it? What is at stake in what we know? In presenting this account, I stress not politics and personalities but issues of the sources and how they are to be read. I do not review the existing literature or supply a bibliographical essay. Rather, I turn first to examples of the inherited ways of studying formative Judaism and forthwith turn to the sources and the issue of how they are now to be read: what is important about them and what do we learn from them in answer to the questions that, these days, prove urgent?

I

From Judaism
to Judaisms

Learning a Half-Century Ago: What Did We Know
and How Did We Know It?

In 1950 everybody assumed that in the first seven centuries A.D.[1] there was a single Judaism, corresponding to a single Christianity. That Judaism was a linear continuation of the Hebrew Scriptures, or "Old Testament," the original intent and meaning of which that Judaism carried forward. That same Judaism was normative, everywhere authoritative and accepted. Its canon was so uniform that any holy book, whenever edited, testified equally as any other book to the theological or normative position of that single, unitary Judaism. The allegations of the canonical documents about things that people said or did were, in general, accurate, or had to be assumed to be accurate unless proved otherwise.[2] True, a rational, skeptical attitude treated with caution obviously miraculous or otherwise "impossible" allegations, for example, about rabbis turning people into cows or dust into gold. But, in general, the canonical writings defined Judaism, and, as a matter of fact, Judaism dealt with historical facts. It was true, because its facts were true, and its representation of the meaning of Scripture accorded with the original intent and sense of the authors of Scripture as well. Today, not a single one of these principles of scholarship stands.

But for most of this century, New Testament scholars in quest of the "Jewish background" or "the Jewish roots of Christianity" thought they could rely upon this literature of the one and only Judaism to tell them about that single, uniform Judaism to which earliest Christianity referred. If a sentence, taken out of context, in a seventh-century writing seemed to intersect, or even say the same thing as, a statement of Paul, then Paul could be assumed to have drawn upon "his Judaism" in making the statement that he did. And if people wanted to know the meaning of what Jesus said and could locate a pertinent statement in a fourth-century Babylonian rabbi's mouth, well, then, that tells us what "Rabbi Jesus" had in mind.

It is no surprise, therefore, that people commonly interpreted a passage of the New Testament by appeal to what that "single Judaism" taught. The holy books of that single Judaism, whenever and wherever they reached closure, told us what that one, unitary, harmonious Judaism had to say. So we could cite as evidence of opinions held in the first century writings edited in the sixth—a longer span of time than separates us from Columbus! Not only so, but everybody assumed that all Jews, except a few cranks or heretics, believed and practiced this single, unitary Judaism, which therefore was not only normal but normative. The Judaism of Jesus, in A.D. 30, was pretty much the same as the Judaism of Ezra, in 450 B.C., and of Aqiba, in A.D. 130, and the Judaism of the Land of Israel (also called "Palestine") of the first century was the same as the Judaism of the Greek-speaking Jews of Alexandria at that same time or of the Aramaic-speaking Jews of Babylonia five hundred years later.

What then did we know and how did we know it? In 1950 we knew pretty much what people said, thought, and did. We knew it because the rabbinic sources reported what they said and did. If sources were not redacted or edited until sometime after the event, well, then, people had access to oral traditions, which they preserved word for word and handed on until they were written down wherever and whenever (and it did not matter). And since we knew lots of historical facts, we could write history in the way in which people assumed history should be written: the story of what happened, in order and sequence, beginning to end; the tale of what great men (rarely women) taught; the lessons to be learned from facts.

Scholarship then consisted of mainly the study of the meanings of words or phrases or sentences. If you knew the meaning of a sentence, then you knew what the person to whom that sentence was attributed really said and thought; and since everybody was assumed to hold the same views, or at least talk about the same things, you could then write what "Judaism" taught about this or that. What happened if you had an unclear reading? You consulted manuscripts—written a thousand years later, to be sure—and these would answer your question and make your history possible. So these three issues predominated: the study of the critical reading of a passage, the inquiry into the critical philology or the meaning of words, and the critical exegesis, or the meaning of sentences, all done against the background of the preparation of critical texts. To dismiss a person who disagreed with your view, you would call him or her (there were very few women!) either uncritical or, better still, ignorant. Scholarly debate then was meant to discredit the other person, not to disprove a position contrary to one's own or even to help solve a problem held in common.

Today few scholars ignore or neglect the results of the century of work on text criticism, philology, and exegesis. We still need well-crafted versions of documents, formed out of the broad array of manuscript evidence, thoughtfully reworked. True, the century that closed in 1950 never witnessed the preparation of the required critical texts for most of the documents of the Judaic canon; but they were working on it. We of course need our dictionaries, and if the entire span of positivist study of Judaism failed to yield a decent Aramaic dictionary, even now one is coming. So the report card of the hundred years of positivist historicism shows many incompletes.

But in 1950, people took for granted, that same evaluation would contain unquestioned judgments in favor of excellence. For however partial the fulfillment of the great tasks—no definitive dictionaries, no critical texts for the most important writings—still, there were the achievements in critical history. After all, people contended, we no longer believe all those fables; now we bring to the documents' allegations a thoroughly critical spirit. In context, people were entirely right. For they looked back on the age prior to their own—just as we do—and where they remembered credulity, they now discerned honest independence of spirit, and a critical eye examined all claims. But the premises of the long period of historical-critical scholarship corresponded, in their way, to the foundations of the age of faith: these documents yield history, meaning, an accurate picture of what pretty much everybody was thinking, saying, and doing. So when you have done your work right, (meaning that you have established a critical text), determined a critical definition of the meanings of words, phrases, and sentences, examined the appropriate "parallels" (meaning other presentations of pretty much the same theme), then you could say what the text meant. And that statement took the form of history writing: what people said and did and thought then. That premise explains the questions people asked: how they defined what they wished to know. To put matters in a plain way: they wanted to know what they thought they already knew—only better.

Archaeology and the Demise of "Normative Judaism"

What called into question the fundamental positive-historical suppositions about the character of the literary evidence was not the discovery of other literary evidence, for example, the Dead Sea Scrolls or the Nag Hammadi library. The Dead Sea Scrolls presented us with the writings of a Judaic religious community possibly identified with the Essenes; but prior to the discovery of the library of the community, we had no writings of that group. Nag Hammadi, in Egypt, yielded a vast library in Coptic of Gnostic Christianity, of which, beforehand, we had scarcely a hint. Literary evidence of one kind could readily be accommodated with literary evidence of some other kind. Nobody in the decade after the discoveries at the Dead Sea and in Nag Hammadi called into question the accepted consensus concerning the character of the literary evidence overall. That is to say, there really was one Judaism, the one about which the rabbinic canon informs us; Qumran simply showed us a heretical sect. What really shook the foundations was the accumulation of evidence that there really was not a single Orthodox Judaism at all, only diverse Judaisms. And that evidence derived from not writing but material and concrete data: archaeology.

Specifically, most synagogues built from the third to the seventh century, both in the Land of Israel and abroad, had decorated floors or walls. Some symbols out of the religious life of Judaism or of Greco-Roman piety occur nearly everywhere. These include the symbols for the festival of Tabernacles. Other symbols, available, for example, from the repertoire of items mentioned in Scripture, or from the Greco-Roman world, never make an appearance at all. The symbols of Pentecost, for instance, are rare indeed. A *shofar*, a *lulab* and *ethrog*, a *menorah*, all of them Jewish in origin, but also such pagan symbols as a Zodiac, with symbols difficult to find in Judaic written sources—all of these form part of the absolutely fixed symbolic vocabulary of the synagogues of late antiquity. By contrast, symbols of other elements of the calendar year, at least as important as those which we do find, turn out never to make an appearance. And, obviously, a vast number of pagan symbols proved useless to Judaic synagogue artists. It follows that the artists of the synagogues spoke through a certain set of symbols and ignored other available ones. That simple fact makes it highly likely that the symbols they did use meant something to them, represented a set of choices, delivered a message important to the people who worshiped in those synagogues.

Because the second commandment forbids the making of graven images of God, however, people have long taken for granted that Judaism should not produce an artistic tradition. Or, if it does, it should be essentially abstract and nonrepresentational, much like the rich decorative tradition of Islam. But from the beginning of the twentieth century, archaeologists began to uncover in the Middle East, North Africa, the Balkans, and the Italian peninsula synagogues of late antiquity richly decorated in representational art. For a long time historians of Judaism did not find it possible to accommodate the newly discovered evidence of an ongoing artistic tradition. They did not explain that art, they explained it away. One favorite explanation was that "the people" produced the art, but "the rabbis," that is, the religious authorities, did not approve it or at best merely tolerated it. That explanation rested on two premises. First, because talmudic literature—the writings of the ancient rabbis over the first seven centuries of the common era—made no provision for representational art, representational art was subterranean and "unofficial." Second, rabbis are supposed to have ruled everywhere, so the presence of iconic art had to indicate the absence of rabbinic authority.

Aware of the existence of sources that did not quite fit into the picture that emerged from talmudic literature as it was understood in those years or that did not serve the partly apologetic purposes of their studies, scholars such as George Foot Moore in his *Judaism in the First Centuries of the Christian Era: The Age of the Tannaim*[3] posited the existence of "normative Judaism," which is to be described by reference to talmudic literature and distinguished from "heretical" or "sectarian" or simply "nonnormative" Judaism of "fringe sects." Normative Judaism, exposited so systematically and with such certainty in Moore's *Judaism,* found no place in its structure for art, with its overtones of mysticism (except "normal mysticism"), let alone magic, or salvific or eschatological themes, except within a rigidly reasonable and mainly ethical framework; nor did Judaism as these scholars understood it make use of the religious symbolism or ideas of the Hellenistic world, in which it existed essentially apart and at variance. Today no informed student of Judaism in late antiquity works within the framework of such a synthesis, for this old way is no longer open. The testimony of archaeology, especially of the art of the synagogues of antiquity, now finds a full and ample hearing.

At stake was the conviction that the rabbinic canon was normative and tells us how things were everywhere. Once the archaeological evidence had made its impact, however, people came to recognize diversity where they had assumed uniformity and harmony. Then the conception of a single, normative Judaism, the same through five hundred years, uniform wherever Jews lived, and broadly confessed by almost all Jews almost everywhere, fell of its own weight. Scientific studies on "Talmudic Judaism," which had begun about a century ago, had rested on the presupposition that talmudic literature might by itself yield a whole and accurate view of Judaism in the early centuries of the Common Era. Iconic evidence was simply ignored.

When the diversity of Jews in antiquity came to be recognized, then the other premises of the received tradition of learning lost the standing of self-evident truths. If there was no single, unitary, harmonious Judaism, then (1) the sources that portrayed that picture could no longer be taken at face value. If the sources stood only for their authors' opinions, not for broadly held norms, then (2) we could no longer assume that all sources everywhere, without regard to when they were redacted, attested to that same, single Judaism. And if people differentiated between a given document and the worldview and way of life of the Jews everywhere and through a half-millennium or more, then (3) they had also to differentiate among the documents themselves. These three challenges to scholarship today outline not only what we now do not think we know. They also point toward what we think we know and how we think we know it; they account for the kinds of questions we now investigate. But it will take the rest of this book to spell out in detail the way in which the new learning reads the canonical writings and to account for the questions that today appear both urgent and accessible to sustained scholarly research: what we think we know and how we think we know it.

From "Normative Judaism" to Judaisms:
The Beginning of the New Learning

Today no sophisticated student of Judaism in late antiquity works within the framework of the firmly established scholarly orthodoxy of 1950. The path to a conception of a single "normative Judaism" was closed by a number of scholars and by the infusion of new attitudes.[4] First, Saul Lieberman, who, drawing upon[5] the early researches of Samuel Krauss and others, demonstrated how deeply embedded in late Hellenism were the methods and vocabulary of the Rabbis. But Lieberman went much farther. He drew attention to the divisions within Jewry, thus implicitly admitting the existence of more than a single Judaism. In an essay, "Pleasures and Fears," Lieberman stated:

The wisdom of the East [in this context, astrology] could not be entirely ignored. A learned and cultured man of those times could not reject the science of Astrology, a science recognized and acknowledged by all the civilized ancient world. To deny at that time the efficacy of Astrology would mean to deny a well established fact, to discredit a "science" accepted by both Hellenes and Barbarians.[6]

Lieberman goes on to trace the attitude of the Rabbis toward astrology and to show how they mediated between it and Judaism, concluding: "The power of Astrology is not denied, but it is confined to the Gentiles only, having no influence on Israel." What is important here is Lieberman's willingness to take seriously the challenges of Hellenistic science, magic, and religion, not merely in the faith of "assimilated" Jews or in the practices of the "ignorant masses" but in the bastions of the faith and their guardians.

Here we find no effort to explain away embarrassing and irritating contradictions to the prevailing view of a rationalistic and antiseptic this-worldly faith but rather a realistic effort to take all evidence seriously. True, Lieberman did not conclude that there was no single, unitary, harmonious normative Judaism, deriving in a linear path out of the Hebrew Scriptures, or "Old Testament." He did not recognize that there were several Judaisms, each with its own points of special interest and concern, modes of selecting out of the Hebrew Scriptures passages of probative importance. He did not have the conceptual tools for even conceiving such possibilities. But within his framework he did explicitly recognize that there were Jews, in large numbers, not accurately characterized as to their religion by the rabbinic writings at all. Then, so far as learning engaged with the religion of the Jews, not only the theology of some sages, the study of Judaism would have to address evidence of more than one Judaism.

Nor did Lieberman in that early time stand alone. Gershom Scholem's researches[7] on Jewish mysticism in late antiquity demonstrated how both talmudic and extra-talmudic literature point toward the existence of Hellenistic themes, motifs, and symbols deep within the circles of "pious" Jews. Since the rabbinic literature scarcely accounts for the vitality of such themes within the life of Jewry, the existence of more than a single authoritative Judaism once more became a plausible hypothesis in the description, analysis, and interpretation of that religion. But Scholem's grasp of the rabbinic literature in its totality was superficial and conventional. His generative category was "Judaism." He drew no important conclusions from his own allegations, other than that the esoteric doctrines that surfaced in the Middle Ages were rooted in late antiquity. For historicistic positivism, that was not a trivial result. For scholarship on formative Judaism, Scholem led nowhere, with his facts celebrated out of all context. His entire contribution is now in the process of being dismantled and placed in storage. Moshe Idel, the great Israeli historian of religion, has shown Scholem's scholarship to be dated and, in the end, merely ideological.

It was Erwin R. Goodenough,[8] whose major publications came out between 1920 and 1960, studying archaeological remains and Hellenistic literature, who was the first to state the obvious fact that archaeological evidence demanded interpretation within its own framework, as evidence of *a Judaism*— one with its own autonomy. Goodenough identified as distinct the Judaism formed among the circles in which the artifacts bearing pagan symbols, or symbols bearing Jewish values different from those associated with their original pagan setting, were used. Goodenough was the first explicitly to posit the existence of more than one Judaism. Goodenough's findings may be summarized in this way.

At the period between the first and the sixth century, the manifestations of the Jewish religion were varied and complex, far more varied, indeed, than the extant talmudic literature would have led us to believe. Besides the groups known from this literature, we have evidence that "there were widespread groups of loyal Jews who built synagogues and buried their dead in a manner strikingly different from that which the men represented by extant literature would have probably approved, and, in a manner motivated by myths older than those held by these men." The content of these myths may never be known with any great precision, but they suggest a Hellenistic-Jewish mystic mythology far closer to the Qabbalah than to Talmudic Judaism. In a fairly limited time before the advent of Islam, these groups dissolved. This is the plain sense of the evidence brought by Goodenough, not a summary in any sense of his discoveries, hypotheses, suggestions, or reconstruction of the evidence into a historical statement. Clearly, he articulated for the first time a fully exposed theory that there was more than a single Judaism in the formative age.

To see how the matter was put together in a different way from Goodenough's, toward the end of the 1950s, by the time at which Lieberman, Scholem, and Goodenough had set forth their findings, we turn to Morton Smith. Smith pointed out the striking convergence of the scholarly results of several distinct inquiries, results based upon disparate sources and produced by scholars who, though aware of one another's work, specialized in a single body of evidence. But Smith did not then draw the proper conclusion:

> It is amazing how the evidence from quite diverse bodies of materials, studied independently by scholars of quite different backgrounds and temperaments, yields uniform conclusions which agree with the plain sense of these discredited passages. Scholem's study of the materials in the hekhalot tradition, for instance, has just led us to conclusions amazingly close to those reached by Goodenough from his study of the archaeological remains: to wit, the Hellenistic period saw the development of a Judaism profoundly shaped by Greco-Oriental thought, in which mystical and magical . . . elements were very important. From this common background such elements were derived independently by the magical papyri, Gnosticism, Christianity, and Hellenistic and Rabbinic Judaism.[9]

The integration of these bodies of evidence into a coherent picture of, if not one Judaism, then multiple Judaisms, has yet to take place. But it is clear that the history of Judaism in late antiquity will tell the story of convergence and divergence.[10] Smith further states:

> Of all these four bodies of evidence—the works of the Biblical tradition, the Jewish literature of pagan style, the testimonia concerning Jews, and the archaeological material—no one is complete by itself. Each must be constantly supplemented by reference to all the others. And each carries with it a reminder that the preserved material . . . represents only a small part of what once existed. . . . Yet even this preserved material . . . testifies consistently to the hellenization of ancient Judaism.[11]

But at stake is not so much "the hellenization," viewed as a single thing, of "Judaism," likewise seen as one thing. Rather, it is the recognition of a variety of Judaisms (and, I take for granted, a variety of phenomena that will stand in various contexts for "hellenization"). Smith had missed the point. He thought a single Judaism had been shown to be different from the way it had been understood. He insisted that all the evidence attested to a single, uniform, harmonious Judaism:

"Each must be constantly supplemented by reference to all the others" indeed!

But Smith's failure of interpretation, requiring the evidence to be harmonized rather than analyzed, obscured the simple fact that each body of evidence tells us what it tells us: about the people of whom it speaks but not (necessarily) about anybody else. Smith then marks the final chapter in the 150-year story of the critical-historical reading of the canonical (and other) sources about the Jews and their Judaism, purporting to tell us pretty much what happened, what there was, and assuming that, once we know what happened and what there was, we can say what Judaism was (and, for Jews, is even now). Still, the demise of the received paradigm took place not only because of the intellectual failures of a generation of mere erudites but also because new people, working in different institutional settings, asked new questions and used new methods in finding the answers. And this they did because they found the received questions and methods insufficient.

When we examine more closely the way in which the critical-historical method was used and the results it produced, we realize it was not only not at all critical but also not very historical; its results turn out to border upon gibberish. To see the intellectual travesty that marked the end of the old, we turn to the movement from yeshiva to a supposedly critical and modern setting on the part of Saul Lieberman.

II

From Yeshiva and Seminary to University

Learning in Movement: Arrival at the Academy

Goodenough was a man of the university, and his independence of mind and outlook, though gifts of his own, found appreciation there in a way in which, in theological and rabbinical schools, such gifts are not treasured. Nearly all scholarship on Judaism before the last part of the twentieth century was conducted by Jews working in institutions sponsored by the Jewish community; most of the very few university-endowed chairs had been paid for by Jews. Employment was open to only a very few, and the institutions were controlled by a handful. Jewish-sponsored scholarly journals provided the principal medium for discussing results, the academic ones dismissing Judaic learning as trivial and unimportant. Opportunities for publishing books were equally restricted. Under such conditions of institutional control of learning, questioning of the received consensus, its methods and premises, opened no paths to gainful employment. Nor in consequence would new perspectives elicit a reply; the established medium for dealing with challenge was called *Todschweigen*, the penalty of death through silence. Goodenough's great *Jewish Symbols in the Greco-Roman Period*[1] was read in not a single course in the Jewish Theological Seminary in the 1950s, when it began to appear. With nearly total control of scholarly discourse in the hands of the proponents of the received paradigm, *Todschweigen* worked. Under such circumstances, fresh perspectives gained access only with difficulty.

The movement of learning into the academy changed all that by breaking the several monopolies—those governing employment, publication, book reviewing, access to a fair hearing. And that is to be expected. For in the shift in a field of learning from one institutional setting to another, the field's paradigms, the modes of thought, programs for identifying and educating future scholars thought not only able but also personally appropriate, as well as the manner of framing and testing hypotheses, the very thing that scholars want to find out about the subject at hand—all undergo drastic changes. For the institutional definition of what is important about a subject derives its norms not from the inner logic of the evidence of the subject, its sources and their structure, but rather from the institutional program itself. What the scholars and the students wish to know about a subject will define their selection of data, their formulation of problems, and their judgment of hypotheses worth entertaining or worthy of neglect.

Younger people in the time of shifts of paradigm, both institutional and intellectual, face the difficult task of moving from the old to the new world of learning. In doing so, they have to define for themselves a new approach to familiar knowledge. One solution to the problem is to ask new questions of old documents, or to do in a new way a task ordinarily done in some other, old way. Reading a familiar text in an unprecedented manner, the new generation then builds a bridge from the known but rejected to the unfamiliar but inviting mode of learning. Writing history in a fresh way, for instance, critically and skeptically instead of gullibly and credulously, or defining the historical agenda in new categories altogether represents a parallel way across what is in fact an unbridgeable abyss.

We see therefore that in the twentieth century a very ancient tradition of learning found itself in a new institutional setting and, furthermore, attracted to itself scholars bearing an unprecedented burden of interests. New kinds of people raised new questions and answered them in new ways, communicating their ideas in new media of discourse and in new settings altogether. That field of learning is called "Jewish scholarship," meaning systematic study of the holy books of Judaism produced, after the Hebrew Scriptures of ancient Israel, from the second through the seventh century. These holy books, the Mishnah, a law code of ca. A.D. 200, various compilations of exegeses of Scripture, and, finally, the Talmud of Babylonia, a systematic exegesis of both the Mishnah and the Hebrew Scriptures, of ca. A.D. 600, had been studied in yeshivas ("sessions") where law was studied and the theory of law evolved. Jewry constituted a political entity, and the institutions of learning served the polis. There the commentaries, codes of law, and basic texts formed the center of legislation and government, in theory and in practice, of the Jewish People. The institutional analogue to the yeshiva ("session") can be imagined if we set the Supreme Court judges onto the faculty of George Washington University, covering all subjects, not only law, and, furthermore, declare them, or those subject to their authority, to be also the U.S. Congress, the executive offices and heads of federal agencies and departments, and on and on. The entire government of Israel, the Jewish People, consisted of these scholar-administrator-clerk-judges. The premises of their education and, consequently, scholarly study derived from the political responsibilities of these central figures and centered upon the amplification and theory of the law.

Now when the Jews en masse entered into the politics of the West they carried forward the study of their received holy books. But the institutional basis shifted radically, for the political tasks entrusted to the scholars no longer pertained in Europe and in the United States (but they do, of course, continue in the State of Israel). Now the holy books were deemed part of the religious-theological or cultural heritage of the Jews, not to constitute political facts as the constitution and bylaws of a nation. Scholars addressed themselves to the study of the history and culture contained in those books, to the discovery of the correct text, the meanings of their words in historical context, and similar questions familiar from nineteenth-century critical learning. A second and distinct task, connected to but not continuous with the first, required the scholars to carry on their studies not only or mainly in institutions sustained by the Jewish community—teachers' seminaries and rabbinical schools, for example—but also in universities. A new address for scholarship invited inquiry into questions of common intelligibility, in place of those issues particular to Judaic discourse that had defined discourse in the Jewish institutions for Jewish learning. The paradigm shift involved, therefore, both institutional and intellectual changes of a fundamental order. Here we inquire about the transitional generation, important figures born in one circumstance but active in the other.

Generation of Transition: The End of the Old or the Beginning of the New

I argue, through an exemplary figure, that the transitional generation, saluted in its day as a harbinger of the new, turns out in retrospect not altogether successful in its enterprise of adaptation or renovation. For a paradigm shift is just that: a

fundamental change in how learning proceeds, for what purposes, and under what auspices—even in what kind of language. The advent of a subject into a new institutional setting
presents what is in fact an insoluble problem before those who
have studied the subject under different conditions. Assuming
that they know the old and have now to bring to bear the disci-
plines of the new, they turn out to grasp little of the new and
only to go through motions they do not fully understand, like
an untrained clog dancer attempting a pirouette. The end of
the old does not mark the beginning of the new. Where, how,
and when the new generation undertakes its labors within the
discipline of a new paradigm and a new institutional sponsorship for its subject, it derives from the immediately prior, supposedly transitional figures no useful model at all.

The paradigm shift and the advent of a different institutional
sponsorship for learning—these signal an abyss beyond all
bridging, separating traditions of learning that address a single
subject in common. So I shall argue by way of one interesting
specimen: the case of Saul Lieberman.[2] It is entirely proper to
look closely at him in particular, because, in his time, he was
regarded as a revolutionary figure, and, further, the man was
deemed the premier scholar of Judaism of his generation. In
retrospect, he will appear to be intellectually limited and in
some measure scarcely competent to do what he wished and
rightly assumed the academy expected. His career supplies testimony (as if it were needed) to the transience of political pre-
ferment. His reputation has scarcely survived his demise. But it
is as an intellectual example of the age of transition that he
remains of some interest even now.

What was new and what was old? Saul Lieberman read an
inherited ("traditional") document not ordinarily studied in
the old institutions, but he did so in accord with essentially the
same exegetical and paraphrastic protocol in which he had
been educated, and when he tried a (to him) new discipline,
namely, history, he proved incapable of mastering it. The reason is that he was unable to think in those propositional and
philosophical patterns which historical study required; he was
all footnotes, no text. Still, what we learn from the transitional
figure is that, when you leave home, you not only cannot go
back, you also cannot go anywhere else. For the true paradigm
shift takes place not with the transitional figures. It makes its
impact upon intellectual life only with those who, from birth
and through their education, prove to be utterly at home in the
new world of intellect and institutional setting alike. There is
no transition; no bridge extends across the abyss. The transi-

tional generation marks only the end of a tradition of intellect that is always available for replication and recapitulation in terms of its own paradigm. But, in terms of a new paradigm, the old tradition forever remains beyond adaptation, let alone renewal.

Born in 1898 Motol, near Pinsk, in Byelorussia, Lieberman studied traditional Jewish sciences, the exegesis of the Babylonian Talmud and related documents for instance, in the yeshivas of Malch and Slobodka. Leaving that subject, Lieberman went on to medicine at the University of Kiev in the 1920s, went to what was then Palestine and promptly left for France, where he continued his studies. He again settled in Jerusalem, in 1928, and reverted to his original subject, particularly talmudic philology. But he added to his curriculum Greek language and literature, and this represented what was new. For it was not common for Talmud scholars to introduce classical philology into talmudic exegesis, though from the time of Samuel Krauss's *Griechische und lateinische Lehnwörter im Talmud, Midrasch, und Targum* (1898–1899),[3] it was generally recognized that talmudic philology required knowledge of Greek. Accordingly, what Lieberman did was new for someone of his origins and interests but was commonplace for learning.

In the yeshiva world, only one of the two Talmuds, the Babylonian, was subjected to study. In defining the new approach to the received literature, Lieberman chose to concentrate on the other, the Talmud of the Land of Israel, also called the Yerushalmi (for "Jerusalem Talmud"). To do so, he turned first to the Tosefta, a supplement and commentary to the Mishnah, ca. A.D. 300, and effected a strikingly original and important treatment of its textual and also exegetical problems. This he did at the Hebrew University, where he was appointed lecturer in Talmud in 1931. From 1934 he was dean at the Harry Fischel Institute for Talmudic Research in Jerusalem. His appointment at the Hebrew University terminated,[4] in 1940 he emigrated to the United States, where he became professor of Palestinian literature and institutions (meaning the Talmud of the Land of Israel, or Yerushalmi) at the Jewish Theological Seminary of America, a rabbinical school for the education of rabbis for Conservative Jewish congregations. In 1949 he was appointed dean and in 1958 rector.

Lieberman's first book was called simply "On the Palestinian Talmud,"[5] and in it he emended texts and conducted a set of lower critical studies. While unconventional for the yeshiva world, the intellectual enterprise—bits and pieces of novellae on isolated texts—hardly represented a new definition of work.

As we shall see, when Lieberman did undertake work that was new in its very morphology, he proved unable to do it. A further set of studies, also mostly of a literary and philological character, followed. As I said, his greatest work was a systematic study of the Tosefta, in four volumes in *Tosefet Rishonim* (1937–1939),[6] a compilation of sayings in the name of authorities who occur, also, in the Mishnah. His analytical and exegetical work, covering the entire, sizable document, both proposed textual revisions based on a diversity of manuscript representations and on citations of the work in medieval commentaries and also supplied explanations for numerous difficult passages.[7]

When Lieberman came to America, at first he took for himself the program of writing in English and also of writing on subjects of broad interest to his new scholarly environment, for example, historical and cultural topics. His work in English concerned historical and cultural problems. *Greek in Jewish Palestine* (1942) and *Hellenism in Jewish Palestine* (1950)[8] dealt with a number of concrete cultural matters, and his one important historical effort, on the history of the Jews in Palestine, will presently occupy our attention. He abandoned the effort to address the larger academic world of America because, as I shall argue, he could not accomplish that task of reframing not only his mode of address but also his mode of thought. In any event, in the 1950s and for the remainder of his life Lieberman reverted to Tosefta exegesis, done in Hebrew of course, vastly expanding it into many volumes.

The work of the 1940s therefore captures Lieberman's effort at moving from one world to another, one country to another, and one paradigm of learning to a new one. Lieberman represents the transition from one institution to two others: specifically, from the old-world yeshiva, which pursued the exegetical study of commentaries to, and codes of, the law of Judaism, beginning with the Talmud of Babylonia, to, first, an Israeli university and, second, an American non-Orthodox rabbinical seminary. In making that move, he sought a fresh program of inquiry into the received literature. He found it in making use of classical philology for the exegesis of words and phrases of the Talmud and related writings, on the one side, and presenting a compendious commentary to a critical text of some of those same writings, on the other.

So when he laid the foundations for his abortive career at the Hebrew University, he continued in a German-model university the philological work he was trained to do in the yeshiva world, but he did it on a broader basis and drew upon a wider range of information. That is to say, in the move from Eastern European yeshiva to the Hebrew University, founded as it was on the German model, he studied the old books in new ways. The American move then challenged him to study new subjects in ways new to him, that is to say, topics of history and culture. That he could not do. Lieberman's move from yeshiva to university in the German tradition and onward to an American rabbinical seminary carried him over considerable territory.

Modes of Thought, Old and New

Here we can deal with only one dimension of Lieberman's intellectual journey. At issue is simply the received mode of thought concerning the making of connections and the drawing of conclusions, and the mode of thought characteristic of Lieberman's intellectual work, as represented by a single exemplary article of his. What we shall now see is the faulty, indeed uncomprehending, replication, without any real understanding, of a rich logical tradition. To explain the way in which Lieberman, in making his move from a traditional to a modern intellectual climate, preserved the form, but not the substance, of a received logic of cogent discourse, I have to explain one paramount principle of cogency in the literature studied in the yeshiva world and also in the university and seminary to which Lieberman moved. The Babylonian Talmud, paramount document for yeshiva study, exhibits two traits of the mind in making connections and drawing conclusions, one familiar, the other not. And it is the unfamiliar one—specifically, the mode of connecting one thing to something else in a well-composed and coherent statement of some dimensions—that will occupy our attention.

The first trait of cogent discourse in the Babylonian and Palestinian Talmuds is appeal to what is familiar indeed to us: rigorous propositional argument at the middle range of forming sentences into paragraphs. That is to say, when authors within the Talmud of Babylonia wish to make connections and draw and present conclusions, they compose statements and construct arguments in precisely the ways that we do in the Western philosophical tradition. They present a proposition, amplify, illustrate, test, prove, argue for it, just as we do. That is how they produce what we should call "paragraphs" or "chapters" of thought. But there is a second principle of cogency operative in the Talmud of Babylonia. It is one not familiar to us. It concerns the composition, out of well-formed propositions, of a sustained discourse, which we might call a chapter, that is to say, several paragraphs that flow in correct, logical order, one from the next, and make a single cogent point.

The (to us unfamiliar) logic of setting forth a sequence of propositions in the Talmud of Babylonia I call "the logic of fixed association." Two or more propositions, unrelated to one another, may be set side by side because a text external to them both is thereby amplified. The association between paragraph A and paragraph X then is not because the one leads to the other and coheres in sense or meaning but because both paragraphs join to a common text, which each one illuminates in its distinct way. The association between the two paragraphs then is extrinsic, supplied, conventional, and always fixed by a third, received statement, a text that is commented upon. When in the Talmud of Babylonia, therefore, an author wishes to join two or more propositions, that is to say, paragraphs of sizable discourse, the author may well affix both of those propositions or paragraphs to a fixed text, in succession to one another, even though the two propositions have not the slightest connection to one another. I call this rather odd way of joining ideas a "logic of fixed association."

What I mean is that an extrinsic protocol permits the association of two or more completed thoughts or propositions, even when those thoughts bear no intrinsic or logical connection. In the Talmud of Babylonia, organized as it is as a commentary to a prior law code, the Mishnah, it is the order of topics (sentences, propositions) of that prior law code, and not of the unfolding and orderly argument in successive stages, that dictates the joining of this to that. This mode of thought then appeals to an *a priori* principle of connection, via fixed associations defined in a manner extrinsic to the proposition, at the broad horizon.

Now what can go wrong with this logic of fixed association is obvious. When the discipline of the protocol of fixed association is broken, what is left is merely *free* association. The faulty understanding of the logic of fixed association proves the key, since, when misunderstood, fixed yields free association. For if the logical sequence of propositions that connect and relate in an unfolding argument do not dictate connection between two facts or among three or more facts, so that the presentation of a statement encompasses facts, argument, and conclusion, then what does? In the received intellect, framed by study of the Talmud of Babylonia, it is the text that joins facts together within its own structure. For those who do not grasp the logic of fixed association that dictates what belongs and what does not, what is left is mere association without proposition. That association beyond all rationality is what we call free association: there was this, and then, by the way, I just thought of that—but the other thing too comes to mind, and so forever and ever.

Training in the logic of fixed association did not teach Lieberman how to compose coherent arguments made up of sentences joined together in the service of a common syllogism, for example. In fact, he showed himself capable of exegesis of words and phrases but unable to write history and treatises on culture. In this way, Lieberman shows us how, at the end of the received paradigm of learning, in the movement from one institutional setting to another, the *forms* of the old system persist but are not understood and so enter a stage of decadence. Misunderstanding the received discipline of thought, he simply took for granted that sustained, continuous discourse, with one thought joined by proposition and logical sense to the next, defined no perquisite of cogent discourse. But then he found, in his progress out of the yeshiva world, no alternative principle of cogent discourse to take the place of the fixed association that, in the yeshiva world, made sense and provided self-evident connections between thought and thought. The result was that, when he had to address a Western reader and produce a set of coherent generalizations, for example, of a historical order, he blundered and, after a few efforts, gave up the effort entirely. What he was left to do, after the 1940s, was to revert to work he had already done, in the 1930s, and do it over again, only bigger and better.

Lieberman shows in a concrete way how the logic of fixed association yielded to mere free association in the case of one who misunderstood the remarkably *disciplined* character of the paramount logic of fixed association. Lieberman of course recapitulated the form of fixed association, that is to say, the commentary. For if we review the literary form indigenous to the logic of fixed association, we note that the commentary or exegesis serves better than any other literary medium for expressing the discourse generated by that logic. The reason, self-evidently, is that once we have a fixed association defined by a text, then we do well to exploit what we have in hand, joining sentences one after the other not through shared propositions, nor even through a common teleological enterprise, but merely through appeal in common to an imputed cogency. But then, he also shows us what would happen when the entire conception of argument and proposition fell away, and when even the notion was lost that discourse of fixed association would register points, concerning the base text, that were susceptible to generalization and systematic propositional statement. What would be left, then, would be simply the collecting and arranging of information pertinent to a given sequence of statements, for instance, a list of words or clauses or even whole sentences.

History or Gibberish: Lieberman's Case

In attempting to write a historical article for the American university setting,[9] Lieberman found himself unable to conduct historical study and never again attempted to write a book or even an article on a historical problem. Nor, indeed, do we find in Lieberman's corpus of writing much further effort to compose propositional discourses of a sustained character; his other work in English is essentially lexicographical and by nature episodic; the vast assembly of information in his Tosefta commentary is conceptually chaotic and bears no propositional character extending beyond two or three successive sentences. Over vast stretches of dreary fact-mongering, it is mere erudition, collecting and arranging lacking all logic. When we examine the sequence of topic sentences of the sample at hand and secondary developments of paragraphs on an announced subject, we see how limited was the intellectual equipment provided to an exemplary figure of learning by training principally in the received canonical writings, secondarily in philology pertinent to them. Lieberman wishes to present an argument on "taxation and imaginary religious persecutions."[10] A survey of his topic-sentences of sequential paragraphs yields the following:

We read in Aboth de R. Nathan, "Therefore shalt you serve . . . "

Similarly, we read in the Palestinian Talmud . . .

Here again the precariousness of riches at the beginning of the third century is well demonstrated.

We have already lost the topic "taxation," and persecution is not at stake. The point of joining the three topic sentences, of course, is that Lieberman appeals to an implicit text, or sequence of texts deemed to relate to one another, thus a fixed association, if one lacking an explicit text. So the procedure is not topical, even though the form is. But we proceed to recover the announced topic. Lieberman says, "The burden of *leitourgiai* of the third century is also well mirrored in rabbinic literature." Here the matter of taxation does emerge. We proceed to Lieberman's next topic sentences:

R. Johanan himself summarized the situation.

Besides the liturgies, rabbinic literature of the time mentions a great number of taxes.

Similarly, Graetz gives a Midrash which demonstrates the crooked ways of the Roman legal procedure in trying the Jews.

Again, we read in the Palestinian Talmud: "Diocletian oppressed the inhabitants of Paneas."

The petition of the people of Paneas was probably worded according to the usual formula.

Similarly, we read in the Midrash: . . .

Again, we read in the Palestinian Talmud: . . .

I think it very probable that the purpose of Proclus' entering Sepphoris is revealed in another passage of TP [the Yerushalmi].

Moreover, the rabbis were not unaware of the fact that the Romans tried to put a face of legality on their robberies.

An interesting discrimination between the arbitrary and the "legal" actions of the officials is noted in the following passage: . . .

It is obvious from the names of the rabbis who visited the Hot Springs of Gadara that the question was raised in the first half of the third century.

Herein lies the main point of the discussion of the rabbis in the above passage of the Palestinian Talmud.

The Jews were in exactly the same situation as the other provincials.

The topic headings of Lieberman's paragraphs leave the strong impression that we deal with a kind of stream of consciousness, not with a program and a well-crafted argument. The topic sentences do not produce the outline of a program, a propositional argument, a systematic inquiry—even a discussion of a sustained and orderly character. The topic sentences attest to a stream of consciousness that in other circumstances we call free association. It is just this, that, and the other thing, starting somewhere, ending somewhere else. What has happened is that the dialectical argument as a mode of sustained discourse yields only the dialectic—the movement. The argument is lost, or left behind, or simply forgotten in the onrush of information and episodic, ad hoc observation concerning this and that.

That is not to suggest that Lieberman invariably proved incapable of composing a sustained argument, setting forth a well-composed statement with a beginning, a middle, and an end. Nor is it to claim that all he had to offer was an enormous mass of disorganized information, given some semblance of order by essentially meretricious appeal to a topic ("persecution," "taxation") or a text (the Tosefta). It is only to show that Lieberman exhibited an infirm grasp on the requirements of propositional discourse and relied rather heavily upon imputed connections which, a glance at his rather odd sequence of topic sentences suggests, look suspiciously like the outcome of little more than, "First there was this, and then, by the way, I just thought of it, also there was that." So much for the composition of a large-scale discussion, the counterpart to the resort to fixed association by the mind of Judaism.

Let us then turn to the other principal mode of thought, the propositional, within the limits of a completed unit of thought, a paragraph. Here too we see the same evidence of a limited grasp, on Lieberman's part, of the mixed modes of thought of the received intellectual discipline in which Lieberman was educated and which he was widely held to embody better than anyone else in his time.

The reader may find patience to work through a sequence of two complete paragraphs, in which the full flavor of Lieberman's writing shows us how free association leads hither and yon but never to a cogently stated proposition, at best only to an implicit and somewhat confused one:[11]

> [1] We conclude our short survey with the position of the Patriarch and the Jewish scholars in the Roman system of taxation. [2] The role of the former in the distribution of the tax-burden and his responsibility towards the government are [*sic*] not clear. [3] However, it is certain that the Patriarch had to pay vast sums to the government and offer gifts to the officials. [4] The Midrash relates that the Patriarch asked R. Simeon b. Laqish to pray for him, because "the government is very wicked," and this is demonstrated by the following episode: "A woman brought the Patriarch a small salver (*diskarion*) with a knife on it. He took the knife and returned the salver to her. Then a courier (*beredarios, veredarius*) of the government came and he saw it, coveted it, and took it."

I have numbered the sentences so that the simple point may be visibly clear. Numbers 1–3 form a cogent statement. The break at number 4 is stunning. In fact, we have no paragraph at all, only a set of generalizations followed by a case that in no way proves commensurate with, or even congruent to, the generalizations and, in my judgment, has not been demonstrated to be even relevant to the issue.

Let us conduct the same analysis of the following paragraph in context, for we shall see precisely the same problem exhibited by Lieberman's writing in sustaining a thought and mounting an argument at the intermediate level of discourse, that of a propositional character, that we noted in mounting a cogent statement at the large level of discourse, that in accord with the logic of fixed association:

> [1] As for the scholars, there is enough evidence to show that they were at certain periods . . . exempt from some taxes and especially from *leitourgias*. [2] But it is unlikely that all scholars enjoyed the tax immunities. [3] It is much more probable that only the ordained scholars benefited from this privilege, scholars who could be placed in the category of priests, *sacerdotes*. [4] From the Palestinian Talmud we learn that Simeon b. Abba was not ordained because he happened to be in Damascus when an opportunity to ordain him presented itself. [5] We also find that R. Jonah refused to be ordained prior to his teacher, R. Zeminah.

I simply point out that between sentence 3 and sentence 4 is an abyss, another between 4 and 5. So the paragraph consists of three absolutely unrelated thoughts—and no proposition joins the thoughts. The pattern in both paragraphs is manifestly the same. Lieberman starts with something very like a generalization, then resorts immediately to a "case." But the case stands on its own. There is no clear connection between the case and the generalization. In the first paragraph, the "wickedness of the government" is not very clearly linked to the generalization, and Lieberman's reason for introducing the case is scarcely made explicit, nor are the conclusions we are to draw. But his persistent introduction of the Greek and Latin for the Hebrew counterparts suggests that a secondary motive was simply to show off knowledge of the Greek and Latin counterparts for the Hebrew, since that information plays no role whatsoever in making the point, if any, that he wished to make. In Lieberman's defense, I have to point out that the next paragraph refers back to "these incidents" and alludes to this and that, so that, if we stay the course, we can get some sense out of the whole.

But it seems to me amply demonstrated that Lieberman found exceedingly difficult the composition of a cogent paragraph, with a beginning, a middle, and an end, and that he was remarkably adept at collecting and posting interesting pieces of information. These pieces of information manifestly lacked all cogency between and among themselves but were joined to some larger whole only by reason of an assumed composition, an implicit set of unstated associations of an other than propositional character. With no evidence of an available program of fixed associations (except as Lieberman's own mind defined for him the points of contact or intersection between one thing and the next), we have to conclude that the Judaic mind of the Bavli in our own day is imitated but not understood. For Saul Lieberman, exemplary of the world which received this kind of writing (whether in English or in Hebrew) and valued it, and Lieberman's audience too, obviously took for granted that free association, when executed by a scholar of sufficient public notoriety or political influence in the limited world at hand, constituted logical discourse. And that is not at all how the mind of Judaism was meant to think.

The Intellectual Failure of Critical Exegesis

In his move from yeshiva to an American setting, Lieberman faced the task of shifting from one intellectual paradigm to another. The former involved a somewhat modernized continuation of the exegetical-philological modality of the inherited system of thought. Just as in studying the Talmud, people read words and phrases and said things about them, so the so-called scientific (i.e., *wissenschaftliche*) students of the Talmud did the same. They added attention to variant readings and they learned languages not ordinarily learned in yeshivas. But what they did with what they knew was not different in morphology, in fundamental mode of logical discourse, from what people in yeshivas did. When he moved from Slobodka to Jerusalem, Lieberman moved to a world that was different from, but intellectually continuous with, the world in which he originated. When he left Jerusalem and came to New York, he encountered a different world altogether. He tried to meet its challenges but did not have the intellectual equipment to do so, and so he turned back to his earlier success with the Tosefta and recapitulated it. And as to the prior hope, namely, to present the Talmud of the Land of Israel with a critical text and an ample commentary, so opening it for contemporary study, beyond his earliest efforts, and excepting only some bits and pieces of apercus on this and that, Lieberman never even tried. Nor did he encourage anyone else to.

To state the matter simply, what we find in Lieberman is simply the incapacity either to generalize or to compose a competent paragraph, that is to say, present a propositional statement of a cogent character in which connections between two facts are made to yield a conclusion. Fixed association has in Lieberman's mind, as shown in his writing, given way to free association. He presents us with an exemplary figure who excelled at the hunting and gathering, the collecting and arranging of information, which is always best presented—predictably—in the form of a commentary. Even within the units of thought of the commentary, for example, on the Tosefta, Lieberman found it exceedingly difficult to state two or more cogent thoughts in not only succession but cogent relation. But Lieberman in English presents us with an accurate portrait of the workings of the mind.

What was at stake in Lieberman's (exemplary) failure to replicate the received logic? For him and those around him, what would happen, concretely, was that fixed association, with its remarkably subtle mode of effecting connection, was misunderstood as a license for *free* association in which nothing joined anything to anything else. Merely collecting and arranging vast quantities of information, without a semblance of a point or a proposition, is not the same thing as collecting what pertains immediately and directly to a sequence of words, phrases, or topics that stand in a fixed and precise relationship with one another. The logic of fixed association dictated not only what fit but also what did not. Reduced to a scheme of collecting and arranging masses of information composing a whole of a merely thematic order, the logic of free association ended up no logic at all, because no one could say what did not belong to discourse. Everything fit as well as everything else, because, in a logic of free association, nothing was to be excluded on principle, on logic.

The long-term result was to yield public discourse, in the Judaic sciences, lacking all cogency, a mode of setting forth sentences in which beginnings and endings of paragraphs, that is to say, of whole discourses or expositions of ideas, played no role and served no purpose. For in free association, not only does any thing enter or leave merely as a matter of whim but the very notion of connection is lost. And that forms the end of logic, of cogent discourse of a public character that, in one way or another, produces if not propositions, then a kind of discourse deemed cogent and sensible with rules of intelligible exchange of thought, public laws governing what one may say and what is forbidden, in all, a syntax and structure of mind. In our own day the world made by the Bavli tended to lose sight of the discipline and order implicit in the logic of fixed association and to understand as the principle of intelligible discourse generated by the Bavli the legitimacy of utter free association. And that, by the way, was why Lieberman also could not write history.

But despite his influence in his time, and despite even the claques ever ready to applaud his every word, Lieberman marked the end of an era, for he never defined an intellectual career that anyone afterward would follow. Lieberman produced no students at all, never directing a doctoral dissertation that in any way carried forward work that he himself initiated—for example, in Tosefta exegesis, in Yerushalmi studies, and the like—and the work that he undertook ended with his death. He continued the received tradition that learning means exegesis of texts but did not fully master the logic of that received tradition and so distorted it.

The End of the Old, the Beginning of the New

In the age of change in the institutional and conceptual setting in which the ancient tradition of Jewish learning would go forward, what we see in the most important figure of the transitional generation is only the end of the old, not the beginning of the new. The new generation in the subject in fact would have no past, and the successors, none of them continuators, unanimously—a few explicitly, but most merely tacitly—acknowledged no continuity with an intellectual past. And they were right. There was none. The new learning began like archaeology, which leaps over centuries of silence to renew dialogue with the detritus of vanished ages. The archaeologist is no more a continuator of discourse in the languages of Sumer or Akkad or the Rosetta Stone than the contemporary scholar of Judaic studies carries forward the conversation of the Talmud in the language of thought of the Talmud. Once the sands cover the monuments, only the steel spade of another age can reveal them again—but only for the inquiry of that new age, lacking all precedent in its separation from the old, whether by one year or by one generation or by a millennium. And so too when intellectual paradigms shift, the old order passes into oblivion.

But when the new begins, it is born *ex nihilo,* in the minds and intellects of scholars without a past. New people, working in new settings, asked new questions, produced new answers, and so inaugurated a new appreciation for the scholarly enterprise. We now turn to ask, What did the new generation want to know, and how did that generation claim to find out?

III

What Do We Now
Want to Know About Judaism
in the First Six Centuries A.D.?

The Beginnings of the Critical Enterprise:
The Recognition of the Religious Dimension

What changed between 1950 and 1990 was the development of new interests, a new program of inquiry altogether. A reforming program, using philology and exegesis as instruments of change, had treated as secular—a matter of positive-historical fact—writings with another focus altogether, and, in the last half of this century, the writings again were read as the canon, the coherent statement of a religious system, a Judaism comprising a worldview, way of life, and theory of the social entity, Israel. Once people recognized that no single Judaism had predominated in the first six centuries A.D., they found the task of discerning Judaisms engaging. What the century and a half of scholarship on Judaism had ignored came to the fore, which is, the religion, Judaism. People now asked, in particular, about the religious world that Jews made for themselves, trying to understand the relationship between the ideas they held and the society they comprised.[1]

In doing so, scholarship on Judaism addressed issues of deep concern to the academic social sciences and humanities of the West: the interplay between ideas and society.[2] A typical statement of that program that prevails now is as follows:

> There can be no serious history of ideas that is not also the history of the social experience of the people who have them. Apart from that experience, where their meaning is grounded, ideas may have a chronology, but not a history.[3]

Writing not on the history of formative Judaism in the first century but on the life of William Lloyd Garrison the American abolitionist in the nineteenth, R. Jackson Wilson expresses the exact program that has taken shape: the study of Judaisms in the context of the social world of those Jews who through those Judaisms answered the questions they found urgent: ideas in the social context of the people who have them.

Setting forth self-evidently valid answers to those ineluctable questions in the worldview, way of life, and theory of themselves as the social entity, Israel, producing books deemed canonical or art regarded as fully representative, those Jews set forth their various Judaisms. All meaning is grounded in the social world of those Judaisms; apart from the compelling and urgent questions raised by their encounter with the politics and society of their place and time, the canonical writings do not yield even the chronology of ideas but rather, dogmatic theology.

If, then, the task of learning is to ask a fresh set of questions, the ones provoked by the recognition of the religious dimension of the social world, who found these questions compelling? Jews, Roman Catholic and Orthodox Christians, and other believers. The reason these newcomers pursued accounts of religion and the social order is not that the Protestant academic ascendancy exhibited less piety or pursued a secular program but because its conception of religion stressed issues of faith viewed in their own terms. Issues of theology and matters of faith took second place to other matters altogether. At stake in religion was something other than the introspective conscience and its propositional faith; rather, the fate of society before God: religion as something that "we" do together. The study of religion took up the questions of religion and society, how religion addresses the issues of the social order, for example, and these questions framed for the canonical writings (and the iconic expressions as well) a quite fresh program: new questions, new answers, a new hermeneutic.

From History to History of Religion and Society: The New Paradigm and Its Formation

Translating Wilson's statement into terms appropriate for the study of ancient Judaism allows a succinct account of what is at stake. When he says, "There can be no serious history of ideas that is not also the history of the social experience of the people who have them," we may read, "There can be no serious study of religion ("history of religion") that is not also the study of the interplay between the religious ideas that people have held and the social world in which they think they live. A brief outline of what I claim to have contributed to this paradigm shift is required for this primer of what I think we know and how I think we now know it. Pretending merely to describe, when as a matter of fact I passionately advocate, a particular program for the study of formative Judaism would form an act of bad faith with the reader. Saying up front what my own position has outlined will place in perspective my account of the way to proceed.

If I had to specify what I think I have given, it is this: (1) the recognition that the canonical writings of Judaism are fundamentally religious books, framing an account of a Judaic religious system; and (2) the insistence that a religious system deals in a fundamental way with an urgent and ineluctable question that faces a social entity, and that that system provides an answer deemed self-evidently valid to the question that people confront. The Judaisms of late antiquity then have formed for me a laboratory case for the examination of religion and society: religion as something people do together to solve their problems.[4]

In these books as I read them, people have made statements about how they have worked out answers to critical and urgent problems that faced them. Read properly, the canonical writings tell us history of a different sort from the account of persons and events that earlier was thought to emerge. In more general terms, conceiving that religion is the work of real people working together to solve pressing problems, I have worked out, for Judaism, a particular way of addressing the canonical writings. I read them within the hermeneutics serviceable for religious writings that set forth the (to their authors) self-evidently valid answers that they have found to these problems. Read each on its own and then all together, the canonical writings form an account of the worldview, way of life, and theory of the social entity, the "Israel," that realizes the worldview in its everyday life, that we may call a Judaism. So the problem of the right reading of the canon is to discern the religion that the authors of documents meant to set forth for us. That is the framing of the matter that I claim to have innovated.

If these statements seem banal, it is not because, to me, to begin with they were obvious. It took me many years to form them. And the angry controversy precipitated by the changes I have wrought in the study of formative Judaism suggests they are not banal even today.[5] I have spent nearly thirty-five years, from 1954 to the present, studying a literature not widely accessible in the humanities and the social sciences. I have aimed

to move that literature, its history and religion, into the main-
stream of academic learning and so to make that literature useful to specialists in a variety of fields within the academic study
of religion as well as in ancient history and culture and Near
and Middle Eastern Studies. My work has concerned the exemplary classics of Judaism and how they form a cogent statement. These classical writings, produced from the first to the
seventh centuries A.D., form the canon of a particular statement of Judaism, the Judaism of the dual Torah, oral and written. That was only one Judaism among many, but the canon
defined the Judaism that flourished in both Christendom and
Islam from the seventh century to the present. The circumstances of its formation, in the beginnings of Western civilization, the issues important to its framers, the kind of writings
they produced, the modes of mediating change and responding
to crisis—these form the center of my interest.

Autonomy, Connection, Continuity

In the past thirty years I have translated and reread for historical purposes nearly all of the classic documents of the Judaism that took shape in the first through the sixth century A.D.
and that has predominated since then, the Judaism of the dual
Torah.[6] These documents—the Mishnah, Tosefta, Midrash
compilations, the two Talmuds—represent the collective statement and consensus of authorships (none is credibly assigned
to a single author and all are preserved because they are
deemed canonical and authoritative) and show us how those
authorships proposed to make a statement to their situation—
and, I argue, upon the human condition. What I do in this
reading of the canonical literature of Judaism is divided into
three stages.

Autonomy: My work proceeds in a systematic way, document by document. First, I place a document on display in its
own terms, examining the text in particular and in its full particularity and immediacy. Here I describe the text from three
perspectives: rhetoric, logic, and topic (the received program of
literary criticism in the age at hand). Reading documents one
by one represents a new approach in this field, though it is
commonplace in all other humanistic fields. Ordinarily, in
studying ancient Judaism people have composed studies by citing sayings attributed to diverse authorities without regard to
the place in which these sayings occur. They have assumed that
the sayings really were said by those to whom they are attributed, and, in consequence, the generative category is not the

document but the named authority. But if we do not assume that the documentary lines are irrelevant and that the attributions are everywhere to be taken at face value, then the point of origin—the document—defines the categorical imperative, the starting point of all study.

Connection: Second, I seek to move from the text to that larger context suggested by the traits of rhetoric, logic, and topic shared between one document and some other. Here I compare one text to others of its class and ask how these recurrent points of emphasis, those critical issues and generative tensions, draw attention from the limits of the text to the social world that the text's authorship proposed to address. Here too the notion that a document exhibits traits particular to itself is new with my work, although, overall, some have episodically noted traits of rhetoric distinctive to a given document, and, on the surface, differences as to topic—observed but not explained—have been noted. Hence the movement from text to context and how it is effected represents a fresh initiative on my part.

Continuity: Finally, so far as I can, I want to find my way outward toward the matrix in which a variety of texts find their place. In this third stage I want to move from the world of intellectuals to the world they proposed to shape and create. That inquiry defines as its generative question how the social world formed by the texts as a whole proposes to define and respond to a powerful and urgent question, that is, I read the canonical writings as response to critical and urgent questions. Relating documents to their larger political settings is not a commonplace in Judaic studies; moreover, doing so in detail— with attention to the traits of logic, rhetoric, and topic—is still less familiar.

These three categories correspond, in general terms, to the study of the canonical writings as literature, religion, and theology. Read autonomously, they exhibit indicative traits. Interpreted as points of entry into the mentality of the authors, these indicators guide us toward the religious worldview of the authors. Seen as continuous with other writings of the canon, the whole then requires reading in the framework of a coherent theological discourse.

My work goes forward in systematic dialogue with the readings of these same canonical writings produced by others before our own day as well as by colleagues today. I have read not only the sources but nearly the whole of the scholarly corpus that has taken shape around them, both of an exegetical and of a historical character. With my students I have provided in a systematic way full accounts of prior readings of these same writings, introduced in the volumes of studies and bibliography edited by me, for example, *The Formation of the Babylonian Talmud, The Modern Study of the Mishnah,*[7] *The Study of Ancient Judaism,*[8] and the like. Full state-of-the-question studies have been accomplished by myself and coworkers, and, from these, colleagues can follow up other readings of these writings overall and, obviously, exegetical results of episodic passages, philological achievements, critical texts, and accounts of the sense of passages—all of these literary achievements of the past fifteen hundred years of reading these same documents retain enormous interest and value, though all in the nature of things have to be sorted out afresh in the light of the documentary reading of the canonical writings.

Reframing the Paradigm

Mine is a constructive exercise in scholarly inquiry, not a transaction of a political character in shifting the paradigm of a field of learning (although, as a matter of fact, I have done just that).[9] That brings us to the systemic approach,[10] which, in this area, I have invented.[11] Spelling it out is not difficult.

Writings such as those of the Judaic canon have been selected by the framers of a religious system, and, read all together, those writings are deemed to make a cogent and important statement of that system, hence the category "canonical writings." I call that encompassing, canonical picture a "system" when it is composed of three necessary components: an account of a worldview, a prescription of a corresponding way of life, and a definition of the social entity that finds definition in the one and description in the other. When those three fundamental components fit together, they sustain one another in explaining the whole of a social order, hence constituting the theoretical account of a system. This is the point at which we recall my initial insistence upon seeing religion as people solving problems together. A religious system answers an urgent question with truth deemed self-evidently valid by members of the social entity that lives in accord with the way of life posited by the system and sees its society in accord with the worldview of the system and interprets its collective existence within the systemic framework as well: " 'we' are 'Israel.' "

Judaic systems—Judaisms—defined in this way therefore work out a cogent picture, for those who make them up, of *how* things are correctly to be sorted out and fitted together, of *why* things are done in one way rather than in some other, and of *who* they are that do and understand matters in this particular way. When, as is commonly the case, people invoke God as the foundation for their worldview, maintaining that their way of life corresponds to what God wants of them, projecting their social entity in a particular relationship to God, then we have a religious system. When, finally, a religious system appeals as an important part of its authoritative literature or canon to the Hebrew Scriptures of ancient Israel, or "Old Testament," we have a Judaism.[12]

I recognize that in moving beyond specific texts into the larger worldview that they join to present, I may be thought to cross the border from the humanistic study of classical texts to the anthropological reading of those same texts. I therefore emphasize that I take most seriously the particularity and specificity of each document, its program, its aesthetics, its logic. I do not propose to commit upon a classic writing an act of reductionism, reading a work of humanistic meaning merely as a sociological artifact. Further, as between Max Weber and his critics, I take my place with Weber in maintaining that ideas constitute, in their context and circumstance, what sociologists call independent variables, not only responding to issues of society but framing and giving definition to those larger issues. In this way I make a stand, in the systemic reading of the classic writings of Judaism in its formative age, with those who insist upon the ultimate rationality of discourse.

Religions form social worlds and do so through the power of their rational thought, that is, their capacity to explain data in a (to an authorship) self-evidently valid way. The framers of religious documents answer urgent questions, framed in society and politics to be sure, in a manner deemed self-evidently valid by those addressed by the authorships at hand. For at stake in this *oeuvre* is a striking example of how people explain to themselves who they are as a social entity. Religion as a powerful force in human society and culture is realized in society, not only or mainly theology; religion works through the social entity that embodies that religion. Religions form social entities—"churches" or "peoples" or "holy nations" or monasteries or communities—that, in the concrete, constitute the "us" as against "the nations" or merely "them."[13] And religions carefully explain, in deeds and in words, who that "us" is—and they do it every day. To see religion in this way is to take religion seriously as a way of realizing, in classic documents, a large conception of the world. But how do we describe, analyze, and interpret a religion, and how do we relate the contents of a religion to its context? These issues of method are worked out through the reading of texts and, I underline, through taking seriously and in their own terms the particularity and specificity of texts. This I accomplish by special reference to problems in studying Judaism in particular.

Viewing Religions as Systems, Illustrated by Cases Drawn from Judaism

Now that I have focused upon the central role of specific documents, let me explain the movement from text to context and matrix that is signaled by use of the word "system." For reading a text in its context and as a statement of a larger matrix of meaning, I propose to ask larger questions of systemic description of a religious system represented by the particular text and its encompassing canon. Colleagues who work on issues of religion and society will find familiar the program I am trying to work out.[14] But, I underline, the success of that program is measured by its power to make the texts into documents of general intelligibility for the humanities, to read the text at hand in such a way as to understand its statement within, and of, the human condition. That seems to me not only the opposite of reductionism but also a profoundly rationalist mode of inquiry.

Systems begin in the social entity, whether one or two persons or two hundred or ten thousand—there and not in their canonical writings, which come only afterward, or even in their politics. The social group, however formed, frames the system, the system then defines its canon within and addresses the larger setting, the *polis* without. We describe systems from their end products, the writings. But we have then to work our way back from canon to system, not to imagine either that the canon is the system or that the canon creates the system. The canonical writings speak, in particular, to those who can hear, that is, to the members of the community, who, on account of that perspicacity of hearing, constitute the social entity or systemic community. The community then comprises that social group, the system of which is recapitulated by the selected canon. The group's exegesis of the canon in terms of the everyday imparts to the system the power to sustain the community in a reciprocal and self-nourishing process. The community through its exegesis then imposes continuity and unity on whatever is in its canon.

While, therefore, we cannot account for the origin of a successful religious-social system, we can explain its power to persist. It is a symbolic transaction, as I said just now, in which social change comes to expression in symbol change. That symbolic transaction, specifically, takes place in its exegesis of the systemic canon, which, in literary terms, constitutes the social entity's statement of itself So, once more, the texts recapitulate the system. The system does not recapitulate the texts. The system comes before the texts and defines the canon. The exegesis of the canon then forms that ongoing social action that sustains the whole. A system does not recapitulate its texts, it selects and orders them. A religious system imputes to them a cogency, one to the next, that their original authorships have not expressed in and through the parts, and through them a religious system expresses its deepest logic, *and it also frames that fit which joins system to circumstance.*

The whole works its way out through exegesis, and the history of any religious system—that is to say, the history of religion writ small—is the exegesis of its exegesis. And the first rule of the exegesis of systems is the simplest, and the one with which I conclude: *The system does not recapitulate the canon. The canon recapitulates the system.* The system forms a statement of a social entity, specifying its worldview and way of life in such a way that, to the participants in the system, the whole makes sound sense, beyond argument. So in the beginning are not words of inner and intrinsic affinity but (as Philo would want us to say) the Word: the transitive logic, the system, all together, all at once, complete, whole, finished—the word awaiting only that labor of exposition and articulation which the faithful, for centuries to come, will lavish at the altar of the faith. A religious system therefore presents a fact not of history but of immediacy, of the social present.

The issue of why a system originates and survives, if it does, or fails, if it does, by itself proves impertinent to the analysis of a system but of course necessary to our interpretation of it. A system on its own is like a language. A language forms an example of language if it produces communication through rules of syntax and verbal arrangement. That paradigm serves full well however many people speak the language or however long the language serves. Two people who understand each other form a language community, even, or especially, if no one understands them. So too by definition religions address the living, constitute societies, frame and compose cultures. For however long, at whatever moment in historic time, a religious system always grows up in the perpetual present, an artifact of its day, whether today or a long-ago time. The only appropriate tense for a religious system is the present. A religious system always *is*, whatever it was, whatever it will be. Why so? Because its traits address a condition of humanity in society, a circumstance of an hour—however brief or protracted the hour and the circumstance.

When we ask that a religious composition speak to a society with a message of the *is* and the *ought* and with a meaning for the everyday, we focus on the power of that system to hold the whole together: the society the system addresses, the individuals who compose the society, the ordinary lives they lead, in ascending order of consequence. And that system then forms a whole and well-composed structure. Yes, the structure stands somewhere, and, yes, the place where it stands will secure for the system either an extended or an ephemeral span of life. But the system, for however long it lasts, serves. And that focus on the eternal present justifies my interest in analyzing why a system works (the urgent agenda of issues it successfully solves for those for whom it solves those problems) when it does, and why it ceases to work (loses self-evidence, is bereft of its "Israel," for example) when it no longer works. The phrase "the *history* of a *system*" presents us with an oxymoron. Systems endure—and their classic texts with them—in that eternal present which they create. They evoke precedent, they do not have a history. A system relates to context, but, as I have stressed, exists in an enduring moment (which, to be sure, changes all the time). We capture the system in a moment, the worm consumes it an hour later. That is the way of mortality, whether for us one by one, in all mortality, or for the works of humanity in society. But systemic analysis and interpretation require us to ask questions of history and comparison, not merely description of structure and cogency. So in this exercise we undertake first description, that is, the text; then analysis, that is, the context; and finally, interpretation, that is, the matrix, in which a system has its being.

Explaining an *Oeuvre*

The methodological problem that has occupied my mind since I completed my Ph.D. in 1960 therefore derives from my chosen discipline. It is history of religion, and my special area, history of Judaism in its formative period, the first six centuries A.D.[15] I am trying to find out how to describe a Judaism in a manner consonant with the historical character of the evidence, therefore in the synchronic context of society and politics, and not solely or mainly in the diachronic context of theology which, until now, has defined matters.

The inherited descriptions of the Judaism of the dual Torah

(or merely "Judaism") have treated as uniform the whole corpus of writing called "the oral Torah." The time and place of the authorship of a document played no role in our use of the allegations, as to fact, of the writers of that document. All documents have ordinarily been treated as part of a single coherent whole, so that anything we find in any writing held to be canonical might be cited as evidence of views on a given doctrinal or legal or ethical topic. "Judaism" then was described by applying to all of the canonical writings the categories found imperative, for example, beliefs about God, life after death, revelation, and the like. So far as historical circumstance played a role in that description, it was assumed that everything in any document applied pretty much to all cases, and historical facts derived from sayings and stories pretty much as the former were cited and the latter told.

What We Want to Know About Judaism: What Is Worth Knowing?

It is time to say quite simply that much that the inherited agenda of learning has produced is trivial, merely antiquarian, not much worth knowing. For Lieberman, on the one side, and the dreary succession of credulous historians whom we shall meet in chapter IV, on the other, rarely ask what is at stake in their inquiries and, consequently, celebrate self-validating knowledge ("for its own sake"). If they are right in everything they say, then Lieberman still yields gibberish instead of history, and the pseudo-historians we presently shall encounter tell us information out of context. By contrast, I want my contribution assessed by the weight of the questions I have formulated: in the case I make, the arguments I amass, and the evidence I adduce, are the stakes trivial or high? So if I had to specify a single charge against the received scholarly tradition, it would not be intellectual incompetence, on the one side, or mere gullibility, on the other, but rather something much simpler: triviality. If they all are right in everything they say, so what? And my answer: so nothing.

I offer in place a history of a Judaism in its historical and social setting. I am not alone in undertaking the social study of Judaisms—the way in which a Judaism sets forth its conception of the social order. Many now recognize that systems of thought concerning the social order work out a cogent picture, self-evidently true for those who make them up, of *how* things are correctly to be sorted out and fitted together, of *why* things are done in one way rather than in some other, and of *who* they are that do and understand matters in this particular way. These systems of thought then are composed of three elements: ethics, ethos, ethnos, that is, worldview, way of life, and an account of the social entity at hand. Such systems need not fall into the category of religion or invariably be held to form religions, and it is the fact that not all religions set forth accounts of the social order. But when, as has often been the case, people invoke God as the foundation for their worldview, maintaining that their way of life corresponds to what God wants of them, projecting their social entity in a particular relationship to God, then we have a system. And when, finally, a religious system appeals as an important part of its authoritative literature or canon to the Hebrew Scriptures of ancient Israel, or "Old Testament," we have a Judaism.

In the renewal of the academic engagement with the study of religion, we find our purpose for the study of formative Judaism. When we ask that a religious composition such as the Mishnah or a Midrash compilation or one of the Talmuds speak to a society with a message of the *is* and the *ought* and with a meaning for the everyday, we focus on the power of that system to hold the whole together: the society the system addresses, the individuals who compose the society, the ordinary lives they lead, in ascending order of consequence. And that system then forms a whole and well-composed structure.

I conceive this project of the social study of the formation of Judaism to form a chapter in the study of the rise of Western civilization. Just as Max Weber understood the issue, Why has the West defined the world? so I want to explain in what ways Judaism has formed a Western religion and in what ways it has not. Just as Weber asked questions of comparison and contrast in finding out what is particular and what common, so I want to find points of commonality and difference in the study of Judaisms.

The given of my inquiry is that religion is what social science calls an independent variable, that is to say, a factor that explains other things but is not explained by other things. Religion I see as the single most powerful force in the making of human civilization: it is why we are what we are, for good or ill. When I describe, analyze, and interpret the evidence of Judaisms in late antiquity, therefore, I work my way into the formative power in the life of Israel, the Jewish people, and I furthermore aim at setting forth the Judaic part of the world-defining power of Western civilization, which is the creation of Judaism, Christianity, and Islam.

Why do I conceive this work to demand continuators in the

twenty-first century? The reason is simple. At issue in academic debate in the next half-century will be the place of the West in the world. Since, as a matter of fact, everywhere in the world, people aspire to those material advantages which flow—uniquely, I think—from the modes of social organization that the West has devised—the West's economics, its science and technology, and also, let us say it straight out, its politics and also its philosophy as modes of thought and inquiry, I think it is time to stop apologizing and start analyzing what has made Western civilization the world-defining power that it has become. When Weber asked why no capitalism in India, China, or Judaism, he opened, in that exemplary manner, a much broader set of questions. When, nowadays, people rightly want to find a place, in the study of civilization that the academy sustains, for Africa, Asia, peoples indigenous to every region and land, we all need to frame a global program of thought and reflection. And if we are not merely to rehearse the facts of this one and that one, we shall require modes of comparison and in particular the comparative study of rationalities.

Hence sustaining questions, applying to all areas because of their ubiquitous relevance—why this, not that?—have to come to definition. And since the simple fact of world civilization is that the West has now defined the world's economy, politics, and philosophy, and since all social systems measure themselves by Western civilization in its capacity to afford to large masses of people both the goods of material wealth and the services of political power, the indicative traits of the West demand close study. These are, I think, in politics, mass distribution of power in political structures and systems, in economics, capitalism, and in philosophy, the modes of thought and inquiry we call scientific. That explains why I have now undertaken to revise the entire program of the study of the Jews and Judaism. And, it is self-evident, what I mean to do is to provide a model for others to follow in the study of all other social entities and their social systems. So the stakes in this scholarly program of mine are as high as I can make them. But in saying what I think is at stake and in explaining why I want to know what I investigate, I have moved away from our problem, which is to explain what we know and how we know it. Let us now start back with the problem of historical knowledge.

IV

Historical-Critical Method in the Study of Formative Judaism

The Move from Gullibility to Criticism

Learning begins with facts: precisely what do we think we know and how do we think we find it out? In the world of Judaic learning over the past half-century, it is now clear, the very identification of the facts has been at stake: what do we know, how do we know it, and why does it matter? For in historical debate, we gain access to no knowledge a priori. All facts derive from sources correctly situated, for example, classified, comprehensively and completely described, dispassionately analyzed, and evaluated. Nothing can be taken for granted. What we cannot show, we do not know.

These simple dogmas of all historical learning go back to the very beginnings of Western critical-historical scholarship, to the age of the Renaissance. When the Donation of Constantine was proved false, all received facts of a historical character, based on certain kinds of information, stood at risk. These same principles—that "the things that you're liable to read in the Bible . . . ain't necessarily so"—emerged with new sharpness from the mind of Spinoza, who founded modern critical biblical scholarship. They passed through the purifying skepticism of the Enlightenment, which learned—because it had to—how to laugh. But gullibility suffered a still further blow in the nineteenth century's refounding of historical science. Systematic skepticism illuminated the founders of historical sciences in the nineteenth century. They serve as commonplace models in the twentieth. Anyone who claims to tell us what happened a long time ago obeys these simple rules, and no one who ignores them can properly use the past tense.

At issue is not personal conviction—fundamentalism, in a theological sense, concerning matters that in any event lie beyond the limits of historical knowledge. At stake are public principles of professional inquiry, matters of public inquiry, not available for idiosyncratic and private apologia through a mere "I believe." When the fundamentalist states, "I believe," he makes a statement of profound consequence. When a scholar claims that the "burden of proof is on the doubter," and frames questions that we can ask only if we assume that the sources contain factual information about what people really said and did, he violates the language rules of his professed field and says something that is merely silly.[1]

But in the historical study of the Jews and Judaism in late antiquity, credulity has proved fundamental, leading scholars to take not only as fact but at face value nearly everything in the holy books. "Judaism"—so they tell themselves—is special and need not undergo description, analysis, and interpretation in accord with a shared and public canon of rules of criticism. "We all know" how to do the work, and "we" do not have to explain to "outsiders" either what the work is or why it is important. It is a self-evidently important enterprise in the rehearsal of information. Knowing these things the way "we" know them explains the value of knowing these things.

That is, however, the mentality of a ghetto, a closed circle,[2] and the generality of Jewish scholars of Judaism in late antiquity have not left the ghetto, nor do they even admit to themselves that they presently reside therein. People who are gullible generically believe everything they hear, and gullibility as generic generates belief in whatever the holy books say. If, therefore, a canonical ("holy") book says a holy man said something, he really said it, and if the book says he did something, he really did it. That is gullibility.

Scholarship in the service of gullibility frames questions that implicitly affirm the accuracy of the holy books, asking questions, for example, that can only be answered in the assumption that the inerrant Scriptures contain the answers— therefore, as a matter of process, do not err. By extension, holy books that tell stories produce history through the paraphrase of stories into historical language: this is what happened, this is how it happened, and here are the reasons why it happened. The gullibility of which I speak, moreover, characterizes not solely Orthodox believers, from whom one can ask no better, but Conservative, Reform, and national-secular Israeli scholars, who claim to be "critical" and who probably believe they are, as well as non-Jewish scholars, in the New

Testament in particular, who approach the same sources for
their own purposes.

Why, you may ask, should a primer of the study of formative
Judaism review these obvious propositions? The reason is that
nearly all scholars work on the premise that if the Talmud says
someone said something, he really said it, then and there. That
premise, moreover, dictates their scholarly program, for it permits them to describe, analyze, and interpret events or ideas
held in the time in which that person lived. Some of these
scholars would deny the charge, and all of them would surely
point, in their writing, to evidence of a critical approach. But
the questions they frame, to begin with, rest on the assumption
that the sources respond. The assumption that if a story refers
to a second-century rabbi, then the story tells us about the second century proves routine. And that complete reliance merely
on the allegations of sayings and stories constitutes gullibility:
perfect faith in the reality of fairy tales. That is gullibility, not a
new kind but a very old kind. The only difference is that the
current generation of scholars claims to know better—and
should know better.

As I said in the Prologue, moreover, the results attract the
interest of scholars in adjacent fields—New Testament, early
Christianity, ancient history, and classics, for instance. But the
newest practitioners of gullibility redivivus cannot work on the
subjects of their choice if they confront the critical program of
the day. So they generally pretend to accept that program,
while in fact ignoring it. In this respect the old fundamentalists
showed greater candor. These judgments cannot make any
reader happy; they do not give me joy in writing them. But the
scholars' words themselves in every case prove my judgment
accurate, indeed moderate. The judgments invariably pertain
to what people say, not who or what they are, which is not
at issue. Let me then restate the question of method in two
aspects:

1. How do you know exactly what was said and done, that is,
the history that you claim to report about what happened long
ago? Specifically, if the document assigns a saying to a sage,
how do you know he really said it?

2. And if you do not know that he really said it, how can you
ask the question that you ask, which has as its premise the
claim that you can say what happened or did not happen?

The second question is as important as the first. If you want
to know the premises of a scholarly article or book, do not start
with the use of evidence. Rather ask, What does this scholar
take for granted about the character of the evidence? Specifi-

cally, can this scholar have asked the question he purports to answer if that author did not take for granted the facticity of the sources pertinent to the question? The character of the question is the key.

The generality of history and biography concerning formative Judaism rests on false premises as to the character of the evidence and therefore asks the wrong questions and produces worthless answers. Total gullibility about what ancient sources tell us, the incapacity critically to analyze those sources—these traits of mind presently characterize the use, for historical purposes, of the documents of Judaism in late antiquity. Believing Jews of Orthodox or Conservative or Reform, or secular, origin, whether young or old, use these sources in ways that no reputable scholar of the Old or New Testaments would condone in the scholarly reading of the biblical writings. Eminent scholars take for granted that we may ignore biblical criticism—indeed, the entire critical program of biblical learning. So the study of ancient Judaism in its formative centuries produces results in no way based on the principles of scholarship universally honored. There has been no revolution in the study of the history and biography of Jews and Judaism in late antiquity, only a rather lonely call for one on my part.

Can we draw an analogy to how things would be done in biblical studies if the same epistemological premise governed? Indeed we can. Working along the same lines, in like manner Old Testament scholars would analyze tales of conversations between Moses and Aaron or Pharaoh as if they really took place, and not as the imaginary compositions of great writers of religious fiction. The scholars, young and old, from whom we shall hear at some length, invoke arguments from the *plausibility* of the contents of a statement for the veracity of that statement. New Testament scholars following that program would tell us that Jesus really made such and such a statement, because it sounds like something he would say. So the *"If I were a horse, I'd like to eat oats too"* school of anthropology finds company in the great stables of Jewish scholarship. The scholars under discussion furthermore invoke the claim that they can identify the point of origin of a statement, without also telling us how they would know if they were wrong. The works of scholarship under discussion recapitulate the mode of historical thought of the Talmud—"since this statement uses this language, it must have been said before such and such a point, after which such language cannot have been used." So they blunder into minefields of pure guesswork. An analogy in biblical studies? In like manner, biblical scholars would tell us that such and such a proposition has the ring of truth; or "if such and such a proposition is true, then we can solve a further problem," or, "since text X knows nothing of the rule in text Y, therefore text X must come before text Y." That may be so— but not on the basis of argument alone. At some point, evidence must make its contribution, not to mention tests of falsification and verification. Otherwise we shall never know whether we are right. Deductive logic untested by evidence and unchallenged by skeptical analysis rules supreme.

To state matters simply: if biblical history were written the way the history of the Jews and Judaism in late antiquity (which used to be called "talmudic history") is written today, the histories of ancient Israel would begin with the creation of the world—in six days, of course. If complete indifference to the history of the writings in hand were to characterize New Testament scholarship, as that indifference governs talmudic-historical scholarship, we should be reading more and more harmonies of the Gospels. For the recognition that the four Evangelists preserve viewpoints distinctive to themselves should never have shaped the interpretation of the Gospels, and we should be left with ever more complicated restatements of the Diatesseron. New Testament scholars know full well that when they come to the rabbinic sources, they tend to use them in ways in which they do not utilize the New Testament. But, as I shall now show, they may take comfort in the simple fact that since the specialists in the talmudic writings read the documents in a fundamentalist way, the New Testament scholars do no worse. Nonetheless, both Old and New Testament scholarship, with its keen interest in questions of formulation and transmission of sayings, composition of sayings into documents, preservation of documents, and other critical issues, must find primitive and alien the traits of mind to which I shall now point. In contemporary Judaic studies, we routinely deal with premises last found plausible in biblical studies more than 150 years ago.

The prevalent scholarly premise is this: If a source says Rabbi X said something, he really said it. Without that premise, not a single paragraph I shall present can have been conceived and written. If we did not know in advance that whatever is assigned to an authority represents a view held by that person in the time in which, in general, we assume that person lived, none of the scholars at hand can have formulated and asked the questions they ask and provided the answers they give. Since that premise is manifestly unacceptable as the starting point of historical scholarship, which always starts by asking *how* ancient writers know what they tell us and analyzes sources and their usefulness prior to framing questions—for instance, reporting what really happened—it must follow that all of the work of the sample I shall survey is, from a critical-historical viewpoint, a mere curiosity. And no understanding of the paradigm shift that now affects studying ancient Judaism—fully set forth in chapters V through IX—can be gained without a clear picture of the alternative way of reading the canon of this Judaism. So let us follow, in detail, the language and arguments of those within the now-passing paradigm.[3]

He Really Said It

To show how history is written when you believe that all attributions are valid and that all narratives record things that really happened I give a single example. Unless readers see with their own eyes how the work is done in detail, they may well doubt that unalloyed fundamentalism characterizes scholarship on formative Judaism. My single example is Lawrence H. Schiffman, *Who Was a Jew? Rabbinic and Halakhic Perspectives on the Jewish-Christian Schism.*[4] He states:

> Since Second Temple times, there have been four basic requirements for conversion to Judaism: (1) acceptance of the Torah, (2) circumcision for males, (3) immersion, and (4) sacrifice (no longer required after the destruction). These requisites are explained in a statement attributed to Rabbi Judah the Prince in Sifre Be-Midbar 108:
>
>> Rabbi says: Just as Israel did not enter the covenant except by means of three things—circumcision, immersion, and the acceptance of a sacrifice—so it is the same with the proselytes.
>
> This statement is based on a series of 'aggadot to the effect that Israel was circumcised shortly before the eating of the first paschal lamb, was immersed, and offered sacrifices in preparation for the giving of the Torah at Mount Sinai. Rabbi Judah the Prince understands the entire conversion procedure as an opportunity for the proselyte to celebrate his own reception of the Torah as Israel did at Mount Sinai, for only through sharing in this historic religious experience could the convert become a Jew.
>
> The conversion procedure and ceremony is described in a long baraita' in B. Yevamot 47a–b:
>
>> Our Rabbis taught: A proselyte who comes to convert at this time, we say to him: "Why did you decide to convert? Do you

not know that Israel at this time is afflicted, oppressed, downtrodden, and rejected, and that tribulations are visited upon
them?" If he says, "I am aware, but I am unworthy," we accept him immediately, and we make known to him a few of
the lighter commandments and a few of the weightier commandments, and we make known to him the penalty for transgression of gleaning (the poor man's share), the forgotten
(sheaves), the corner, and the poor man's tithe. And we make
known to him the punishment for violating the commandments. . . . And just as we make known to him the punishment for violating the commandments, so we also make
known to him the reward for their observance. . . . We are not
too lengthy with him nor are we too detailed. If he accepts
(this), we circumcise him immediately. . . . Once he has re-
covered, we immerse him immediately. And two scholars
stand over him and make known to him some of the lighter
and some of the weightier commandments. If he immersed
validly, he is like an Israelite in all matters. (In the case of) a
woman, women position her in the water up to her neck, and
two scholars stand outside and make known to her some of
the lighter commandments and some of the weightier
commandments.

*From the language of our baraita', with its stress on the perse-
cution and downtrodden nature of Israel, it is most likely to have
been composed in its present form in the aftermath of either the
Great Revolt of 66–74 c.e. or the Bar Kokhba Revolt (132–35 c.e.).*
[Italics mine.]

The passage I have italicized makes the point. The language
permits us to date the passage, pure and simple. Since the language says thus and so, the passage *"is most likely to have been
composed in its present form . . . ."* The language on its own
tells us facts. Schiffman then knows that the sage really said
what is assigned to him. Without attention to the document
that presents the language, the context of that document, or
any other variables—and a person can think of many—Schiffman adduces in evidence for the facts at hand merely what the
text alleges—that alone. I cannot imagine a more blatant expression of gullibility.

I do not exaggerate the matter, since Schiffman is clear in
claiming "composed in its present form." He proceeds to state:

Regardless of which of these two dates is correct, the baraita'
reflects the legal rulings prevalent among the tannaim by the
Yavnean period, as will be seen below. That the baraita' does not

represent the procedure as followed before 70 C.E. is certain from
the absence of mention of the sacrifice which would have been
included had the Temple cult still been functioning.

This argument appeals to what the passage says, and does not
say, as evidence for the facts of the matter. Nor does Schiffman
leave himself room for maneuver. He states simply, " . . . is
certain from the absence of mention." He tells us that we can
learn the facts of the matter from the content of the passage—
and that without regard to a single question of critical importance. What I have reviewed is not a lapse in an otherwise
critical study. Quite to the contrary, Schiffman could not have
written this book without the principle I have shown he
invokes.

What is wrong here is not that Schiffman cannot be right. It
is that he has no way of telling whether he is wrong, therefore,
of testing, and permitting others to test, the validity of his
proposition. When I accuse Schiffman of believing everything
the sources tell him, I can point to the simple fact that he takes
for granted that Eleazar ben Zadok really said what is assigned
to him, at the time the Temple stood, so we now have a fact
about the state of the halakhah in the time of the Temple. The
fact that other sources attribute the saying to much later authorities makes no difference; we simply record that fact, without taking it seriously. We have what we want. Schiffman
argues as follows:

> On the one hand, we have failed to establish a definite attestation
> of our tradition at an early date. *On the other hand, the transmis-*
> *sion of this statement in the names of three separate tannaim*
> *indicates that it was widespread, and we may therefore take it as*
> *reliable evidence that the dispute of the Hillelites and Shammaites*
> *circulated from the Yavnean period on in the schools of the tan-*
> *naim.* [Italics mine.]

To three different names the saying is imputed, so Schiffman
concludes not that we have three versions of one saying but
that the saying was widespread. Schiffman is not alone in
equating recurrence of a story with circulation of that story;
others we shall shortly read will draw the conclusion that the
event portrayed by the story happened very often. That is an
undoubted fact. But so what? We may therefore take it as reliable evidence. Once more, true. But evidence as to what? What
is the force of the "therefore"?

The only reliable evidence I see is that the same saying is
imputed to three names. I do not know what, on that basis, the

dispute circulated broadly or circulated at all. Nothing in hand even pertains to that matter. We know only that the same thing is assigned to three names, and that proves, on the face of it, that no one was sure who said what. That does not seem to me reliable evidence of any proposition except one: people were confused. Just because different sources say different people made the same statement, we cannot imagine that a lot of people said the same thing—except in the never-never land of talmudic history, Talmud style.

Let us hear Schiffman's conclusions, on the basis of the passage at hand and in direct sequence from the foregoing:

> What can now be said about the evidence for the dating of immersion as a requirement for conversion? First, it seems that it is necessary to date it before the time of John the Baptist and the rise of Christianity in order to understand the background against which baptism comes to the fore. Second, tannaitic evidence, although admittedly lacking early attestation, also lends support to the claim that immersion was already a necessary requirement for conversion in late Second Temple times. Nonetheless, we cannot prove that immersion was a sine qua non for conversion before the early first century C.E.

Schiffman is satisfied that he has made his point. He now meretriciously invokes an entirely critical, contemporary rhetoric. He claims this baptism was required by *the halakhah* in particular in the last century before the destruction. Schiffman admits he cannot prove that baptism was required *before* that time. But the proof that it was required in "the halakhah" in the period before A.D. 70 rests on our accepting as fact one among several attributions of rules maintaining that immersion is necessary. If the cited rabbi really made the statement, then we know as fact that that rabbi held that opinion—no more than that.

New Testament Scholarship on History and Biography

Two traits of mind define academic gullibility. A currently prominent New Testament scholar will show us how they work. One is believing everything you read. The second is free-associating about what you read, without the control of a test of right or wrong. If I believe without asking how the author of this text knows that the things he imputes to an authority really were said by that authority, hence at the time that that authority lived, I am a fundamentalist. In the setting of the rabbinic writings of late antiquity, if I take for granted that what is attributed to a given rabbi really was said by him, in his day, when he lived, and recorded verbatim from that day until it was written down, and if—and this proves the premise on which I work—on that basis I say what happened in that rabbi's time, then I am credulous. And if not, then I am not.

Ignoring the scholarly canons of his own field of research, the New Testament specialist Helmut Koester states:

> **Hillel.** What would give to later rabbinic Judaism its characteristic mark was the practice of legal interpretation in the Babylonian synagogue. Hillel (who lived until about 20 CE) came from Babylon. He may have also studied in Jerusalem, but his exegetical principles, which together with his humaneness became determinative for rabbinic Judaism, reveal the diaspora situation, for which legislation related to the temple cult and to living conditions in an overwhelmingly Jewish country was of only academic interest. This perspective as well as his great gifts as a teacher made Hillel the father of rabbinic Judaism—much more so than his famous exegetical rules, like the conclusion a minore ad maius and the conclusion from analogy. In contrast, his often-quoted opponent Shammai represents a branch of Pharisaism which was closely related to the temple. Shammai is aristocratic, severe, and nationalistic. But Gamaliel I, Hillel's successor as the head of his school (probably a son of Hillel), had also become a member of the Jerusalem aristocracy. He was a member of the Jerusalem sanhedrin who became famous for his wisdom (and as such he appears in Acts 5:34–39), though he may have distanced himself sometimes from the prevailing opinion of that institution, as is indicated by the report of the Book of Acts. However, Gamaliel's son Simeon became the leader of the Pharisaic war party and was associated with the first government of the revolutionaries, although he later had to make room for a more radical leadership. This Pharisaic war party can be largely identified with the Shammaites with whom Simeon, grandson of Hillel, perished in the chaos of the Jewish war.[5]

Koester presents a pastiche of allusions to references to Hillel in a diverse body of writings, some of them separated from the time in which Hillel lived by only two hundred years, others by much longer. For example, "Hillel the Babylonian" and merely "Hillel" do not occur side by side. Should we not ask whether, overall, "Hillel the Babylonian" references present a viewpoint about Hillel different from the "merely Hillel" sources? "His" exegetical principles are assigned to him only in sources of the fourth century and beyond—four hundred years

later. Does Koester describe the life of Jesus on the basis of
statements of fourth-century church fathers? I think not. The
conclusion *a minore ad maius*, for example, is a commonplace
in Scripture and not Hillel's invention. I can direct him to
chapter and verse, both in Scripture and in the later rabbinic
exegesis of Scripture. For more than a few passages in the
canon of Judaism recognize that fact. Koester is copying what
he read somewhere. He even favors us with the gentle and humane Hillel, in the tradition of the stories, obviously partisan,
that contrast the humane Hillel and the captious Shammai—
stories that, in the main, circulated only in the latest parts of
the canon, redacted at ca. A.D. 500–600, for instance. Then,
with "But Gamaliel . . . " we jump into a different body of
sources, now drawing on Josephus and Acts for the rest of the
tale. So we mix up a rather diverse group of sources, some from
the first century and some from the seventh, believing whatever
we find in any one of them and forming the whole into a harmonious statement: pure gullibility.

When the Question You Ask Shows Credulity
About the Answers You Expect to Find

More to the point, when you believe that the sources answer
historical questions, you ask historical questions. A rather
complex but telling case of the act of pure faith in the framing
of issues derives from Shaye J. D. Cohen. To appreciate the
character of his argument, we start with his own précis of his
chapter, which is as follows:

> After the destruction of the second temple in 70 C.E. the rabbis
> gathered in Yavneh and launched the process which yielded the
> Mishnah approximately one hundred years later. Most modern
> scholars see these rabbis as Pharisees triumphant, who define
> "orthodoxy," expel Christians and other heretics, and purge the
> canon of "dangerous" books. The evidence for this reconstruc-
> tion is inadequate. In all likelihood most of the rabbis were Phar-
> isees, but there is no indication that the rabbis of the Yavnean
> period were motivated by a Pharisaic self-consciousness (con-
> trast the Babylonian Talmud and the medieval polemics against
> the Karaites) or were dominated by an exclusivistic ethic. In con-
> trast the major goal of the Yavnean rabbis seems to have been
> not the expulsion of those with whom they disagreed but the
> cessation of sectarianism and the creation of a society which tol-
> erated, even encouraged, vigorous debate among members of the
> fold. The Mishnah is the first work of Jewish antiquity which

ascribes conflicting legal opinions to named individuals who, in spite of their disagreements, belong to the same fraternity. This mutual tolerance is the enduring legacy of Yavneh.[6]

Let us proceed to ask how Cohen uses the evidence, investigating the theory of the character of the sources that leads him to frame his questions in one way and not in some other. What we shall see, first of all, is that Cohen takes at face value the historical allegation of a source that a given rabbi made the statement attributed to him. Cohen states:

> The text narrates a story about a Sadducee and a high priest, and concludes with the words of the wife of the Sadducee:
> A. "Although they [= we] are wives of Sadducees, they [= we] fear the Pharisees and show their [= our] menstrual blood to the sages."
> B. R. Yosi says, "We are more expert in them [Sadducean women] than anyone else. They show (menstrual) blood to the sages, except for one woman who was in our neighborhood, who did not show her (menstrual) blood to the sages, and she died [immediately]" (Bab. Niddah 33b).[7]

Cohen forthwith states, "In this text there is chronological tension between parts A and B. A clearly refers to a woman who lived during second temple times, while B has R. Yosi derive his expertise about Sadducean women from personal acquaintance." Why Cohen regards that "tension" as probative or even pertinent I cannot say. Now we may wonder whether Cohen believes that Yose really made the statement attributed him. We note that Cohen does not specify the point at which "the text" was redacted. The fact that the Babylonian Talmud reached closure in the sixth or seventh century makes no difference. *If the text refers to Yosé, then it testifies to the second century, not to the seventh.* We shall now hear Cohen treat the text as an accurate report of views held in the time of which it speaks. How does he know? Because the text says so: it refers to this, it refers to that. What we have is a newspaper reporter, writing down things really said and giving them over to the National Archives for preservation until some later reporter chooses to add to the file: gullibility of a vulgar order indeed. Here is Cohen again, in the same passage, starting with the pretense of a critical exercise of analysis:

> In this text there is chronological tension between parts A and B. A clearly refers to a woman who lived during second temple times, while B has R. Yosi derive his expertise about Sadducean women from personal acquaintance. He recalls a Sadducean

woman who lived in his neighborhood and died prematurely because (R. Yosi said) she did not accept the authority of the sages
to determine her menstrual status.

To this point Cohen simply paraphrases the text, and now he
will verify the story. It seems to me that Cohen takes for
granted that Yosé really made the saying attributed to him;
moreover, that saying is not only Yosé's view of matters but
how matters really were. He says so in so many words: "This
baraita clearly implies that R. Yosi is referring to contemporary Sadducean women. If this is correct, R. Yosi's statement
shows that some Sadducees still existed in the mid-second century but that their power had declined to the extent that the
rabbis could assume that most Sadducees follow rabbinic
norms."
     It seems to me beyond doubt that Cohen takes for granted
that what is attributed to Yosé really was said by him, and,
more interesting, Yosé testifies to how things were not in one
place but everywhere in the country. "If this is correct," Cohen
concludes not that Yosé *thought* there were still a few Sadducees around but that there *were* still a few Sadducees around.
There is a difference. Cohen does not tell us what conclusions
he draws *if this is not correct,* because, in point of fact, that
possibility he declines to explore. Nonetheless, he wants to verify the story. How? By finding another text that tells the same
story. He states:

> The version of the Tosefta is similar:
>   A. "Although we are Sadducean women, we all consult a
>   sage."
>   B. R. Yosi says, "We are more expert in Sadducean women
>   than anyone else: they all consult a sage except for one who
>   was among them, and she died" (Tosefta Niddah 5:3).
> The Tosefta does not identify Pharisees with sages, a point to
> which we shall return below, and omits the phrase "who was in
> our neighborhood." Otherwise, it is basically, the same as the
> Babylonian version.

Now the reader may rightly wonder whether perhaps Cohen
intends something other than historical narrative about views
Yosé held or opinions he taught. Cohen leaves no doubt as to
his intention. Let us listen as he tells us what *really* happened:
since Yosé made his statement, Yosé's statement tells us about
the second century. Then Yosé's statement proves that there
were Sadducees in the mid-second century but they had no
power. I find no evidence whatsoever that Cohen grasps the

critical problem of evaluating the allegations of sources. He looks into a source and comes up with a fact. If he finds two versions of the same story, the fact is still more factual. Gullibility, pure and simple! And, if that were not enough, he gives us the "proof" of "according to rabbinic tradition." That tradition suffices: "They always failed, of course, but they resisted; by the second century they stopped resisting." Let us review those clear statements of his:

> This baraita clearly implies that R. Yosi is referring to contemporary Sadducean women. If this is correct, R. Yosi's statement shows that some Sadducees still existed in the mid-second century but that their power had declined to the extent that the rabbis could assume that most Sadducees follow rabbinic norms. Contrast the Sadducees of the second temple period who, according to rabbinic tradition, tried to resist rabbinic hegemony (see below). They always failed, of course, but they resisted; by the second century they stopped resisting. This is the perspective of R. Yosi.

The "if this is correct" changes nothing. As soon as the "if" has been said, it is treated as a "then." "Then" it is correct, so Cohen here tells us the story of the Sadducees in the first and second centuries. In the first century they resisted "rabbinic norms," whatever they were, but in the second century they gave up. This is Cohen's conclusion, based on his failure to ask how the Bavli and the Tosefta's compilers or the author of the story at hand knew the facts of the matter. The sole undisputed fact is that they represent the facts one way rather than some other. But that does not suffice. Thus far we have seen a use of evidence entirely as gullible as that of Koester. Now, again, let us give Cohen his due. Any fair-minded reader may claim that what we have is a mere lapse. Cohen may have made a minor lapse that we should forgive. So let us see how he analyzes sources. He says:

> Rabbinic tradition is aware of opposition faced by Yohanan ben Zakkai at Yavneh but knows nothing of any expulsion of these opponents (Bab. Rosh Hashanah 2b). Yohanan ben Zakkai was even careful to avoid a confrontation with the priests (Mishnah 'Eduyyot 83).[8]

Now what have we here? "Rabbinic tradition" indeed. What can that possibly mean? All rabbis at all times? A particular rabbi at a given time? Church historians these days rarely base their historical facts on "the tradition of the church." Would that we could write a life of Jesus based on the tradition of the

church! How many problems we could solve! Cohen does not
favor us with an exercise in differentiation among the sources.
His is an undifferentiated harmony of the Jewish Gospels. Indeed, to the opposite, he looks into "rabbinic tradition," undifferentiated, unanalyzed, and gives us a fact: *Bab. Rosh
Hashanah 2b.* What can that be? It is a story about someone.
What does the story tell us? Is it true? Why should we think so?
Cohen does not ask these questions. He alludes to a page in the
Talmud, and that constitutes his fact, on which, it goes without
saying, he proposes to build quite an edifice. So the Talmud is a
kind of telephone book, giving us numbers through which we
make our connections. In no way does he establish a critical
method which tells us why he believes what he believes and
disbelieves what he rejects.

But he does have a clear theory of matters. Where sources
concur with Cohen's thesis, he accepts them, and where not,
not. Cohen wants to prove that earlier there were disputes,
later on disputes ended. Now some sources say that earlier
there were no disputes, later on there were disputes. *So Cohen
rejects the historicity of the sources that say there were no disputes earlier and accepts that of the ones that say there were no
disputes later.* This sleight of hand I find on p. 48. Here he cites
T. Hagigah 2:9: "At first there was no dispute in Israel." He
proceeds to point to an "irenic trend," M. Yebamot 1:4 and M.
Eduyyot 4:8, which alleges that while the Houses disputed various matters, they still intermarried and respected each other's
conformity to the purity rules. Then Cohen says:

> But this wishful thinking cannot disguise the truth. The two
> Talmudim find it almost impossible to understand this state-
> ment. The Houses could not marry or sup with each other. They
> were virtually sects—kitot the Palestinian Talmud calls them
> (Yer. Hagigah 2:2). At Yavneh sectarian exclusiveness was re-
> placed by rabbinic pluralism, collective authority was replaced
> by individual authority.[9]

What Cohen has done is to reject the statements in *earlier*
sources—Mishnah, Tosefta—and adopt those in *later* ones (the
Palestinian Talmud). He has done so simply by fiat. He cites
what they say, and then he calls it wishful thinking. The truth,
he discovers, is in the judgment of the Palestinian Talmud. I
find this strange, for two reasons. First, it is odd to reject the
testimony of the earlier source, closer to the situation under
discussion, in favor of the later. Second, it is not entirely clear
why and how Cohen knows that the Mishnah's and Tosefta's
statements represent wishful thinking at all. Had he cited the

talmudic discussions of the passage, readers would have found that the problem confronting the later exegetes is not quite what Cohen says it was. The Talmuds do not say that the parties were "virtually sects." That statement, it is true, occurs where Cohen says it does—but that is not on the passage of M. Yeb. 1:4 etc. that Cohen is discussing. It is on another passage entirely. The talmudic discussion on the Mishnah passage and its Tosefta parallel is a legal one; the sages are troubled by the statement that people who disagree on laws of marriage and of purity can ignore those laws. The talmudic discussion in no way sustains Cohen's statement. If now we reread the sequence of sentences, we find an interesting juxtaposition:

1. The two Talmudim find it almost impossible to understand this statement.

2. The Houses could not marry or sup with each other. They were virtually sects—*kitot* the Palestinian Talmud calls them.

3. At Yavneh sectarian exclusiveness was replaced by rabbinic pluralism, collective authority was replaced by individual authority.

It would appear that Saul Lieberman's disease—his incapacity to frame a coherent argument, made up of sentences that follow from one another—has infected another generation. For, self-evidently, sentence 3 does not follow from sentence 2, unless sentence 2 has had something to do with "sectarian exclusiveness" replaced by "rabbinic pluralism." But the passage cited by Cohen does not say that, it has no bearing on that proposition. Cohen writes as though the evidence supports his thesis, when, in fact, the evidence has no bearing on that thesis. The sentences in fact do not follow from one another. Number 1 is factually inaccurate. Number 2 makes the valid point that the Yerushalmi calls the sects *kitot*. That is an undisputed fact. It, however, bears no consequences for the statements fore or aft. And number 3 is parachuted down, Cohen's own judgment. So, to repeat, he believes what he wishes to believe, the *later* sources' allegations, disbelieves what he does not wish to believe, the *earlier* sources' statements, finds in a source not related to anything a statement he wishes to believe, cites that, then repeats—as though it had been proved—the fundamental thesis of his paper. I find this confusing.

It follows that Cohen's reading of the source begins with a generous view of the a priori accuracy of his own convictions about what the source is saying. Yohanan's "care" in avoiding a confrontation is Cohen's allegation, for the source does not quite say that. It says, in point of fact, not that he avoided confrontation, but that he did not think he could force the priests to do what they refused to do. Cohen simply cites the tractate and its chapter and paragraph number, and lo, another fact, another proof. I shall now show that Cohen can tell us "the truth," because *he* knows which source is giving us facts and which source is giving us fancies. That explains why what gets a question mark "(at Yavneh?)" half a dozen lines later loses the question mark and becomes a fact "At Yavneh sectarian exclusiveness was replaced by rabbinic pluralism." On what basis? Let us hear. For this purpose we review the materials just now set forth. He says:

> Some of the rabbis were aware that their ideology of pluralism did not exist before 70. "At first there was no dispute (mahloqet) in Israel" (Tos. Hagigah 2:9 and Sanhedrin 7:1). How did disputes begin? According to one view in the Tosefta, disputes were avoided by the adjudication of the great court which sat in the temple precincts and determined either by vote or by tradition the status of all doubtful matters. In this view, when the great court was destroyed in 70, disputes could no longer be resolved in an orderly way and mahloqot proliferated. According to another view, "once the disciples of Hillel and Shammai became numerous who did not serve [their masters] adequately, they multiplied disputes in Israel and became as two Torahs." In this view Jewish (i.e., rabbinic) unanimity was upset by the malfeasance of the disciples of Hillel and Shammai, a confession which would later be exploited by the Karaites. What happened to the disputes between the Houses? They ceased at Yavneh, how we do not know. Amoraic tradition (Yer. Yevamot 1:6 [3b] and parallels) tells of a heavenly voice which declared at Yavneh, "Both these [House of Hillel] and these [House of Shammai] are the words of the living God, but the halakha always follows the House of Hillel." As part of this irenic trend someone (at Yavneh?) even asserted that the disputes between the Houses did not prevent them from intermarrying or from respecting each other's purities (Mishnah Yevamot 1:4 and 'Eduyyot 4:8; Tos. Yevamot 1:10–12) but this wishful thinking cannot disguise the truth. The two Talmudim find it almost impossible to understand this statement. The Houses could not marry or sup with each other. They were virtually sects—*kitot* the Palestinian Talmud calls them (Yer. Hagigah 2:2 [77d]). At Yavneh sectarian exclusiveness was replaced by rabbinic pluralism, collective authority was replaced by individual authority. The new ideal was the sage who was ready not to insist upon the rectitude of ("stand upon") his opinions. The creation of the Mishnah could now begin.[10]

When Cohen says "were aware," he treats the thesis of his article as the fact of the matter. Who were these rabbis? And how do we know of what they were, or were not, aware? Did they live at Yavneh, in A.D. 70? Or did they live in the early third century, when the Mishnah had reached closure, or did they live a hundred years later, when the Tosefta was coming to conclusion? Cohen does not tell us. But he clearly thinks that their awareness is evidence of historical fact. Now these in the aggregate constitute historical statements, for example, "the Houses were virtually sects." Why Cohen valorizes Y. Hag. 2:2—a late source—and dismisses the evidence of the Mishnah and the Tosefta is something that causes a measure of surprise. In fact, he has set out to prove at the end of his paragraph the very point he takes for granted at the outset of his paragraph. Philosophers call that begging the question.

Cohen's review of the stories makes a feint toward criticism. He cites diverse views, balancing one view against another. But from Cohen we do not have a history of people's opinions, we have facts. "What happened to the disputes between the Houses? They ceased at Yavneh, how we do not know." Materials deriving from the period after the Bar Kokhba war are particularly rich in allusions to Houses' disputes that take up moot principles otherwise debated entirely in the age beyond Bar Kokhba's war. We clearly have mid-second-century literary conventions. I do not mean to suggest that the names of the Houses served as more than literary conventions; I demonstrated that they served at least as literary conventions. Why? Were there "Houses of Shammai and Houses of Hillel" in the time of Yosé, in the mid-second century? Is that why so many sayings about the relationships among the Houses are assigned, in fact, to mid-second-century authorities? But the assignments of those sayings occur in documents edited only in the third century, at which point (some stories have it) the patriarch Judah discovered that he descended from Hillel. So perhaps the disputes of the Houses served a polemical purpose of the patriarchate, since the ancestor of the patriarchate—everyone knew—kept winning the disputes. These are only possibilities. In answering the question as Cohen phrases it, all we have are possibilities, few of them subject to tests of falsification or validation.

Cohen knows facts, the unbelieving among the rest of us, only possibilities. But why in particular much more than half a century beyond the point at which Cohen knows the Houses went out of business: "They ceased at Yavneh, how we do not know." Well, just what ceased at Yavneh, if the names of the

Houses persisted as literary conventions and points of polemic for a hundred years and more? It must follow that Cohen's claim of knowledge of an "irenic trend" rests on nothing more than two things: first, the source's claim of such a trend; second, Cohen's opinion as to the facts. This is proved by the stories cited from M. Yeb. 1:4 and M. Ed. 4:8 and so on. Let us review in sequence Cohen's statements:

> [1.] But this wishful thinking cannot disguise the truth.
> [2.] At Yavneh sectarian exclusiveness was replaced by rabbinic pluralism, collective authority was replaced by individual authority.
> [3.] The new ideal was the sage who was ready not to insist upon the rectitude of his opinions.
> [4.] The creation of the Mishnah could now begin.

All of these statements may well be true. But in the paragraph that I have cited, in which these statements occur, not a single source, not a single piece of evidence, proves any such thing. I cite number 1 to prove that Cohen claims to make a historical statement. Number 2 then tells us he sees a movement from sect to church (though he does not appear to have read Max Weber, who saw much the same movement). Cohen has not proved that the "new ideal" of the sage antedates the Mishnah, in which it is said that that is the ideal. But he has ignored the fact that the Mishnah imputes that irenic position to none other than the House of Hillel—who lived long before "Yavneh." And what all of this has to do with "the creation of the Mishnah" only Cohen knows.

So, in a climax of total confusion, if a passage in the Mishnah refers to the time of the Houses, but Cohen thinks that the fact does *not* apply to the time of the Houses, he ignores the allegation of the Mishnah's passage. If a passage in the Yerushalmi, two hundred years later, refers to the earlier period and says what Cohen thinks was the fact, then that later passage is true, while the earlier one is not. What does he do in the case at hand? He assigns that allegation neither to the context of the age of the Mishnah itself, as, to begin with, I would find plausible, nor to the age of which the passage itself speaks, namely, the time of the Houses (before A.D. 70, so Cohen), as other believers, consistent in their gullibility, would insist.

In Cohen's mind, the passage testifies to an age of which it does not speak and also in which the document that contains the passage was not redacted. This is pure confusion, and I can find, in the rest of Cohen's article, still more utter chaos. But Cohen is consistent if he does not think something happened, then he also will not believe sources that say it happened, even though they are early sources. We already have noticed that if a passage in a later rabbinic document refers to an earlier time and Cohen does think the fact applies to that early time, then he of course produces the source to prove the point that, to begin with, he wishes to make. So he prefers the later source that conforms to his thesis over the earlier one that does not. Let us not forget where we started. Does Cohen believe that if the source says that someone said something, then that person really said it? Well, yes, on the one side Cohen does believe it, when the source says something Cohen thinks the source should have said the man said, as in the case of Yosé. But no, on the other side Cohen does not believe it, when the source says something Cohen thinks the source should not have said the man (or group) said, as in the case of the Houses when they are represented in an irenic mode. So Cohen's scholarship emerges as rather credulous except when he is confused. And let us at the end not miss the simple point that Cohen's thesis to begin with rests on the conviction that the sources as we have them present us with the facts we require to test—and prove—a thesis of that order and not some other. That framing of the question attests to a profound gullibility indeed.

From Honest Gullibility to Pseudo-Criticism: The Younger Generation

Cohen's credulity lies beneath the surface, one mode of avoiding the issue of whether historical research in the canonical writings of Judaism can yield results of professional quality. But a new generation has come on the scene, claiming explicitly to address the critical issue. But it is pseudo-criticism, since, as we shall see, the question is not asked, it is only evaded. That forms the one new methodological development in the past quarter-century. Rosalie Gershenzon and Elieser Slomovic, in their article "A Second Century Jewish-Gnostic Debate: Rabbi Jose ben Halafta and the Matrona," introduce the rhetoric of a critical approach to learning but not the substance of that approach.[11] In fact, they evade the question while pretending to answer it.

First, one mark of gullibility is to translate theological conviction into literary and historical fact. A principal conviction of Judaism is that God revealed one whole Torah, in diverse media, to Moses at Sinai. Consequently, all components of that one whole Torah contribute equally, and with slight differentiation, along with all others. For the fundamentalist historian, the upshot is simple. We ignore the point of origin of all stories and sayings. Anything in the canon bears equal weight with anything else, and that without the slightest regard for the particular document in which a saying or story makes its appearance. The received theology states, "There is no consideration of priority or anachronism in the Torah," and so, for the fundamentalists, the same applies. Gershenzon and Slomovic cite a broad range of stories about a second-century rabbi, *at no point differentiating among those stories by the criterion of their point of documentary origin!* For example, they do not tell us that story A appears in a document closed in the second century, story B in one in the third, story C in one in the fourth, and so on. Everything is the same as everything else.

Second, the two authors insist that all the stories at hand not only speak about the second-century rabbi—who ever doubted it?—but also testify to ideas *held at the time he lived.* The basis for that insistence marks them as fundamentalists. It is that they invoke the contents of the stories to justify the second-century dating of the stories. Specifically, they argue that at the time Yosé lived Gnosticism flourished, so Yosé's statements (even though they do not allege that he *really* said them) require interpretation in the context of debates between Gnostics and rabbis.

But if Yosé did not make the sayings attributed to him, then why should we read those sayings in the setting of the second century in particular? If the name of Yosé did not appear in those sayings—and if in our mind the appearance of that name did not carry *prima facie* weight that he really made those statements—we could as well have read what is attributed in the context of some other time altogether. The two authors go on: in fact—so their circular argument goes—(1) when we read these stories knowing that Yosé was arguing with Gnosticism, (2) sure enough, he is arguing with Gnosticism. The fact about Gnosticism is established.

But is that the only possibility? Where are the others? The two authors do not rigorously examine other possibilities, so they rest their case on the argument from content: it sounds right, so it is right, and the old ring of truth sounds loud and clear. We come back to the original observation, that the two authors ignore the time of the appearance of the documents that contain the stories they cite, paying attention only to the contents of the stories but not to their provenance. On that basis, as I said, they immediately leap into the second century—when Yosé lived. So two distinct strands of gullibility intertwine: first, the argument from contents; and second, the argument that it does not matter where the saying in his name now is preserved.

The upshot is simple. (1) The two authors ignore the age *in* which the document that contains a story was closed but immediately introduce the traits of the age *to* which the story refers. (2) The two authors announce a thesis but do not test their thesis against contrary possibilities. They are enormously pleased with their thesis, and that is that. And why not? For the contents of the stories conform to the requirements of their thesis. So here is a fresh and complex version of gullibility, in four aspects:

First, second-level gullibility about attributions ("he did not really say it but someone in his day did").

Second, indifference to the differentiation among documents and insistence that everything is pretty much the same as everything else.

Third, appeal to the contents of a story in validation of its historicity (which is the first again).

Fourth, failure to validate a theory by constructing a test of falsification.

Lest readers think I have exaggerated the intellectual follies of these two young authors, let us hear them speak for themselves:

> Two anticipatory questions arise: can the midrashim in question, embedded in contextual layers which cannot themselves be reliably dated, be ascribed with any certainty to R. Jose? Can the entire polemic be regarded as a historical encounter between two actual antagonists, rather than as a conventional literary vehicle in which the ostensible literary opponent is merely a fiction mouthing widely known arguments?

I give the answer whole and complete and then come back and analyze its parts:

> After all, many of the questions raised by the matrona were regarded as legitimate exegetical problems within the rabbinic schools. Our proposal that these midrashim be treated as a unit does not depend on a demonstration—obviously impossible— that they reflect actual encounters between specific individuals. Whatever the historical and literary impetus for enclosing their contents in this unusual polemical frame work, we believe that they record the major arguments in the second century Gnostic-Jewish debate, as preserved by Jewish spokesmen. Later redactors may no longer have recognized Rabbi Jose's opponent as a

Gnostic, but they recognized and preserved the language of religious polemic and the second century Galilean provenance.

There are several a priori reasons for treating this group of midrashim as a unit. First, although a wide variety of encounters between sages and matronas is reported in the literature, both in Palestine and in Rome itself, the passages involving R. Jose are unique. They are the only ones which present a straight forward religious polemic in query-answer format. The polemical approach is almost invariably exegetical, a pattern which appears to be characteristic of early refutations of heretical doctrine. All the other passages are anecdotal or episodic, and some have cautionary or legendary overtones. Second, the passages under consideration share distinctive features of style and tone, most notably the homely, almost banal illustrations utilized by R. Jose, and the surprisingly friendly mood of the argument. These features will become apparent upon closer acquaintance. Finally, a brief examination of religious, social and political conditions in second century Galilee suggests that at that time and place an encounter between a leading Jewish sage and an educated Roman aristocrat with Gnostic leanings was, if not routine, quite plausible. Indeed, almost no other time and place could have been more suitable. Let us briefly examine some of these contributing factors.

Now let us review these paragraphs. First, the question:

[1.] Can the entire polemic be regarded as a historical encounter between two actual antagonists, rather than as a conventional literary vehicle in which the ostensible literary opponent is merely a fiction mouthing widely known arguments?

[2.] After all, many of the questions raised by the matrona were regarded as legitimate exegetical problems within the rabbinic schools.

Second, the answer:

[3.] Our proposal that these midrashim be treated as a unit does not depend on a demonstration—obviously impossible—that they reflect actual encounters between specific individuals.

Clearly, the authors see a connection between the question and the answer:

[1.] Can the entire polemic be regarded . . . ?
[2.] After all, many of the questions . . .
[3.] Our proposal . . .

But—here we go again!—what, exactly, is the connection between sentences 1 and 2 and sentence 3? I see none at all. The authors win our trust by asking the critical question, How do we know the stories really took place in the second century, involving Yosé in particular? But then they make a statement that has no bearing whatsoever on the question.

Let me unpack this matter with some care. First they say they do not attribute the stories to Yosé in particular. Then they talk, rather, about grouping the stories. What connection between the one (1, 2) and the other (3), the question and the answer? The question has not been answered by the answer, because the answer has nothing to do with the question. The answer evades the question, denying its relevance. But there is the implicit premise, denied by the evasion at hand. I can expose the implicit premise simply by a question of my own: Why leap into the second century? It is because, as the authors explicitly say, "We believe that they record the major arguments in the second century Gnostic-Jewish debate." But why the second century in particular, *if not because Yosé is their protagonist?* As I said in the beginning, if not Yosé, then I should think that the third or the fourth centuries offer themselves as candidates. And, again, if not the second century, then why Gnostic-Jewish debate in particular? Why not a debate *within* the Jewish community? We could as well interpret the stories as evidence of opinions held within the Jewish community as outside its borders. The results of scholarship on the rhetoric of disputations in ancient times points time and again to the invention of an antagonist as testimony to issues vital within the community of readers, not at the outside. Whether Justin's Trypho or Aphrahat's "sage of Israel," the other side turns out to speak to concerns of Justin's and Aphrahat's readers: Christians. Trypho and the "sage" tell us about what Christians, not Jews, were thinking: so all scholarship has concurred for a long time.

The upshot may be stated very simply but requires emphasis *If it is not the historical Yosé in particular, then it is another Jewish spokesman whose name just happened to be Yosé.* We have once more crossed the border into the land of make-believe. But, failing to read carefully and ask how one sentence logically produces the next, and how a concluding sentence flows logically from the preceding sentences, we are supposed to concede that the authors have taken up the critical agenda. They have not even touched it. Let us now reread the concluding paragraph and see:

(1) arguments from content, and

(2) the prevailing, but denied, premise that, after all, Yosé really said these things, because

(3) other things Yosé said (not imputed to Yosé) "share distinctive features of style and tone" with these sayings, and, anyhow,

(4) in second-century Galilee, Gnostics and sages kept meeting, so "almost no other time and place could have been more suitable." So to conclude the dreary tale, we once more examine *ipsissima verba*:

> There are several a priori reasons for treating this group of midrashim as a unit. First, although a wide variety of encounters between sages and matronas is reported in the literature, both in Palestine and in Rome itself, the passages involving R. Jose are unique. They are the only ones which present a straight forward religious polemic in query-answer format. The polemical approach is almost invariably exegetical, a pattern which appears to be characteristic of early refutations of heretical doctrine. All the other passages are anecdotal or episodic, and some have cautionary or legendary overtones. Second, the passages under consideration share distinctive features of style and tone, most notably the homely, almost banal illustrations utilized by R. Jose, and the surprisingly friendly mood of the argument. These features will become apparent upon closer acquaintance. Finally, a brief examination of religious, social and political conditions in second century Galilee suggests that at that time and place an encounter between a leading Jewish sage and an educated Roman aristocrat with Gnostic leanings was, if not routine, quite plausible. Indeed, almost no other time and place could have been more suitable. Let us briefly examine some of these contributing factors.

What shows closet gullibility? Let me conclude by underlining the main points.

1. The fact that a number of similar *stories* occur in a number of documents is turned into "a wide variety of *encounters* between sages and matronas is reported in the literature." That is not the fact. The fact is that the similar stories occur a number of times. If we turn that fact into "a wide variety of *encounters*," we are making things up, just as the sages of the Talmud turned two versions of a saying into two stages in Yohanan ben Zakkai's career. The stories may speak of a number of different events. Or they may speak of only one event, told in a number of different ways. Or they may speak of nothing that really happened but only of something that someone imagines happened. The counterpart in New Testament studies

was the discovery of the Sermon on the Mount and the Sermon on the Plain—and not many people preach about that anymore.

2. The argument from style is this: the stories share distinctive features of style. But what else does that fact prove? I am baffled. If now the authors do not wish to suggest that Yosé really said these things, then what historical fact do they hope to demonstrate by showing that fixed and shared literary conventions characterize the genre of story at hand? I imagine they can show a literary fact—like Cohen, recognizing a convention of genre, but I do not know what *historical* event they therefore allege they have uncovered. What sounds authentic is authentic—another argument not much used in Christian pulpits, still less in Christian scholarship.

3. The argument from content: this is how we imagine things should have taken place anyhow, so "quite plausible," generates "No other time and place could have been more suitable." But how do we know unless we compare one proposed context with some other? In fact, this is no more than part of the large-scale evasion. I look in vain for any sustained investigation of other times and places. If Gershenzon and Slomovic imagine such possibilities, they do not take them up and show they do not serve, or do not serve so plausibly, as the one at hand. Pseudo-criticism gives us, if not the historical Yosé, then someone else named Yosé.

The Bankruptcy of Historical-Critical Method

No primer on the study of formative Judaism can ignore the way in which historical studies are carried forward. It is the simple fact that, outside of a very small circle, historical-critical method in the study of Judaism and the history of the Jews in late antiquity is typified by the New Testament scholar and the older and younger scholars of the Jews and their religion whom I have cited here. Numerous others can have supplied still more striking examples of what can only be called intellectual bankruptcy. It is not as though alternatives have not been laid before the scholarly world. For my part I have raised the issues in work after work for fifteen years. But when we speak of a paradigm shift, we must remember, what is involved is not merely new results or new questions addressed in the old way to familiar sources.

A paradigm shift such as I have claimed has taken place is marked by a fresh range of questions, deriving from a different perception of the evidence and what it tells us. That shift further redefines what is at stake in the very enterprise of learning. The movement from a historical to a religious-historical reading of the same sources has taken place, as I shall show in the next chapter. If the historical gullibility of the study of Judaism, its positivism and naive notion that we know exactly what happened, have not yet found an honorable place in a museum for ancient notions, the results, as we have seen, prove not very compelling. Not only so, but interest in this sort of information wanes, as we begin to see much more engaging questions emerging. Reading the sources as holy books, which portray a religious system, produces more interesting results—so many have concluded—than reading those same sources for such information as they give us about precisely what was going on in the time to which those sources refer.

It remains to ask, What price gullibility?—and What is at stake here? The cost to the study of the texts at hand—which the believers claim to prize—is incalculable. For the believers insist on asking questions the holy books do not answer, and they also do not wish to listen to the answers the holy books give to questions the holy books do address. So the Orthodox, the religious fundamentalists, the credulous and the believers, the Israeli talmudic historians, and the other believers, whatever their belief, reject what the sources at hand wish to teach and impose a program of inquiries for which the sources scarcely serve. We cannot ask religious texts that by no reasonable standard can tell us what really happened on a given day long before the texts' own redaction to report to us about "that day." Nor can we demand that that authorship record what Yosé really thought or how "the rabbis" said this or did that or changed their policy in such and such a way.

Texts written down centuries beyond the point purportedly under discussion cannot have much information on those matters. We can and should ask the texts to give us their messages and to convey their meanings. But the believers do not want to listen to those messages, and that is a loss—to the holy books. For the true believers do not want to pay attention to the convictions important to the authorship of the holy books. The victim of the sin of gullibility is the canon that the believers claim to hold dear. They want what the sources do not give, and they do not want what the sources provide in abundance. And that is the principal cost. In the next two chapters I shall show what is to be gained by letting holy books speak of holy Israel's encounter with God.

V

From History
to Religion

Why History and Biography Are Irrelevant to Judaism:
(1) Biography

Christians naturally want to know more about the life and teachings of Jesus, because in the context of Christian faith he is unique. Biography presupposes that the named individual bears traits that are particular to himself or herself. But what if the purpose of telling stories about a given sage or holy woman or miracle-man is not to preserve the record of a distinctive and singular person? Then stories will be told for some other purpose altogether, and, it will follow, biographies will not be written. Christianity is rich in biographical literature—books comprising lives of Jesus, holy deeds of the saints, stories of the martyrdom of this one or that one. Not only so, but individual authors most commonly signed their names to their books or signed apostolic names to gain acceptance for their books. Both of these traits of literature point toward a trait of the religious worldview that, beginning with Jesus himself, values the distinctive traits of the individual, sees the incarnate God in the particularities of one man. That is why, in consequence, people will write biographies and even autobiographies, and it also explains why authors will sign their books.

In the Judaic systems represented by the writings collected as "apocrypha and pseudepigrapha," by contrast, to gain authority people signed the names of others rather than their own name: Adam, Abraham, Moses, and the like. In the rabbinic canon, for its part, not a single book bears the name of its author, if it had an individual author. Most documents are anonymous and thereby are represented as deriving from the consensus of collective authorships. Not only so, but in all of the canonical writings there is not a single sustained biography, with a beginning, a middle, and an end.

That fact was appreciated by William Scott Green in his landmark essay "What's in a Name? The Problematic of Rabbinic 'Biography.' "[1] Green asks:

> Is it likely that studies which focus exclusively on the traditions ascribed to a single master will result in an authentic biography of that figure, in the story of his life? . . . If we cannot produce rabbinical "lives," what kinds of things can be known, for instance, about the historical Eliezer b. Hyrcanus or Joshua b. Hananiah? If such studies will not produce biographies, what problems, if any, can they solve, and what is the place of their problematic within the larger critical investigation of rabbinic Judaism?[2]

Green answers these questions negatively: "The literature of rabbinic Judaism offers no systematic or coherent biographies of its important sages." There were no hagiographies, no lives of saints, and no literary form uniquely suited to that enterprise.[3] That is not to suggest that the writings emerged out of chaos or that individuals played no role in making them, only that the role of individuals was subordinate in the textual community that stands behind the documents of Judaism. The anonymity—the opposite of biography—is inherent and intrinsic, so Green:

> These documents appear to be not accidental, inchoate collections, but carefully and deliberately constructed compilations. Each document has its own ideological or theological agendum, and it is axiomatic that the agendum of any document . . . ultimately is the creation of the authorities, most of whom are anonymous, who produced the document itself. They have determined the focus, selected the materials, and provided the framework. . . . The features of these documents suggest that their agenda surpass the teaching of any individual master.[4]

The documents do not attribute material deemed authoritative, only that which is personal opinion; they are not constructed around sayings attributed to individuals but follow a thematic plan. So Green concludes, "We know about early rabbinic figures what the various authorities behind the documents want us to know, and we know it in the way they want us to know it." The upshot is simple. Biography not only does not serve but cannot serve, and if we wish to compose biographies, the character of the sources opposes our work. Biography is not possible, because the Judaism under examination did not want to produce distinguished individuals, only those exemplary of common and usual virtue.

Why History and Biography Are Irrelevant to Judaism: (2) Events in Judaism

If not the unique person, then how about the unique event? History—at least, as narrative historians who have written about the history of the Jews in ancient times have conceived history—is composed of such events, each requiring description, analysis, and interpretation in the context of all others. But what if the rabbinic canon does not recognize unique and one-time events? Then the presumption that out of those sources we can write history, or chapters of a history, fails; without events, there can be no history, and the Judaism of the dual Torah knows nothing of events as unique and one-time happenings. What must follow is not that out of the canonical literature of Judaism we cannot write history, it is that we *should* not write it. It is inappropriate to do so, a violation of the premises and character of the canonical writings—therefore a profound error, a misinterpretation.

In an exact sense, "event" has no meaning at all in Judaism, since Judaism forms culture through other than historical modes of organizing existence. Without the social construction of history, there also is no need for the identification of events, that is, individual and unique happenings that bear consequence, since, within the system and structure of the Judaism of the dual Torah, history forms no taxon, assuredly not the paramount one, and, it must follow, no happening is unique, and, on its own, no event bears consequence. These statements rest upon modes of the analysis of history as the fabrication of culture, including a religious culture, and require us to review the recent formation of thought on history as culturally ordered and on the event as "contingent realization of the cultural pattern," for it is only in that context that we may make sense, also, of the representation of both history and its raw materials, events, in Judaism in its definitive canon.

Until modes of historical thinking of a social-scientific character got under way, narrative history served as a medium for organizing and explaining perceived experience. That kind of history enjoyed the status of objective truth, a principle of explanation bearing self-evident validity. When people contemplated the past, it was because they proposed through such precise knowledge to explain whatever mattered in the present.

What they chose to interpret in the present then defined their curiosity about the past. They then identified out of the unlimited agenda of the past those things which mattered, and these they called events, occasions of consequence, as distinct from undifferentiated and unperceived happenings—from eating breakfast to losing one's keys—which of course bear no material consequence in the explanation of the world.

Now it hardly mattered, in the long era during which historical study predominated as the medium for the explanation of the social order, that the received manner of doing history as a mode of organizing and explaining experience involved a series of logical fallacies. Explaining the outcome by reference to a sequence of ordered events, after all, formed an intellectually legitimate way of appeal to the intellectually illegitimate argument, *post hoc, ergo propter hoc.* So too, explanation without verification through a process of generalization, interpretation without a process of comparison and contrast, analysis as mere paraphrase of received accounts—these traits of historical learning did not attract attention.

Historical explanation of the world, specific and ad hoc and episodic, found no competition and enjoyed the standing of self-evident truth. The notion that the mere paraphrase of "happenings," identified by ourselves, as a matter of fact, as events, could account for the perceived present demands for credulity an innocence so childlike that we must wonder how historical explanation of society and culture served for as long as it did.[5] All the more reason to admire the towering intellects whose independence of mind impelled them to ask, Why so? when everyone held, indeed, Why not? and How otherwise? But they persisted. In consequence we now understand that the very notion of an "event," and with it the vast superstructure of the ordering of intellect and the explanation of society built upon historical explanation of sequences of events, then to now, there to here, all rational, all obvious, all self-evidence, come to us as the gifts of naive credulity, such as the preceding chapter has shown us.

It would carry us far afield to trace the long history of historical explanation of the social order by appeal to the definition, selection, and sequence of events. Chronicles, of course, go back to remote antiquity. But history as arbiter of truth, history as mediator of sensibility and source of explanation— these honored roles in the court of intellect came to history only in the formative centuries of our own civilization. As I said earlier in these pages, we should have to trace the path back to the Protestant Reformation, with its insistence on the priority of historical fact, deriving from a mythic age of perfection, in dictating the legitimacy of social reality in the present moment. Cutting through the detritus and sediment of the long centuries of increment and accumulation, therefore appealing not to *Listenwissenschaft* ("the science of lists"), but to a different, more autonomous kind of judgment altogether, for the logic of their discourse, the Reformation theologians identified history, the record of what happened (in this case) in Scripture, as the instrument for the validation of reform. Reform then would accomplish the renewal of times past, times perfect, appealing therefore to the court of appeal formed by history.

But history of a particular order, events of a very specific character, reaching their definition in the second way station, beyond the Reformation, in our quest for the self-evidence of history as a medium of social explanation. And, as I have already suggested, that, of course, is the nineteenth century with its interest in historical explanation of not merely the life of faith but the reality of society, above all, the formation of the nation. History, with its canon of well-chosen events, in explanation of the social order, this time, the "we" of the nation, the otherness of other peoples, served the intellectual program of the romantic nationalism of the nation-state. If history with its proof texts in self-evidently probative events served the purpose of religious reform, it provided a still more abundant source for explaining the self-evidence of the nation-state.[6]

History as a Cultural Indicator

Now as we approach the third millennium we have begun to recognize that history forms a discourse of contemporary taste and judgment. Events become eventful only because we make them so. *History is culturally ordered,* a statement of an intensely contemporary perception. It follows, we now understand, that all histories are the creation of an eternal present. And, with that understanding well in hand, fully recognizing that history is one of the grand fabrications of the human intellect, facts not discovered but invented, explanations that themselves form cultural indicators of how things are in the here and now, we find ourselves no longer historians of ideas of history, or analysts of the history of culture, let alone practitioners of the dread narrative history that makes of historical writing a work of elegant imagination. Rather, we find ourselves archaeologists, working, from the surface that is known, through the detritus of the unknown, in quest of a material understanding of a reality that is not known but for its artifacts, not susceptible of explanation and understanding except in categories and terms that are defined by those same artifacts. And that quest is, we all recognize, not a very smooth one.

The metaphor of archaeology for historical study is jarring, because, after all, nearly all historical evidence is in writing, and we are used to thinking of archaeology in terms of the pick and the shovel. But it is an apt metaphor, nonetheless, for it teaches us how to examine the written evidence on which most of us work in our cultural analysis of we know not what. The archaeologist (in theory at least) peels back from the surface to the underneath, and so must we. The archaeologist knows no categories other than the boundaries of the dig and the strata of the dig, knows no categories, imposes no categories, invents no categories that are not there. Then the things dug up define the categories and impose their own questions, their location *in situ* defining their "text," by which I mean their circumstance, their relationships with other artifacts *in situ* defining their context, their stratum *in situ* dictating the matrix of interpretation. For us, the site is the document, and our task is to treat the document as not a candidate for paraphrase, that is, for descriptive historical study within the premise of explaining how things were and how they got to be the way they are. For us the task is to treat the document as a cultural artifact, evidence for the working out of a social order in small detail.

The definition of events forms an acutely concrete statement of the larger systemic principles, and when we understand how a system defines events, we grasp the working of that system. And what emerges is that, if history is not a category of the Judaism of the dual Torah, religion is. And what, concerning religion, we learn from the consideration of the religious uses of historical events in the rabbinic canon, do we learn? The answer concerns the character of the religious system that identifies a happening as an event, gives the event its form and purpose and context, and draws conclusions from it.

The event is to the composition of history as the atom is to the molecule, the thread to the fabric, or the steel beam to the building. Yet these diverse metaphors reverse matters. The molecule defines the atoms that it wants (to impute teleology to the inanimate, in the manner of historians), the fabric requires that thread and no other, the building dictates the requirements, as to tensile strength, of its beams. And so the culture—in the case of a Judaism, the religious system—is what identifies the events that explain and justify the culture. And, in consequence, we must ask ourselves, are not the literary records of events so constituted as to dictate the shape of the parts by appeal to the necessities of the whole?

It is my view that the system forms its events, not as a matter of mere consciousness, but as a *diktat* of culture. History therefore emerges as not the source for the explanation of culture but rather as the best evidence for the shape, structure, and system that a culture comprises.

An Event as a Contingent Realization
of the Cultural Pattern

Let me offer as my initial instance not Judaism but a different matter altogether, one that gives us perspective on our question, What, in Judaism, is an event, and how, from Judaism, do we learn about the hermeneutics of events? It is the clash of cultures that produced a long-remembered event indeed, the death of Captain Cook in Hawaii two hundred years ago. Marshall Sahlins argues[7] in behalf of the view, adumbrated in my remarks, that "history is culturally ordered, differently so in different societies, according to meaningful schemes of things."[8] Sahlins further cites Clifford Geertz's observation that "an event is a unique actualization of a general phenomenon, a contingent realization of the cultural pattern." Sahlins selects as his probative case the death of Captain Cook, because he is able, through his analysis of exactly what happened, to show the cultural indicators to which "events" testify—and which explain "events."

To state matters briefly: "When the English anchored next year at Kealakekua, Hawaiian priests were able to objectify their interpretation of Cook as the Year-God Lonon, on his annual return to renew the fertility of the land." Then, when Cook came back to repair the broken mainmast, he violated the rules and had to be, and was, killed. Sahlins, in his "Anthropology of History," states the upshot with lapidary clarity: "Different cultural orders have their own modes of historical action, consciousness, and determination—their own historical practice."[9] That is not to argue in favor of historical, let alone intellectual, relativity. It is only to insist upon the study of what a culture, as represented by its documents, defines as its past the events, their order and connection, the meanings to be derived from them.

History in the Cultural Heritage of a Judaism

When we come to the case of Judaism, we bring with us a substantial intellectual heritage, composed, as a matter of fact, of misinformation or no information. First, we wrongly take for granted that Judaism (whatever else it may be) is the religion of the Old Testament. Then we have as an established fact the utter misrepresentation that Judaism is a historical religion, in that it appeals for its worldview to not myth about gods in heaven but the history of Israel upon earth—interpreted in relationship to the acts of God in heaven, to be sure. Whether history in this form materially differs from myth in the Greek form is not at issue here. I take it as a broadly held conviction, third, that Judaism is a religion that appeals to history, that is, to events, defined in the ordinary way, important happenings, for its source of testing and establishing truth.

True, what the Old Testament writers deem events is not to be gainsaid: God descending to Sinai surely proves more dramatic than the failure of rain on a village, but to Amos, what does not happen defines an event as rich in revelation as, to the Yahwist, Elohist, and Priestly authors of the strands of the Pentateuch, what does happen defines an event. The fundamentally historical character of the Old Testament narratives, with their beginnings, middles, ends, their lessons and their demonstrations—that basic historical character is so broadly held as not to require comment.

But Judaism, of course, is not only (or even mainly) the religion of the Old Testament, and, as a case in the study of the cultural definition of events, only in its full canonical expression does Judaism serve to show us how culture identifies event through its own cognitive processes. Judaism is the religion of not the Old Testament but the Torah, and the canonical Torah encompasses the Old Testament only as it is reworked, as an object of rewriting and revision, in the vast canon of the two Talmuds and the Midrash compilations that took shape in late antiquity, the first seven centuries A.D., under the title, the Oral Torah. That labor of rewriting and recasting of one thing in the light of something else that produced the Judaism of the dual Torah forms a rich set of cases in cultural transformation, in the determination, by a system, of its own past, in the identification, within a system, of its own resources. For, after all, while a system speaks through its canon, and while theologians commonly read the canon to describe the system, in point of fact it is the canon that recapitulates the system, the system that speaks, in detail to be sure, through the canon.

When, therefore, we can affirm with Sahlins that "the different cultural orders studied by anthropology have their own historicities," the result of that affirmation is not a conclusion (the relativity of historical knowledge) but a question: How shall we frame history into a cultural indicator? In the case of the Judaism of the dual Torah, the answer to that question proves quite accessible, for that Judaism makes ample use of the Old Testament in its account of itself.

We should therefore anticipate that the canon of the dual Torah will encompass narrative history, but it does not. We should expect to find therein accounts of events of not only times past but also the present explained by the past, but we do not. We should go in search of the description of one-time, unique happenings—events in the conventional sense—but, if we did, we should return disappointed. The result will be quite opposite. When we read matters properly, we shall find out how to read. For the archaeology of texts uncovers abstract structure in the identification and explication of the concrete event.[10]

This brings me directly to the problem at hand: What exactly does the Judaism of the dual Torah mean by events? What I shall now show is that events find their place, within the science of learning of *Listenwissenschaft* that characterizes this Judaism's canon, along with sorts of things that, for our part, we should not characterize as events at all. Events have no autonomous standing; events are not unique, each unto itself; events have no probative value on their own. Events form cases, along with a variety of other cases, making up lists of things that, in common, point to or prove one thing. Not only so, but events do not make up their own list at all, and this is what I found rather curious when I first noted that fact. Events will appear on the same list as persons, places, and things. That means that events not only have no autonomous standing on their own but also that events constitute no species even within a genus of a historical order. For persons, places, and things in our way of thinking do not belong on the same list as events; they are not of the same order. Within the logic of our own minds, we cannot classify the city, Paris, within the same genus as the event, the declaration of the rights of man, for instance, nor is Sinai of the same order of things as the Torah.

The Religious Uses of Historical Events

What, then, will you make of a list that encompasses within the same taxic composition events and things? One such list in a canonical document, Song of Songs Rabbah, made up of events, persons, and places, is as follows: (1) Israel at the sea; (2) the ministering angels; (3) the tent of meeting; (4) the eternal house [=the Temple]; and (5) Sinai. That mixtures an event

(Israel redeemed at the sea), a category of sensate being (angels), a location (tent of meeting, Temple), and then Sinai, which can stand for a variety of things but in context stands for the Torah. In such a list an event may or may not stand for a value or a proposition, but it does not enjoy autonomous standing; the list is not defined by the eventfulness of events and their meaning, the compilation of matters of a single genus or even a single species (tent of meeting and eternal house are the same species here). The notion of event as autonomous, even unique, is quite absent in this taxonomy.

Another such list moves from events to other matters altogether, finding the whole subject to the same metaphor, hence homogenized. First come the events that took place at these places or with these persons: Egypt, the sea, Marah, Massah and Meribah, Horeb, the wilderness, the spies in the Land, Shittim, for Achan/Joshua and the conquest of the Land. Now that mixture of places and names clearly intends to focus on particular things that happened, and hence, were the list to which I refer to conclude at this point, we could define an event for Judaism as a happening that bore consequence, taught a lesson, or exemplified a truth. For example, in the present case, an event matters because it is the mixture of rebellion and obedience. But there would then be no doubt that "event" formed a genus unto itself and that a proper list could not encompass both events, defined conventionally as we should, and also other matters altogether.

But the literary culture at hand, this textual community, proceeds, in the same literary context, to the following items: (1) the Ten Commandments; (2) the show fringes and phylacteries; (3) the Shema and the Prayer; and (4) the tabernacle and the cloud of the Presence of God in the world to come. Why we invoke, as our candidates for the metaphor at hand, the Ten Commandments, the show fringes and phylacteries, the recitation of the Shema and the Prayer, the tabernacle and the cloud of the Presence of God, and the mezuzah, seems to me clear from the very catalog. These reach their climax in the analogy between the home and the tabernacle, the embrace of God and the Presence of God. So the whole is meant to list those things which draw the Israelite near God and make the Israelite cleave to God. And to this massive catalog, events are not only exemplary—which historians can concede without difficulty—but also subordinated.

They belong on the same list as actions, things, persons, and places, because they form an order of being that is not to be differentiated between events (including things that stand for

events) and other cultural artifacts altogether. A happening is no
different from an object, in which case "event" serves no better,
and no worse, than a hero, a gesture or action, a recitation of a
given formula, or a particular locale, to establish a truth. It is
contingent, subordinate, instrumental. I can think of no more
apt illustration of Geertz's interesting judgment: "An event is a
unique actualization of a general phenomenon, a contingent realization of the cultural pattern." And why find that fact surprising, since all history comes to us in writing, and it is the culture
that dictates how writing is to take place; that is why history can
only paraphrase the affirmations of a system, and that is why
events recapitulate in acute and concrete ways the system that
classifies one thing that happens as event, but another thing is
not only not an event but is not classified at all. In the present
instance, an event is not at all eventful; it is merely a fact that
forms part of the evidence for what is, and what is eventful is
not an occasion at all but a condition, an attitude, a perspective,
and a viewpoint. Then, it is clear, events are subordinated to the
formation of attitudes, perspectives, and viewpoints—the formative artifacts of not history in the conventional sense but
culture in the framework of Sahlins' generalization that "history
is culturally ordered, differently so in different societies, according to meaningful schemes of things."

To make more concrete the evidence on which I draw, let me
refer to one important compilation of lists, of the sixth century
A.D., Song of Songs Rabbah, a reading of the Song of Songs as a
metaphorization of God's relationship of intense love for Israel
and Israel's relationship of intense love for God. In that document we find sequences, or combinations, of references to Old
Testament persons, events, actions, and the like. These bear the
rhetorical emblem "another matter," in long lists of composites
of well-framed compositions.[11] Each entry on a given list will be
represented as "another matter," meaning another interpretation of reading of a given verse in the Song of Songs. As a matter
of fact, however, that "other matter," one following the other,
turns out to be the same matter in other terms. These constructions form lists out of diverse entries. When in Song of Songs
Rabbah we have a sequence of items alleged to form a taxon,
that is, a classification of things that share a common indicator,
of course what we have is a list. The list presents diverse matters
that all together share, and therefore also set forth, a single fact
or rule or phenomenon. That is why we can list them, in all their
distinctive character and specificity, on a common catalog of
"other things" that pertain all together to one thing.

Since on these lists we find classified within a single taxon events, persons, places, objects, and actions, it is important to understand how they coalesce. The rhetoric is the key indicator, since it is objective and superficial. When we find the rhetorical formula, "another matter," that is, *davar aher,* what follows says the same thing in other words, or at least something complementary and necessary to make some larger point. That is why I insist the constructions form lists. William Scott Green states the matter, in his analysis of a single passage, in these words:

> Although the interpretations in this passage are formally distinguished from one another . . . by the disjunctive device *davar aher* ("another interpretation"), they operate within a limited conceptual sphere and a narrow thematic range. . . . Thus rather than "endless multiple meanings," they in fact ascribe to the words "doing wonders" multiple variations of a single meaning. . . . By providing multiple warrant for that message, the form effectively restricts the interpretive options.[12]

When we have a sequence of *davar aher* passages forming a *davar aher* construction, the message is cumulative, and the whole as a matter of fact forms a sum greater than that of the parts; it will then be that accumulation which guides us to what is at the foundation of matters; there is where we should find that system, order, proportion, and cogency which all together we expect a theology to impart to discrete observations about holy matters.

In general, "another matter" signals "another way of saying the same thing"; or the formula bears the sense, "These two distinct things add up to one thing," with the further proviso that both are necessary to make one point that transcends each one. Not only so, but in Song of Songs Rabbah the fixed formula of the *davar aher* compilation points toward fixed formulas of theological thought: sets of coherent verbal symbols that work together. These "other things" encompass time, space, person and object, action and attitude, and join them all together—for instance, David, Solomon, Messiah at the end of time; this age, the age to come; the exodus from Egypt, Sinai, the age to come all may appear together within a single list. Let me give a single example of the list that makes it possible to redefine "event" into a category of ahistorical valence.

Chapter Five. Song of Songs Rabbah to Song 1:5

V:i.1. A. "I am very dark, but comely [, O daughters of Jerusalem, like the tents of Kedar, like the curtains of Solomon]" (Song 1:5):

B. "I am dark" in my deeds.

C. "But comely" in the deeds of my forebears.

2. A. "I am very dark, but comely":

B. Said the Community of Israel, " 'I am dark' in my view, 'but comely' before my Creator."

C. For it is written, "Are you not as the children of the Ethiopians to Me, O children of Israel? says the Lord" (Amos 9:7):

D. "as the children of the Ethiopians"—in your sight.

E. But "to Me, O children of Israel, says the Lord."

3. A. Another interpretation of the verse, "I am very dark": in Egypt.

B. "but comely": in Egypt.

C. "I am very dark" in Egypt: "But they rebelled against me and would not hearken to me" (Ez. 20:8).

D. "but comely" in Egypt: with the blood of the Passover offering and circumcision, "And when I passed by you and saw you wallowing in your blood, I said to you, In your blood live" (Ez. 16:6)—in the blood of the Passover.

E. "I said to you, In your blood live" (Ez. 16:6)—in the blood of the circumcision.

4. A. Another interpretation of the verse, "I am very dark": at the sea, "They were rebellious at the sea, even the Red Sea" (Ps. 106:7).

B. "but comely": at the sea, "This is my God and I will be comely for him" (Ex. 15:2) [following Simon's rendering of the verse].

5. A. "I am very dark": at Marah, "And the people murmured against Moses, saying, What shall we drink?" (Ex. 15:24).

B. "but comely": at Marah, "And he cried to the Lord and the Lord showed him a tree, and he cast it into the waters and the waters were made sweet" (Ex. 15:25).

6. A. "I am very dark": at Rephidim, "And the name of the place was called Massah and Meribah" (Ex. 17:7).

B. "but comely": at Rephidim, "And Moses built an altar and called it by the name 'the Lord is my banner' " (Ex. 17:15).

7. A. "I am very dark": at Horeb, "And they made a calf at Horeb" (Ps. 106:19).

B. "but comely": at Horeb, "And they said, All that the Lord has spoken we will do and obey" (Ex. 24:7).

8. A. "I am very dark": in the wilderness, "How often did they rebel against him in the wilderness?" (Ps. 78:40).

B.   "but comely": in the wilderness at the setting up of the tabernacle, "And on the day that the tabernacle was set up" (Num. 9:15).

9. A.   "I am very dark": in the deed of the spies, "And they spread an evil report of the land" (Num. 13:32).

B.   "but comely": in the deed of Joshua and Caleb, "Save for Caleb, the son of Jephunneh the Kenizzite" (Num. 32:12).

10. A.   "I am very dark": at Shittim, "And Israel abode at Shittim and the people began to commit harlotry with the daughters of Moab" (Num. 25:1).

B.   "but comely": at Shittim, "Then arose Phinehas and wrought judgment" (Ps. 106:30).

11. A.   "I am very dark": through Achan, "But the children of Israel committed a trespass concerning the devoted thing" (Josh. 7:1).

B.   "but comely": through Joshua, "And Joshua said to Achan, My son, give I pray you glory" (Josh. 7:19).

12. A.   "I am very dark": through the kings of Israel.

B.   "but comely": through the kings of Judah.

C.   If with my dark ones that I had, it was such that "I am comely," all the more so with my prophets.

Vii.5. A.   [As to the verse, "I am very dark, but comely,"] R. Levi b. R. Haita gave these interpretations:

B.   " 'I am very dark': all the days of the week.

C.   " 'but comely': on the Sabbath.

D.   " 'I am very dark': all the days of the year.

E.   " 'but comely': on the Day of Atonement.

F.   " 'I am very dark': among the Ten Tribes.

G.   " 'but comely': in the tribe of Judah and Benjamin.

H.   " 'I am very dark': in this world.

I.   " 'but comely': in the world to come."

The contrast of dark and comely yields a variety of applications; in all of them the same situation that is the one also is the other, and the rest follows in a wonderfully well crafted composition. What is the repertoire of items? Dark in deeds but comely in ancestry; dark in my view but comely before God; dark when rebellious, comely when obedient, a point made at numbers 3 for Egypt, 4 for the sea, 5 for Marah, 6 for Massah and Meribah, 7 for Horeb, 8 for the wilderness, 9 for the spies in the Land, 10 for Shittim, 11 for Achan/Joshua and the conquest of the Land, and 12 for Israel and Judah. But look what follows: the week as against the Sabbath, the weekdays as against the Day of Atonement, the Ten Tribes as against Judah and Benjamin, this world as against the world to come. Whatever classification these next items demand for themselves, it surely will not be that of events. Indeed, if by event we mean something that happened once, as in "once upon a time," then Sabbath as against weekday, Day of Atonement as against ordinary day form a different category; the Ten Tribes as against Judah and Benjamin constitute social entities, not divisions of time; and this age and the age to come form utterly antihistorical taxa altogether.

Events not only do not form a taxon, they also do not present a vast corpus of candidates for inclusion into some other taxon. The lists in the document at hand form selections from a most limited repertoire of candidates. If we were to catalog all of the exegetical repertoire encompassed by *davar aher* constructions in this document, we should not have a very long list of candidates for inclusion in any list. And among the candidates, events are few indeed. They encompass Israel at the sea and at Sinai, the destruction of the first Temple, the destruction of the second Temple, events as defined by the actions of some holy men such as Abraham, Isaac, and Jacob (treated not for what they did but for who they were), Daniel, Mishael, Hananiah and Azariah, and the like. It follows that the restricted repertoire of candidates for taxonomic study encompasses remarkably few events, remarkably few for a literary culture that is commonly described as quintessentially historical!

The Theological Uses of History

Then what taxic indicator dictates which happenings will be deemed events and which not? What are listed throughout are not data of nature or history but of theology: God's relationship with Israel, expressed in such facts as the three events, the first two in the past, the third in the future, namely, the three redemptions of Israel, the three patriarchs, and holy persons, actions, events, what have you. These are facts that are assembled and grouped; in Song of Songs Rabbah the result is not propositional at all, or, if propositional, then essentially the repetition of familiar propositions through unfamiliar data. What we have is a kind of recombinant theology, in which the framer ("the theologian") selects from a restricted repertoire a few items for combination, sometimes to make a point (e.g., the contrast of obedient and disobedient Israel we saw just now), sometimes not. What is set on display justifies the display: putting this familiar fact together with that familiar fact in an unfamiliar combination constitutes what is new and im-

portant in the list; the consequent conclusion one is supposed
to draw, the proposition or rule that emerges—these are rarely
articulated and never important.

True, the list in Song of Songs Rabbah may comprise a rule,
or it may substantiate a proposition or validate a claim; but
more often than not, the effect of making the list is to show
how various items share a single taxic indicator, which is to
say, the purpose of the list is to make the list. The making of
connections among ordinarily not connected things is then
one outcome of *Listenwissenschaft.* What I find engaging in
davar aher constructions is the very variety of things that, on
one list or another, can be joined together—a list for its own
sake. What we have is a kind of subtle restatement, through
an infinite range of possibilities, of the combinations and recombinations of a few essentially simple facts (data). It is as
though a magician tossed a set of sticks this way and that,
interpreting the diverse combinations of a fixed set of objects.
The propositions that emerge are not the main point; the
combinations are.

That seems to me an important fact, for it tells me that the
culture at hand has defined for itself a repertoire of persons and
events and conceptions (e.g., Torah study), holy persons, holy
deeds, holy institutions, presented candidates for inclusion in
davar aher constructions, and the repertoire, while restricted
and not terribly long, made possible a scarcely limited variety of
lists of things with like taxic indicators. The same items occur
over and over again, but there is no pattern to how they recur.
By a pattern I mean that items of the repertoire may appear in
numerous *davar aher* constructions or not; they may keep company with only a fixed number of other items, or they may not.
Most things can appear in a *davar aher* composition with most
other things.[13]

The upshot is simple. List making is accomplished within a
restricted repertoire of items that can serve on lists; the list
making then presents interesting combinations of an essentially small number of candidates for the exercise. But then,
when making lists, one can do pretty much anything with the
items that are combined; the taxic indicators are unlimited, but
the data studied are severely limited. And that fact returns us
to our starting point: the observations on history as a cultural
artifact that form the premise for the study of history within
the archaeology of knowledge. In fact, in Judaism history
serves the theological sciences and therefore cannot be said to
constitute history in any ordinary sense at all; but that is a
trivial and obvious observation. More to the point, *history, in*

the form of events, contributes to a rather odd way of conducting theological science.

For, forming part of the *davar aher* construction, history constitutes one among a variety of what I call, for lack of more suitable language at this point, theological "things"[14]—names, places, events, actions deemed to bear theological weight and to affect attitude and action. The play is worked out by a reprise of available materials, composed in some fresh and interesting combination. When three or more such theological "things"—whether person, whether event, whether action, whether attitude—are combined, they form a theological structure, and, viewed all together, all of the theological "things" in a given document constitute the components of the entire theological structure that the document affords. The propositions portrayed visually, through metaphors of sight, or dramatically, through metaphors of action and relationship, or in attitude and emotion, through metaphors that convey or provoke feeling and sentiment, when translated into language prove familiar and commonplace. The work of the theologian in this context is not to say something new or even persuasive, for the former is unthinkable by definition, the latter unnecessary in context. It is, rather, to display theological "things" in a fresh and interesting way, to accomplish a fresh exegesis of the canon of theological "things."

The combinations and recombinations defined for us by our document form events into facts, sharing the paramount taxic indicators of a variety of other facts, comprising a theological structure within a larger theological structure a reworking of canonical materials. An event is therefore reduced to a "thing," losing all taxic autonomy, requiring no distinct indicator of an intrinsic order. It is simply something else to utilize in composing facts into knowledge; the event does not explain, it does not define, indeed, it does not even exist within its own framework at all. Judaism by "an event" means, in a very exact sense, nothing in particular. It is a component in a culture that combines and recombines facts into structures of its own design, an aspect of what I should call a culture that comes to full expression in recombinant theology.

We have been prepared for such a result by Jonathan Z. Smith, who has made us aware of the recombinancy of a fixed canon of "things" in his discussion of sacred persistence, that is, "the rethinking of each little detail in a text, the obsession with the significance and perfection of each little action." In the canonical literature of Judaism, these minima are worked and reworked, rethought and recast in some other way or order or combination—but always held to be the same thing throughout. In this context I find important Smith's statement:

> An almost limitless horizon of possibilities that are at hand . . .
> is arbitrarily reduced . . . to a set of basic elements. . . . Then a
> most intense ingenuity is exercised to overcome the reduction
> . . . to introduce interest and variety. This ingenuity is usually
> accompanied by a complex set of rules.[15]

The possibilities out of which the authorship of our exemplary document has made its selections are limited not by the metaphorical potential of the Song of Songs (!) but by the contents of the Hebrew Scriptures as the textual community formed of the Judaic sages defined those contents within their Torah.

For every Abraham, Isaac, and Jacob that we find, there are Job, Enoch, Jeroboam, or Zephaniah, whom we do not find; for every sea/Sinai/entry into the Land that we do find, there are other sequences—for example, the loss of the ark to the Philistines and its recovery, or Barak and Deborah—that we do not find. Ezra figures, Haggai does not; the Assyrians play a minor role, Nebuchadnezzar is on nearly every page. Granted, Sinai must enjoy a privileged position throughout. But why prefer Shadrach, Meshach, and Abednego, or Hananiah, Mishael, and Azariah, over other trilogies of heroic figures? So the selection is an act of choice, a statement of culture in miniature. But once restricted through this statement of choice, the same selected theological "things" then undergo combination and recombination with other theological things, the counterpart to Smith's "interest and variety." If we know the complex set of rules in play here, we also would understand the system that makes this document not merely an expression of piety but a statement of a theological structure: orderly, well composed and proportioned, internally coherent and cogent throughout.

The canonical, therefore anything but random, standing of events forms a brief chapter in the exegesis of a canon. That observation draws us back to Smith, who observes:

> The radical and arbitary reduction represented by the notion of
> canon and the ingenuity represented by the rule-governed ex-
> egetical enterprise to apply the canon to every dimension of hu-
> man life is that most characteristic, persistent, and obsessive
> religious activity. . . . The task of application as well as the judg-
> ment of the relative adequacy of particular applications to a
> community's life situation remains the indigenous theologian's
> task; but the study of the process, particularly the study of com-
> parative systematics and exegesis, ought to be a major preoccu-
> pation of the historian of religions.[16]

Smith speaks of religion as an "enterprise of exegetical totalization," and he further identifies with the word "canon" precisely what we have identified as the substrate and structure of the list. If I had to define an event in this canonical context, I should have to call it merely another theological thing: something to be manipulated, combined in one way or in another, along with other theological things.

Have we access to other examples of cultures that define for themselves canonical lists of counterparts to what I have called "theological things"? Indeed, defining matters as I have, I may compare the event to a fixed object in a diviner's basket of the Ndembu, as Smith describes that divinatory situation:

> Among the Ndembu there are two features of the divinatory situation that are crucial to our concern: the diviner's basket and his process of interrogating his client. The chief mode of divination consists of shaking a basket in which some twenty-four fixed objects are deposited (a cock's claw, a piece of hoof, a bit of grooved wood, . . . withered fruit, etc.). These are shaken in order to winnow out "truth from falsehood" in such a way that few of the objects end up on top of the heap. These are "read" by the diviner both with respect to their individual meanings and their combinations with other objects and the configurations that result.[17]

In Song of Songs Rabbah, Abraham, Isaac, Jacob, or the sea and Sinai, or Hananiah, Mishael, and Azariah, are the counterpart to the cock's claw and the piece of hoof. The event, in Judaism, is the counterpart to a cock's claw in the Ndembu culture. Both will be fixed but will combine and recombine in a large number of different ways. But then what of "the lessons of history," and how shall we identify the counterpart to historical explanation? I find the answer in the Ndembu counterpart, the mode of reading "the process of interrogating the client." Again Smith:

> The client's situation is likewise taken into account in arriving at an interpretation. Thus . . . there is a semantic, syntactic, and pragmatic dimension to the "reading." Each object is publicly known and has a fixed range of meanings. . . . The total collection of twenty-four objects is held to be complete and capable of illuminating every situation. . . . What enables the canon to be applied to every situation or question is not the number of objects. . . . Rather it is that, prior to performing the divination, the diviner has rigorously questioned his client in order to determine his situation with precision. . . . It is the genius of the inter-

preter to match a public set of meanings with a commonly
known set of facts . . . in order to produce a quite particular
plausibility structure which speaks directljy to his client's condition, which mediates between that which is public knowledge
and the client's private perception of his unique situation.[18]

That concludes our inquiry, since it draws us to the task of the
exegesis of exegesis. Events then form a problem of exegesis, in
which, we find our way back to the system and structure that
that culture means to form. The work before us will teach us, in
the case of Judaism, how from the study of what are defined as
events to describe the process of interrogation that has produced the result we see before us, this particular plausibility
structure that has persuaded holy Israel, from then to now (as
indeed all the Israels that revere the Song of Songs have been
persuaded), to read the erotic as the best, the only way to express precisely who is God in relationship to Israel and who is
Israel in relationship to God. The theology of this Judaism—
that is to say, our account of the worldview that comes to expression within this literary culture and textual community—
will take shape within the exegesis of that exegesis. What all
this has to do with philology and positive historical facts I cannot say. Then where to begin? As I argued at the outset, it is
with the conception of religion as arbiter of the social system:
Judaism and the social order.

VI

Philosophy and Religion:
The First Two Stages
in the Formation of Judaism

Outlining a Constructive Program

If not history or biography, then what? In this and the next three chapters I set forth the program that has now gotten under way: what we know about the formation of the Judaism of the dual Torah. Here are the answers precipitated by questions of the analysis of religious literature read as the statement of a religious system. Making a powerful commitment to the study of a Judaism through the systematic reading of its sources, the new approach asks about how a Judaism as a system takes shape in the light of its canonical formation. Further, differentiating stages or components of a larger systemic mosaic, we compare and contrast two or more systems set forth by canonical documents, seen as both autonomous of one another (represented, e.g., by separate documents) and also connected with one another.

The formation of the Judaism of the dual Torah worked through three distinct phases, yielding three Judaic systems, the second and third connected to the first and to one another; each is to be characterized in its own terms and also placed in relationship with the others in succession. Comparison shows that the first is to be classified as a philosophical Judaic system ("a Judaism as a philosophy"), the second, a religious Judaic system.[1]

Systemic description begins with the written evidence that points us toward the outlines of the intellectual structure upon which the theory of the social order is constructed. That evidence, when deemed authoritative, forms the canon of the system. The canon recapitulates the system that animates the mentality of both the framers of canonical writers and also the authorities who adopted those writings for a single canonical composition. To study a Judaism, accordingly, we turn to the canon of the Judaism under study to seek its evidence concerning the categories that comprise any account of society: the philosophy, politics, and economics of a Judaism.[2]

The Canonical Writings in Sequence

To begin with, therefore, let us gain perspective on the canon of the Judaism that emerged from ancient times and governed to our own day. That canon, called the Torah, in two parts, written and oral, consisted of the Hebrew Scriptures of ancient Israel (the Old Testament), called in this Judaism "the written Torah," and a set of writings later on accorded the status of Torah as well and assigned origin at Sinai through a process of oral formulation and oral transmission, hence "the oral Torah."

The first of those writings which came to comprise the oral Torah, the single most important one, was the Mishnah, ca. A.D. 200. That document carried in its wake two sustained amplifications and extensions called talmuds, the one produced in the Land of Israel, hence the Talmud of the Land of Israel, ca. A.D. 400, the other in Babylonia, in the Iranian Empire, hence the Talmud of Babylonia, ca. A.D. 600.

The other important part of the Torah, the written part, served analogously to define a framework for (formally) continuous discourse and so received a variety of sustained amplifications, called Midrash compilations. These form three sets, corresponding to the Mishnah, the Talmud of the Land of Israel, and the Talmud of Babylonia.

1. *The Mishnah's Counterparts in Midrash Compilations:* The first, within the orbit of the Mishnah, ca. A.D. 200–300, addressed the books of Exodus, Leviticus, Numbers, and Deuteronomy, in Mekhilta Attributed to R. Ishmael for Exodus, Sifra, for Leviticus, one Sifré to Numbers, another Sifré to Deuteronomy.

2. *The Yerushalmi's Counterparts in Midrash Compilations:* The second, ca. A.D. 400–500, associated with the first of the two Talmuds, took up the books of Genesis and Leviticus, in Genesis Rabbah and Leviticus Rabbah, and the latter begat Pesiqta deRab Kahana in its model.

3. *The Bavli's Counterparts in Midrash Compilations:* The third, ca. A.D. 500–600, identified with the second Talmud, addressed a lectionary cycle of the synagogue, dealing with the

books of Lamentations (read on the ninth of Ab), Esther (read on Purim), Ruth (read on Pentecost), and Song of Songs (read on Passover), in Lamentations Rabbah, Esther Rabbah I (the first two chapters only), Ruth Rabbah, and Song of Songs Rabbah.

The first of the three groups presents marks of transition and mediation from one system to the next.[3] The second, Genesis Rabbah and Leviticus Rabbah, joined by Pesiqta deRab Kahana, with the Talmud of the Land of Israel, attests to that system which I classify as religious. The third, the final Rabbah compilations together with the Talmud of Babylonia, points to the one I classify as theological, and in a moment I shall define the indicative traits of each classification.

The Analytical Program of Systemic Analysis: Description

Now, as is clear, the documentary evidence set forth a system of a very particular kind: one that laid out the components of the social order and explained how they formed a cogent whole. From beginning to end, the Judaic systems attested by the successive parts of the canon defined as their problem the construction of a social world. The categorical structure of each, in succession, framed intelligible thought by appeal to the issues of the world framed, first of all, by a particular ethnos, the social entity (the most neutral language I can find), which was called (an) "Israel." Every Judaic system, moreover, would take as its task the definition of the shared life of (an) Israel: its way of life or (broadly speaking) ethics, its worldview or ethos. So each set forth the account of the social entity, or the "Israel," that realized in its shared and corporate being the ethics (again, broadly construed), and explained that ethos by appeal to the ethos. As a matter of definition, it must follow, a Judaic system is a system that derives its generative categories from the (theoretical) requirements of framing a social order: who "we" are, what we do together, and why we are the corporate body that we are; thus, ethnos, ethics, ethos. And that brings us back to the first of the great Judaic systems that in the end formed Judaism, the system to which the authorships of the Mishnah refer in framing their writing.

The Mishnah set forth in the form of a law code a highly philosophical account of the world ("worldview"), a pattern for everyday and material activities and relationships ("way of life"), and a definition of the social entity ("nation," "people," "us" as against "outsiders," "Israel") that realized that way of life and explained it by appeal to that worldview. Then the successor documents, closed roughly two centuries later, addressed the Mishnah's system and recast its categories into a connected, but also quite revised, one.

Why call them "successors"? Because, in form, the writings of the late fourth and fifth centuries were organized and presented as commentaries on a received text, the Mishnah for the Talmud, Scripture for the Midrash compilations. So the later authorships insisted, in their own behalf, that they (merely) explained and amplified the received Torah. When these documents attached themselves to the Mishnah, on the one side, and the Hebrew Scriptures, on the other, they gave literary form to the theory that the one stood for the oral, the other the written, revelation, or Torah, that God gave to Moses at Mt. Sinai.

Specifically, the Talmud of the Land of Israel, formed around thirty-nine of the Mishnah's sixty-two tractates, and Genesis Rabbah and Leviticus Rabbah (joined by Pesiqta deRab Kahana), addressed the first and third books of Moses, respectively, along with some other documents. The very act of choosing among the Mishnah's tractates only some and ignoring others, of course, represents an act of taste and judgment— hence system-building through tacit statement made by silence. But, as a matter of fact, much of the Talmud as well as of the principal Midrash compilations does amplify and augment the base documents to which they are attached.[4] In choosing some passages and neglecting others, and, more to the point, in working out their own questions and their own answers, in addition to those of the Mishnah, the authorships[5] attest to a system that did more than merely extend and recast the categorical structure of the system for which the Mishnah stands. They took over the way of life, worldview, and social entity, defined in the Mishnah's system. And while they rather systematically amplified details, framed a program of exegesis around the requirements of clerks engaged in enforcing the rules of the Mishnah, they built their own system.

The Analytical Program of Systemic Analysis: Comparison of Systems

At the same time, they formed categories corresponding to those of the Mishnah: a politics, a philosophy, and an economics. But these categories proved so utterly contrary in their structure and definition to those of the Mishnah that they presented mirror images of the received categories. The politics, philosophy, and economics of the Mishnah were joined by what we must call an antipolitics, an antieconomics, and an utterly transformed mode of learning that redefined altogether what was at stake in the intellect and as a matter of fact recast not the issues so much as the very stakes of philosophy or science. The reception of the Mishnah's category formations and their transformation therefore stands for the movement from a philosophical to a religious mode of thinking. For the system to which the Mishnah as a document attests is essentially philosophical in its rhetorical, logical, and topical program. The successor system is fundamentally religious in these same principal and indicative traits of medium of intellect and mentality.

The Mishnah's philosophy, economics, and politics corresponded to the categories worldview, way of life, and social entity, which have already been set forth. The philosophy explained how to think, identified the agenda for sustained thought and learning, and proved a proposition of fundamental importance. Not only so, but in the context of Greco-Roman philosophy the method and proposition are to be classifed as philosophical: Aristotle's method of natural history, Middle Platonism's doctrine of the hierarchical unity of being. The Mishnah's economics set forth a theory of rational action in the face of scarcity and in the increase and disposition of wealth. It corresponded, point by point, with the economics of Aristotle. And the Mishnah's politics laid out an account of precisely how power, encompassing legitimate violence, embodied in institutions and their staff, was to realize in everyday social transactions the social entity, "Israel." The politics in most of its definitive traits corresponded to that of Aristotle as well.[6]

The Talmud of the Land of Israel for the Mishnah, the Midrash compilations Genesis Rabbah and Leviticus Rabbah together with Pesiqta deRab Kahana for Scripture, not only subjected these categories to expansion. These same documents undertook a vast labor of category formation of their own. Their authors set forth their own categories for those served, initially, by philosophy, politics, and economics. When we compare and contrast the Mishnah in its classification as to rhetoric and logic with the successor documents, we find those later writings' category formations not at all like those of the Mishnah. Not only did they accomplish the transformation of the received categories in the initial structure, that is, the Judaic structure of the social order, laid out philosophically. They also set forth categorical reformation of the same structure, that is, once more in categorical terms, the Judaic structure of the social order, now, however, categorized in a fresh way, religiously. The systemic consequence of this transformation was the representation of a Judaism, now as a religious system.

This contrast of a philosophical to a religious classification of a whole system requires me to answer a fundamental question. How do I know whether a system is philosophical or religious? The indicative traits in both instances, to begin with, derive from and are displayed by documents, for—I take it as axiomatic—the mode of the writing down of any system attests to both the method and the message that sustain that system. From how people express themselves, we work our way backward to their modes of thought: the classification of perceived data, the making of connections between fact and fact, the drawing of conclusions from those connections, and, finally, the representation of conclusions in cogent compositions. All of these traits of mind are to be discerned in the character of those compositions, in the rhetoric that conveys messages in proportion and appropriate aesthetics, in the logic that imparts self-evidence to the making of connections, the drawing of conclusions, and in the representation of sets of conclusions as cogent and intelligible, characteristic of writing and expressed in writing.

That is why we turn to analyze the evidence of documents when we ask how people think, here meaning the logic of their intelligible thought and discourse. We further identify the medium by which they frame their message, here meaning the rules of their formal rhetoric. On the basis of these indicators we can account for that union of disciplined rhetoric and logic which comprises the media of expression and the modes of thought of a well-crafted system. From that description the analysis of the system gets under way through the process of comparison and contrast of the traits discerned, to begin with, in documentary inquiry. For the logic, rhetoric, and topical program of one set of writings can be described and compared with the same traits of another. So evidence for the classification of systems that set forth a theory of the social order, their differentiation, for instance, as to philosophy or religion, derives, to begin with, from the use of language, in particular the rules for correct representation of thought, in the right form, that, in general, we know as rhetoric.

From the surface, the rhetoric, we move inward, into the logic of the processes of thought encapsulated in that language. This evidence derives from the argumentation in behalf of a proposition, the kind of evidence and the manner of marshaling that evidence. Since active thought takes place when people see a connection between one thing and something else and determine to explain that connection in one way rather than in some other, we ask what makes a connection self-evident, so that one thing fits with some other, while a third thing does not fit in or make sense at all in connection with the first two things. We have in hand ample evidence, written evidence, of both the decisions that people reached, the ways in which they framed their propositions, and also the expectation that others within the group educated in their writings and manners of thought would find the result compelling.[7]

VII

The Formation of Judaism:
The Mishnah
and Philosophy

The Philosophical Character of the Mishnah's
Method and Paramount Proposition

The Mishnah, seen whole, presents a profoundly philosophical system, one that consistently applies a distinctively philosophical method of analysis to numerous cases to make a single general point, which is also of a philosophical character. The Mishnah's philosophical method derives from the natural history of Aristotle and aims at the hierarchical classification of all things. All things in place, in proper rank and position in the hierarchy of being, point to and stand for one thing. I suppose that, in the context of Scripture, with its insistence that Israel's God is one and unique, we may take as the unarticulated premise a theological position and, it would follow, identify as premise that fundamental and ancient affirmation of Israel.

But we deal with a composition that is everywhere systematically philosophical and only rarely, and then episodically, theological. Two-thirds of all tractates focus upon issues of philosophy, and scarcely a line of the Mishnah invokes the word "God" or calls upon the active presence of God. More to the point, the document at no point addresses such theological questions as the meaning and end of history, the nature of prophecy, nature and supernature, the being of God, miracles, and the like.[1] True, answers to these questions assuredly lie at, or even lay, the foundations for the philosophical structure. But the Judaism attested by the Mishnah asks the questions that philosophers ask, concerning the nature of things, and answers them in the way the philosophers answer them, through an orderly sifting of data in the process of natural philosophy.

The only point of difference is subject matter. But, after all, philosophers in the great tradition took up multiple questions; some worked on this, some on the other thing, and no single question predominated.

The Mishnah's Generative Proposition

To identify the telos of thought in the Mishnah, I state the generative proposition of the Mishnah very simply: In the Mishnah, many things are made to say one thing, which concerns the nature of being, that all being is teleologically hierarchized, to state matters in simple terms. The system of the Mishnah registers these two contrary propositions: [1] many things are one, [2] one thing is many. These propositions of course complement each other, because, in forming matched opposites, the two provide a complete and final judgment of the whole. The philosophy of Judaism must be deemed ontological, for it is a statement of an ontological order that the system makes when it claims that all things are not only orderly but ordered in such wise that many things fall into one classification, and one thing may hold together many things of a single classification.

For this philosophy, rationality consists in a hierarchical order of things. That rationality is demonstrated within the facts of this world by the possibility always of effecting the hierarchical classification of all things: each thing in its taxon, all taxa in correct sequence, from least to greatest. And showing that all things can be ordered, and that all orders can be set into relationship with one another, we transform method into message. The message of hierarchical classification is that many things really form a single thing, the many species a single genus, the many genera an encompassing and well-crafted, cogent whole. Every time we speciate, we affirm that position; each successful labor of forming relationships among species, for example, making them into a genus, or identifying the hierarchy of the species, proves it again. Not only so, but when we can show that many things are really one, or that one thing yields many (the reverse and confirmation of the former), we say in a fresh way a single immutable truth, the one of this philosophy concerning the unity of all being in an orderly composition of all things within a single taxon.

How the Mishnah Demonstrates the Hierarchical Unity of Being

To show how this works, I turn to a very brief sample of the Mishnah's authorship's sustained effort to demonstrate that many classes of things—actions, relationships, circumstances, persons, places—really form one class, or one class forms many. This supererogatory work of classification then works its way through the potentialities of chaos to explicit order. It is classification transformed from the how of intellection to the why and the what for and, above all, the what does it all mean. Recognition that one thing may fall into several categories and many things into a single one comes to expression, for the authorship of the Mishnah, in diverse ways. One of the interesting ones is the analysis of the several taxa into which a single action may fall, with an account of the multiple consequences, for example, as to sanctions that are called into play, for a single action. The right taxonomy of persons, actions, and things will show the unity of all being by finding many things in one thing, and that forms the first of the two components of what I take to be the philosophy's teleology.

Mishnah Tractate Keritot 3:9

A. There is one who ploughs a single furrow and is liable on eight counts of violating a negative commandment:

B. [specifically, it is] he who (1) ploughs with an ox and an ass [Deut. 22:10], which are (2, 3) both Holy Things, in the case of (4) [ploughing] Mixed Seeds in a vineyard [Deut. 22:9], (5) in the Seventh Year [Lev. 25:4], (6) on a festival [Lev. 23:7] and who was both a (7) priest [Lev. 21:1] and (8) a Nazirite [Num. 6:6] [ploughing] in a grave-yard.

C. Hanania b. Hakhinai says, "Also: He is [ploughing while] wearing a garment of diverse kinds" [Lev. 19:19; Deut. 22:11).

D. They said to him, "This is not within the same class."

E. He said to them, "Also the Nazir [B8] is not within the same class [as the other transgressions]."

Here is a case in which more than a single set of flogging is called for. B's felon is liable to 312 stripes, on the listed counts. The ox is sanctified to the altar, the ass to the upkeep of the house (B2, 3). Hanania's contribution is rejected, since it has nothing to do with ploughing, and the sages' position is equally flawed. The main point, for our inquiry, is simple. The one action draws in its wake multiple consequences. Classifying a single thing as a mixture of many things then forms a part of the larger intellectual address to the nature of mixtures. But it yields a result that, in the analysis of an action, far transcends the metaphysical problem of mixtures, because it moves us toward the ontological solution of the unity of being.

The real interest in demonstrating the unity of being lies not in things but in abstractions, and among abstractions *types* of actions take the center stage. Mishnah tractate Keritot works out how many things are really one thing. This is accomplished by showing the end or consequence of diverse actions to be always one and the same. The issue of the tractate is the definition of occasions on which one is obligated to bring a sin offering and a suspensive guilt offering. The tractate lists those sins which are classified together by the differentiating criterion of intention. If one deliberately commits those sins, he is punished through extirpation. If it is done inadvertently, he brings a sin offering. In case of doubt as to whether or not a sin has been committed (hence: inadvertently), he brings a suspensive guilt offering. Leviticus 5:17–19 specifies that if one sins but does not know it, he brings a sin offering or a guilt offering. Then if he does, a different penalty is invoked, with the suspensive guilt offering at stake as well. While we have a sustained exposition of implications of facts that Scripture has provided, the tractate also covers problems of classification of many things as one thing, in the form of a single sin offering for multiple sins, and that problem fills the bulk of the tractate.

Mishnah Tractate Keritot 1:1, 2, 7; 3:2, 4

1:1 A. Thirty-six transgressions subject to extirpation are in the Torah . . .

1:2 A. For those [transgressions] are people liable, for deliberately doing them, to the punishment of extirpation,

    B. and for accidentally doing them, to the bringing of a sin offering,

    C. and for not being certain of whether or not one has done them, to a suspensive guilt offering [Lev. 5:17]—

    D. "except for the one who imparts uncleanness to the sanctuary and its Holy Things,

    E. "because he is subject to bringing a sliding scale offering (Lev. 5:6-7, 11)," the words of R. Meir.

    F. And sages say, "Also: [except for] the one who blasphemes, as it is said, 'You shall have one law for him that does anything unwittingly' (Num. 15:29)—excluding the blasphemer, who does no concrete deed."

1:7 A. The woman who is subject to a doubt concerning [the appearance of] five fluxes,

    B. or the one who is subject to a doubt concerning five miscarriages

    C. brings a single offering.

D. And she [then is deemed clean so that she] eats animal sacrifices.

E. And the remainder [of the offerings, A, B] are not an obligation for her.

F. [If she is subject to] five confirmed miscarriages,

G. or five confirmed fluxes,

H. she brings a single offering.

I. And she eats animal sacrifices.

J. But the rest [of the offerings, the other four] remain as an obligation for her [to bring at some later time]—

K. M'SH S: A pair of birds in Jerusalem went up in price to a golden denar.

L. Said Rabban Simeon b. Gamaliel, "By this sanctuary! I shall not rest tonight until they shall be at [silver] denars."

M. He entered the court and taught [the following law]:

N. "The woman who is subject to five confirmed miscarriages [or] five confirmed fluxes brings a single offering.

O. "And she eats animal sacrifices.

P. "And the rest [of the offerings] do not remain as an obligation for her."

Q. And pairs of birds stood on that very day at a quarter-denar each [one one-hundredth of the former price].

3:2 A. [If] he ate [forbidden] fat and [again ate] fat in a single spell of inadvertence, he is liable only for a single sin offering,

B. [If] he ate forbidden fat and blood and remnant and refuse [of an offering] in a single spell of inadvertence, he is liable for each and every one of them.

C. This rule is more strict in the case of many kinds [of forbidden food] than of one kind.

D. And more strict is the rule in [the case of] one kind than in many kinds:

E. For if he ate a half-olive's bulk and went and ate a half-olive's bulk of a single kind, he is liable.

F. [But if he ate two half-olive's bulks] of two [different] kinds, he is exempt.

3:4 A. There is he who carries out a single act of eating and is liable on its account for four sin offerings and one guilt offering:

B. An unclean [lay] person who ate (1) forbidden fat, and it was (2) remnant (3) of Holy Things, and (4) it was on the Day of Atonement.

C. R. Meir says, "If it was the Sabbath and he took it out [from one domain to another] in his mouth, he is liable [for another sin offering]."

D. They said to him, "That is not of the same sort [of transgression of which we have spoken heretofore since it is not caused by eating a]."

Mishnah Keritot 1:7 introduces the case of classifying several incidents within a single taxon, so that one incident encompasses a variety of cases and therefore one penalty or sanction covers a variety of instances. That same conception is much more amply set forth in chapter 2 of the same tractate. There we have lists of five who bring a single offering for many transgressions, five who bring a sliding-scale offering for many incidents, and the like, so M. Ker. 2:3–6. Then at M. Ker. 3:1–3 we deal with diverse situations in which a man is accused of having eaten forbidden fat and therefore of owing a sin offering. At M. Ker. 3:1 the issue is one of disjoined testimony. Do we treat as one the evidence of two witnesses? The debate concerns whether two cases form a single category. Sages hold that the cases are hardly the same, because there are differentiating traits. M. Ker. 3:2–3 shows us how we differentiate or unify several acts. We have several acts of transgression in a single spell of inadvertence; we classify them all as one action for purposes of the penalty. That at stake is the problem of classification and how we invoke diverse taxic indicators is shown vividly at M. Ker. 3:2 in particular. Along these same lines are the issues of M. Ker. 3:3, 4–6: "There is he who carries out a single act of eating and is liable on its account for four sin offerings and one guilt offering; there is he who carries out a single act of sexual intercourse and becomes liable on its account for six sin offerings," with the first shown at M. Ker. 3:4.

The recognition that one thing becomes many does not challenge the philosophy of the unity of all being but confirms the main point. The main point of Judaism is that God is one, alone, unique. Then if I can show that God is the source of all being, I form out of the facts of this world an argument in favor of the oneness of God, source of all being, to whom all things refer, from whom all things come. And this is a philosophical proposition when it draws upon the facts of this world. The reason is that I appeal not to revelation—Scripture, for example, or the Torah—but to the natural world and its traits. Why do I insist on that proposition? The reason is simple. If we can show that differentiation flows from within what is differentiated—that is, from the intrinsic or inherent traits of things—then we confirm that at the heart of things is a fundamental ontological being, single, cogent, simple, that is capable of diversification, yielding complexity and diversity. The upshot is to be stated with emphasis. *That diversity in species or diversification in action follows orderly lines confirms the claim that there is that single point from which many lines come forth.* Carried out in proper order—(1) the many form one thing, and (2) one thing yields many—the demonstration then leaves no doubt as to the truth of the matter. Ideally, therefore, we shall argue from the simple to the complex, showing that the one yields the many, one thing, many things, two, four. It follows that one thing yields many things, and therefore God, the One, is the source of all being. Many things point to one thing and therefore to God, who holds together and makes one and cogent all of the manifestations of being. So we are dealing with a natural philosophy, one that uses the facts of the natural and social world to make the points of theology.

Mishnah Tractate Shabbat 1:1

1:1 A. [Acts of] transporting objects from one domain to another, [which violate] the Sabbath, (1) are two, which [indeed] are four [for one who is] inside, (2) and two which are four [for one who is] outside.

B. How so?

C. [If on the Sabbath] the beggar stands outside and the householder inside,

D. [and] the beggar stuck his hand inside and put [a beggar's bowl] into the hand of the householder,

E. or if he took [something] from inside it and brought it out,

F. the beggar is liable, the householder is exempt.

G. [If] the householder stuck his hand outside and put [something] into the hand of the beggar,

H. or if he took [something] from it and brought it inside,

I. the householder is liable, and the beggar is exempt.

J. [If] the beggar stuck his hand inside, and the householder took [something] from it,

K. or if [the householder] put something in it and he [the beggar] removed,

L. both of them are exempt.

M. [If] the householder put his hand outside and the beggar took [something] from it,

N. or if [the beggar] put something into it and [the householder] brought it back inside,

O. both of them are exempt.

Mishnah Shabbat 1:1 classifies diverse circumstances of transporting objects from private to public domain. The purpose is to assess the rules that classify as culpable or exempt from culpability diverse arrangements. The operative point is that a prohibited action is culpable only if one and the same person commits the whole of the violation of the law. If two or more people share in the single action, neither of them is subject to punishment. At stake therefore is the conception that one thing may be many things, and if that is the case, then culpability is not incurred by any one actor. The Sabbath exposition appears so apt and perfect for the present proposition that readers may wonder whether the authorship of the Mishnah could accomplish that same wonder of concision of complex thought more than a single time. Joining rhetoric, logic, and specific proposition transforms thought into not merely expository prose but poetry.

Have I given a proof consisting of one case? Quite to the contrary, the document contains a plethora of exercises of the same kind. My final demonstration of the power of speciation in demonstrating the opposite, namely, the generic unity of species and the hierarchy that orders them, derives from the treatment of oaths, to which we now turn. The basic topical program of Mishnah tractate Shabuot responds systematically to the potpourri of subjects covered by Leviticus 5 and 6 within the (to the Priestly author) unifying rubric of those who bring a guilt offering. Leviticus 5:1–6 concerns oaths, an oath of testimony, and one who touches something unclean in connection with the Temple cult, and finally, one who utters a rash oath.

Mishnah Tractate Shabuot 1:1–2; 2:1

1:1 A. Oaths are of two sorts, which yield four subdivisions.
    B. Awareness of [having sinned through] uncleanness is of two sorts, which yield four subdivisions.
    C. Transportation [of objects from one domain to the other] on the Sabbath is of two sorts, which yield four subdivisions.
    D. The symptoms of negas are of two sorts, which yield four subdivisions.
1:2 A. In any case in which there is awareness of uncleanness at the outset and awareness [of uncleanness] at the end but unawareness in the meantime—lo, this one is subject to bringing an offering of variable value.
    B. [If] there is awareness [of uncleanness] at the outset but no apprehension [of uncleanness] at the end, a goat which [yields blood to be sprinkled] within [in the Holy of Holies], and the Day of Atonement suspend [the punishment],
    C. until it will be made known to the person, so that he may bring an offering of variable value.

2:1 A. Awareness of uncleannesses of two sorts, which yield four
      subdivisions [M. 1:lB].
    B. (1) [If] one was made unclean and knew about it, then the
      uncleanness left his mind, but he knew [that the food he
      had eaten was] Holy Things,
    C. (2) the fact that the food he had eaten was Holy Things left
      his mind, but he knew about [his having contracted] un-
      cleanness,
    D. (3) both this and that left his mind, but he ate Holy Things
      without knowing it and after he ate them, he realized it—
    E. lo, this one is liable to bring an offering of variable value.
    F. (1) [If] he was made unclean and knew about it, and the
      uncleanness left his mind, but he remembered that he was
      in the sanctuary;
    G. (2) the fact that he was in the sanctuary left his mind, but
      he remembered that he was unclean,
    H. (3) both this and that left his mind, and he entered the
      sanctuary without realizing it, and then when he had left
      the sanctuary, he realized it—lo, this one is liable to bring
      an offering of variable value.

Mishnah Shabuot 1:1–7; 2:1–5 accomplishes the speciation
of oaths, on the one side, and uncleanness in regard to the
cult, on the other. That work of speciation then joins two
utterly disparate subjects, oaths and uncleanness, so showing
a unity of structure that forms a metaphysical argument for
the systemic proposition on the unity of being. We do so in a
way that is now to be predicted. It is by showing that many
things are one thing, now, as I said, oaths, uncleanness. When
the Priestly author joined the same subjects, it was because a
single offering was involved for diverse and distinct sins or
crimes. When the mishnaic author does, it is because a single
inner structure sustains these same diverse and distinct sins
or crimes. Comparing the Priestly with the Mishnah's strategy
of exposition underlines the remarkable shift accomplished
by our philosophers. Their power of formulation—rhetoric,
logic together—of course, works to demonstrate through the
medium the message that these enormously diverse subjects
in fact can be classified within a simple taxonomic principle.
It is that there are two species to a genus, and two subspecies
to each species, and these are readily determined by appeal to
fixed taxic indicators. An abstract statement of the rule of
classification (and, it must follow, also hierarchization) will
have yielded less useful intellectual experience than the remarkably well balanced concrete exemplification of the rule,

and that is precisely what we have in Mishnah tractate Shabuot 1 and 2.

The main point of differentiation—the taxic indicator—derives from the intersecting issues of a divided sequence of time frames and of awareness. If one knows something at one point in a differentiated process ("the outset," "the meantime," "the end") but does not know that thing at some other point, then we have a grid in two dimensions: sequence of time and sequence of spells of awareness or unawareness. And then the taxic indicators are in place, so the process of speciation and subspeciation is routine. At stake is the power of the taxic indicator. What is stunning is that the same process of speciation and subspeciation is explicitly applied to utterly unrelated matters, which demonstrates for all to see that the foundations of knowledge lie in method, which makes sense of chaos, and method means correct knowledge of the classification of things and the ability to identify the taxic indicators that make classification possible. All of this prepares the way for the treatment of oaths, Mishnah tractate Shabuot 3:1–8:6, that is, the entire tractate.

The God of a Philosophical Judaism

The upshot may be stated very simply. The species point to the genus, all classes to one class, all taxa properly hierarchized then rise to the top of the structure and the system forming one taxon. So all things ascend to and reach one thing. All that remains is for the philosopher as theologian to define that one thing: God. But that is a step that the philosophers of the Mishnah did not take. Perhaps it was because they did not think they had to. But I think there is a different reason altogether. It is because, as a matter of fact, they were philosophers. And to philosophers, as I said at the outset, God serves as premise and principle (and whether or not it is one God or many gods, a unique being or a being that finds a place in a class of similar beings hardly is germane!), and philosophy serves not to demonstrate principles or to explore premises but to analyze the unknown, to answer important questions.

In such an enterprise the premise, God, turns out to be merely instrumental. But for philosophers, intellectuals, God can live not in the details but in the unknowns, in the as yet unsolved problem and the unresolved dilemma. So, I think, in the philosophy of Judaism, God lives, so to speak, in the excluded middle. God is revealed in the interstitial case. God is made known through the phenomena that form a single phenomenon. God is perceived in the one that is many. God is encountered in the many that are one. For that is the dimension of being—that immanental and sacramental dimension of being—that defines for this philosophy its statement of ultimate concern, its recurrent point of tension, its generative problematic.

That then is the urgent question, the ineluctable and self-evidently truthful answer: God in the form, God in the order, God in the structure, God in the heights, God at the head of the great chain of hierarchical being. True, God is premise, scarcely mentioned. But it is because God's name does not have to be mentioned when the whole of the order of being says that name, and only that name, and always that name, the Name unspoken because it is always in the echo, the silent, thin voice, the numinous in all phenomena.

A Philosophical Judaism in Philosophical Context: The Mishnah's System, Aristotle, and Neoplatonism

Among the philosophers of that time and place, which is to say within important components of the philosophical tradition that sustained the Greco-Roman world, however arcane the subject matter of the philosophy of Judaism, the philosophers of Judaism can claim a rightful, and honored, place. I shall now show that among the philosophers, Judaism's philosophy can and should have been perceived not merely as philosophical but, indeed, as philosophy. The basis for that claim is simple: whether or not philosophers can have understood a line of the document (and I doubt that they would have cared to try), the method and the message of the philosophy of Judaism fall into the classification of philosophical methods and messages of the Greco-Roman philosophical tradition. The method is like that of Aristotle, the message, congruent to that of Neoplatonism.[2] To state the upshot of the proposition at hand, Judaism's first system, the Mishnah's, finds its natural place within philosophy first because it appeals to the Aristotelian methods of natural philosophy—classification, comparison, and contrast—and the media of expression of philosophy—*Listenwissenschaft*—to register its position.[3]

As to method, can we classify the taxonomic method—premises and rules—of the sages in the same category as the method of Aristotle? This is the question that yields answers on the methodological context in which the philosophy of Judaism is to be located. And in this setting by "context" we mean something piquantly appropriate to our results: the classification of the philosophy. For, as I shall now show, our back-country philosophers in a fairly primitive way replicated the method of Aristotle in setting forth the single paramount proposition of Neoplatonism.[4]

Having said that, I hasten to add this qualification. The issue is not one of direct connection. None conjures the fantasy and anachronism of the Mishnah's authorship's tramping down a Galilean hill from their yeshiva to the academy in a nearby Greek-speaking town, Caesarea or Sepphoris, for example, there studying elementary Aristotle and listening to the earliest discourses of Neoplatonism, then climbing back up the hill and writing it all up in their crabbed idiom made up of the cases and examples of the Mishnah.

But as a matter of fact, in its indicative traits of message and method, the Mishnah's philosophical system is a version of one critical proposition of Neoplatonism, set forth and demonstrated through a standard Aristotelian method.[5] And that is what an examination of the philosophical context will show us. But—I cannot overstress—these judgments rest not upon a claim of direct connection but upon an exercise of simple, inductive comparison and contrast, that is to say, of mere classification.[6] I propose now only in an entirely inductive manner to classify the system by the indicative traits of philosophical systems. In that simple way I shall show that in one of the two fundamental aspects—method and message—this system shares traits important to systems that all deem to be philosophical. Therefore this system by the criteria of philosophy and in the specific and explicit context of philosophy must be classified as philosophical. That is my simple argument. But it is fundamental to my purpose, which is to show that in the Mishnah's system, both as to mode of thought and as to message, we deal with a philosophy—philosophy in an odd idiom to be sure, but philosophy nonetheless.[7]

Let me ask the question in its simplest form: By appeal to the paramount taxic traits of Aristotelian method, can we classify the method as Aristotelian? If we can, then my purpose, which is to demonstrate that the Judaism of the Mishnah is a philosophy, will have been accomplished. That is as far as we can go: no farther. But it suffices to accomplish the goal of demonstrating that, as to the method of classification, the Mishnah's is philosophical, in the way in which Greco-Roman philosophy, exemplified by Aristotle, is philosophical. True, we cannot show, and therefore do not know, that the Mishnah's philosophers read Aristotle's work on natural history or his reflections on scientific method, for example, the *Posterior Analytics*;[8] we can compare our philosophers' method with that of Aristotle, who also, as a matter of fact, set forth a system that, in part, appealed to the right ordering of things through classification by correct rules.[9]

Now to the specific task at hand. A brief account, based upon the standard textbook picture, of the taxonomic method of Aristotle permits us to compare the philosophical method of the philosophy of Judaism with that of the methodologically paramount natural philosophy of the Greco-Roman world.[10] We begin with the simple observation that the distinction between genus and species lies at the foundation of all knowledge. A. W. H. Adkins states the matter in the most accessible way: "Aristotle, a systematic biologist, uses his method of classification by genera and species, itself developed from the classificatory interests of the later Plato, to place man among other animals. . . . The classification must be based on the final development of the creature."[11] But to classify we have to take as our premise that things are subject to classification, and that means that they have traits that are essential and indicative, on the one side, but also shared with other things, on the other. The point of direct contact and intersection between the Judaism's philosophy of hierarchical classification and the natural philosophy of Aristotle lies in the shared, and critical, conviction concerning the true nature or character of things. Both parties concur that there *is* such a true definition—a commonplace for philosophers, generative of interesting problems, for example, about Ideas, or Form and Substance, Actual and Potential, and the like—of what things really are.[12]

But how are we to know the essential traits that allow us to define the true character of (e.g., to classify) things? And this is the point at which our comparison becomes particular, since what we need to find out is whether there are between Aristotle's and Judaism's philosophies only shared convictions about the genus and the species or particular conceptions as to how these are to be identified and organized. The basic conviction on both sides is this: objects are not random but fall into classes and so may be described, analyzed, and explained by appeal to general traits or rules.

The component of Aristotelianism that pertains here is "the use of deductive reasoning proceeding from self-evident principles or discovered general truths to conclusions of a more limited import; and syllogistic forms of demonstrative or persuasive arguments."[13] The goal is the classification of things, which is to say the discovery of general rules that apply to discrete data or instances. Lorenzo Minio-Paluello states:

> In epistemology . . . Aristotelianism includes a concentration on knowledge accessible by natural means or accountable for by reason; an inductive, analytical empiricism, or stress on experience in the study of nature . . . leading from the perception of contingent individual occurrences to the discovery of permanent, universal patterns; and the primacy of the universal, that which is expressed by common or general terms. In metaphysics, or the theory of Being, Aristotelianism involves belief in the primacy of the individual in the realm of existence; in correlated conceptions allowing an articulate account of reality (e.g., 10 categories; genus–species–individual, matter–form, potentiality–actuality, essential–accidental; the four material elements and their basic qualities; and the four causes–formal, material, efficient and final); in the soul as the inseparable form of each living body in the vegetable and animal kingdoms; in activity as the essence of things; and in the primacy of speculative over practical activity.

The manner in which we accomplish this work is by establishing categories of traits, and these will yield the besought rules or generalizations that make possible both classification and, in the nature of things, therefore hierarchization.

Clearly, when we review some of the more obvious characteristics of Aristotle's logical and taxonomic principles, in specific terms we find only occasional points of contact with the principles we uncover in the Mishnah's philosophical structure. Only in general does the manner in which Aristotle does the work of definition through classification also characterize the way in which sages do the same work. But there are points of intersection. For instance, while the actual and the potential form critical taxic categories for Aristotle, they prove subsidiary, though pertinent, in the Mishnah. While for the Mishnah the matter of mixtures defines a central and generative problematic, for Aristotle the same matter is subsumed into other compositions altogether. It constitutes a chapter in the story of change, which is explained by the passage of elements into one another. That will help us account for the destruction of one element and the creation of another. In this connection J. D. Allan says:

> Aristotle does not mean by "mixture" a mere shuffling of primary particles, as if the seeds of wheat and barley were mixed in a heap, but genuine change of quality resulting in a new "form," towards which each component has made a contribution.[14]

The consideration of the classes of mixtures plays its role in Aristotle's account of the sublunary region; it is not—as represented by Allan—a point at which Aristotle repeatedly uncovers problems that require solution, in the way in which the issue of mixtures forms the source for the Mishnah's solution of urgent problems.

Enough has been said to justify comparing Aristotle's and Judaism's philosophies, but I have yet to specify what I conceive to be the generative point of comparison. It lies in two matters, first, the paramount one of the shared principles of formal logic, which I find blatant in the Mishnah and which all presentations of Aristotle's philosophy identify as emblematic. The second, as is clear, is the taxonomic method, viewed from afar. Let us turn only briefly to the former. When we follow a simple account of the way in which we attain new truth, we find ourselves quite at home. Allan's account follows:

> Induction . . . is the advance from the particular to the general. By the inspection of examples . . . in which one characteristic appears conjoined with another, we are led to propound a general rule which we suppose to be valid for cases not yet examined. Since the rule is of higher generality than the instances, this is an advance from a truth "prior for us" toward a truth "prior in nature."[15]

My representation of the mishnaic mode of presentation of cases that, with our participation, yield a general rule accords with this inductive logic.

The more important of the two principles of sound intellectual method is the taxonomic interest in defining through classification. This definitive trait of natural philosophy is what we find in common between Aristotle's and the Mishnah's philosophical method, and the points in common prove far more than those yielded by the general observation that both systems appeal to the identification of genera out of species. In fact, what philosophers call the dialectical approach in Aristotle proves to be the same approach to the discovery or demonstration of truth that we find in the Mishnah. Joseph Owens sets the matter forth in the following language:

> Since a theoretical science proceeds from first principles that are found within the thing under investigation, the initial task of the philosophy of nature will be to discover its primary principles in the sensible thing themselves.[16]

I cannot imagine a formulation more suited to the method of the Mishnah than that simple statement. For the Mishnah's philosophers compose their taxonomy by appeal to the indicative traits of things rather than to extrinsic considerations of imposed classification, for example, by reference to Scripture.[17] The philosophers whose system is set forth in the Mishnah appeal to the traits of things, deriving their genera from the comparison and contrast of those inherent or intrinsic traits. This I take to be precisely what is stated here.

> In accordance with the general directives of the Aristotelian logic, the process of their discovery will be dialectical, not demonstrative.

This distinction is between genuine reasoning and demonstration.

If the parallels in method are clear, where do we find the difference between Aristotle's system and the Mishnah's? It is that the goal of Aristotle's system, the teleological argument in favor of the unmoved mover, and the goal of Judaism's system, the demonstration of the unity of being, are essentially contradictory, marking utterly opposed positions on the fundamental character of God and the traits of the created world that carries us upward to God. So we establish the philosophical character of the method of the Mishnah's system, only at the cost of uncovering a major contradiction: the proposition that animates the one system stands in direct opposition, as to its premises, implications, and explicit results, with the results of the other. Aristotle's God attained through teleological demonstration accomplished through the right classification of all things and the Mishnah's God, whose workings in the world derive from the demonstration of the ontological unity of all things, cannot recognize each other. And that is the case even though they are assuredly one.

Accordingly, we must ask ourselves, not to whose advantage, but rather *against* whose position, did the Judaic philosophical system propose to argue? When we realize that at stake is a particular means for demonstrating the unity of God, we readily identify as the principal focus the pagan reading of the revealed world of the here and the now, and, it must follow, Judaism as a philosophy stood over against the pagan philosophy of the world of its time and place. The fundamental argument in favor of the unity of God in the philosophy of Judaism is by showing the hierarchical order, therefore the unity, of the world. The world therefore is made to testify to the unity of being, and—to say the obvious with very heavy emphasis—*the power of the philosophy derives from its capacity for hierarchical classification.* When we compare the pagan and the Christian philosophical ontology of God, we see that it is the pagan position, not the Christian one, that forms the target of this system. The Christian position is simply not perceived and not considered.

The comparison of the Judaic, Christian, and pagan systems of Middle Platonism seems to me to be made possible, in a very preliminary way to be sure, by A. Hilary Armstrong:

> The difference here between pagans and Christians . . . is a difference about the degree of religious relevance of the material cosmos, and, closely connected with this, about the relative importance of general, natural, and special, supernatural, divine self-manifestation and self-communication. On the one side, the pagan, there is the conviction that a multiple self-communication and self-revelation of divinity takes place always and everywhere in the world, and that good and wise men everywhere . . . have been able to find the way to God and the truth about God in and through rational reflection on themselves and on the world, not only the heavens but the earth, and the living unity of the whole. On the other side, the Christian, there is indeed a readiness to see the goodness and beauty of the visible cosmos as a testimony to God's creation . . . but the religious emphasis lies elsewhere. Saving truth and the self-communication of the life of God come through the Incarnation of God as a man and through the human . . . society of which the God-Man is the head, the Church. . . . It is only in the Church that material things become means of revelation and salvation through being understood in the light of Scripture and Church tradition and used by God's human ministers in the celebration of the Church's sacraments. It is the ecclesiastical cosmos, not the natural cosmos, which appears to be of primary religious importance for the Christian.[18]

If God is revealed in the artifacts of the world, then, so pagans in general considered, God must be multiple. No, the philosophy of Judaism is here seen to respond. Here we find a Judaic argument, within the premises of paganism, against paganism. To state with emphasis what I conceive to be that argument: *The very artifacts that* appear *multiple in fact form classes of things, and, moreover, these classes themselves are subject to a reasoned ordering, by appeal to this-worldly characteristics signified by properties and indicative traits.* Monotheism hence is to be demonstrated by appeal to those very same data which for paganism prove the opposite.

The medium of hierarchical classification, which is Aristotle's, conveys the message of the unity of being[19] in the this-worldly mode of discourse formed by the framers of the Mishnah. The way to one God, ground of being and ontological unity of the world, lies through "rational reflection on themselves and on the world," this world, which yields a living unity encompassing the whole. That claim, conducted in an argument covering overwhelming detail in the Mishnah, directly faces the issue as framed by paganism. Immanent in its medium, it is transcendent in its message. And I hardly need spell out the simple reasons, self-evident in Armstrong's words, for dismissing as irrelevant to their interests the Christian reading of the cosmos. To the Mishnah's sages, it is not (merely) wrong, it is insufficient.

And yet, that is not the whole story. For the Mishnah's sages reach into Scripture for their generative categories, and, in doing so, they address head-on a Christianity that Armstrong centers, with entire soundness, upon the life of the church of Jesus Christ, God-Man.[20] We do well here to review Armstrong's language: "It is only in the Church that material things become means of revelation and salvation through being understood in the light of Scripture and Church tradition and used by God's human ministers in the celebration of the Church's sacraments."

The framers of the Mishnah will have responded, *"It is in the Torah that material things are identified and set forth as a means of revelation."*

Again Armstrong: "It is the ecclesiastical cosmos, not the natural cosmos, which appears to be of primary religious importance for the Christian."

To this the philosophers of Judaism reply, *"It is the scriptural account of the cosmos that forms our generative categories, which, by the power of intellect, we show to constitute an ordered, hierarchical unity of being."*

So the power of this identification of "the ecclesiastical cosmos" is revealed when we frame the cosmos of the Mishnah by appeal to its persistent response to the classifications and categories of Scripture. If the church, as Armstrong portrays matters, worked out an ecclesiastical cosmos, only later on producing the Bible as it did, for its part the philosophy of Judaism framed a scriptural cosmos—and then read it philosophically in the way in which I have explained matters. We may therefore identify three distinct positions on the reading of the natural world: the pagan, the Christian, and the Judaic. The one reads nature as a source of revelation. The other two insist on a medium of mediation between nature and intellect. For Christianity it is, as Armstrong says, ecclesiastical, and, as I claim, for Judaism the medium of mediation of nature lies through revelation, the Torah.

Why the difference? There is a philosophical reason, which I deem paramount and which explains my insistence, that this Judaism is a philosophy, a philosophy—not a theology—in its message and its mode of thought. It is that by not merely appealing to the authority of Scripture, but by themselves analyzing the revealed truths of Scripture, the intellects at hand accomplished their purposes. By themselves showing the order and unity inherent within Scripture's list of topics, the philosophers on their own power meant to penetrate into the ground of being as God has revealed matters. This they did by working their way back from the epiphenomena of creation to the phenomenon of Creation—then to the numinous, that is, the Creator. That self-assigned challenge forms an intellectual vocation worthy of a particular kind of philosopher, an Israelite one. And, in my view, it explains also why in the Mishnah philosophers produced their philosophy in the form that they chose.

For the form, so superficially unphilosophical in its crabbed and obsessive mode of discourse, proves in the end to form a philosophy. Judaism in the system of the Mishnah is philosophical in medium, method, and message. But then philosophy also is represented as, and within, the Torah in topic and authority. The union then of the Torah's classifications and topics, philosophy's modes of thought and propositions—that marriage produced as its firstfruits a philosophical Judaism, a Judaic philosophy: the Torah as Moses would have written it at God's instructions, were Moses a philosopher. But the offspring of the happy marriage was not to live long, and the presentation of a Judaism in the idiom of philosophy would soon give way to the Judaism of religion and ultimately even theology, and it was the religious Judaism, with its theology, and not philosophy, that dictated the future for a thousand years.

VIII

The Formation of Judaism:
The First Talmud
and Religion

The Reception of the Philosophical System:
Categorical Reformation and the New Structure

Classifying a system as fundamentally religious or essentially philosophical is not a subjective judgment. Objective indicative traits tell us which is which. A philosophical system forms its learning inductively and syllogistically, by appeal to the neutral evidence of the rules shown to apply to all things by the observation of the order of universally accessible nature and society. A religious system frames its propositions deductively and exegetically by appeal to the privileged evidence of a corpus of truths deemed revealed by God.

The authorship of the Talmud of the Land of Israel, the first of the two Talmuds, received the Mishnah and presented whatever they had to say in the form of a commentary to that document. But while connected to the prior one, their system is autonomous of it. We know that is the fact because the Mishnah's categories do not serve the successor system, which forms its own categories to accomplish its own goals of ordering the social world.

Precisely what I mean by calling the second Judaism in literary sequence a religious one must be made clear, since the mishnaic system also was a religious one. But the received system was a religious system of a philosophical character; this world's data are classified according to rules that apply consistently throughout, so that we may always predict with a fair degree of accuracy what will happen and why. And a philosophical system of religion then demonstrates out of the data of the nature and society the governance of God in nature and supernature. This world's data are made to point toward God above and beyond. The God of the philosophical Judaism then sat enthroned at the apex of all things, all being hierarchically classified. Just as philosophy seeks the explanation of things, so a philosophy of religion (in the context at hand) will propose orderly explanations in accord with prevailing and cogent rules. The profoundly philosophical character of the Mishnah has already provided ample evidence of the shape, structure, and character of that philosophical system in the Judaic context. The rule-seeking character of mishnaic discourse then marks it as a philosophical system of religion.

But the successor system saw the world differently and appealed to its own, quite distinctive classifications for the ordering of the facts of reality as it chose those facts. The difference pertains not to detail but to the fundamental facts deemed to matter. Some of those facts lie at the very surface, in the nature of the writings that express the system. These writings were not free-standing but contingent, and that in two ways. First, they served as commentaries to prior documents, the Mishnah and Scripture, for the Talmud and Midrash compilations, respectively. Second, and more consequential, the authorships insisted upon citing Scripture passages or Mishnah sentences as the centerpiece of proof, on the one side, and program of discourse, on the other. But the differences that prove indicative are not merely formal. So while the Mishnah appeals to the data of the natural world and discovers order within them, the Talmud of the Land of Israel appeals to the revealed facts of Scripture—and the Mishnah itself!

More to the point, while the Mishnah's system is steady-state and ahistorical, admitting no movement or change, the successor system of the Yerushalmi and Midrash compilations tells tales, speaks of change, accommodates and responds to historical moments. It formulates a theory of continuity within change, of the moral connections between generations, of the way in which one's deeds shape one's destiny—and that of the future as well. If what the framers of the Mishnah want more than anything else is to explain the order and structure of being, then their successors have rejected their generative concern. For what they, for their part, intensely desire to sort out is the currents and streams of time and change, as these flow toward an unknown ocean.

But these large-scale characterizations in well-crafted systems do not provide the only pertinent evidence. Details too deliver the message. The indicators for each type of system, philosophical or religious, as these are attested in their written testimonies, derive from the character of the rhetorical, logical, and propositional-topical traits of those writings. The shift from the philosophical to the religious modes of thought and media of expression—logical and rhetorical indicators, respectively— come to realization in the recasting of the generative categories of the system as well. These categories were transformed, and the transformation proved to be so thoroughgoing as to validate the characterization of the change as "counterpart categories." The result of the formation of such counterpart categories, already introduced in chapter VI, was to encompass not only the natural but also the supernatural realms of the social order.

From Philosophy to Religion

That is how philosophical thinking gave way to religious, an economics based on prime value assigned to real wealth now encompassed wealth of an intangible, impalpable, and supernatural order, but valued resource nonetheless, and a politics formerly serving to legitimate and hierarchize power and differentiate among sanctions by appeal to fixed principles now introduced the variable of God's valuation of the victim and the antipolitical conception of the illegitimacy of worldly power, the opposite of the Mishnah's this-worldly political system altogether. In all three ways the upshot is the same: The social system, in the theory of its framers, now extends its boundaries upward to heaven, drawing into a whole the formerly distinct, if counterpoised, realms of Israel on earth and the heavenly court above. So if I had to specify the fundamental difference between the philosophical and the religious versions of the social order, it would fall, quite specifically, upon the broadening of the systemic boundaries to encompass heaven. The formation of counterpart categories therefore signals not a reformation of the received, philosophical system but the formation of an essentially new, religious one.

But the critical issue addressed by the new system and the central point of tension and mode of remission thereof, the exegetical focus—these remain to be identified. And, as a matter of fact, the counterpart categories in hand themselves do not help identify the generative problematic that defined the new system and integrated its components. For the issues I have located as the systemic economics and politics—Torah in place of land, the illegitimacy of power and the priority of the absence thereof—while present and indicative in the documentary expression of the system, assuredly do not occupy a principal position within those documents. For the successor documents' categories are not those of philosophy, on the one side, and a politics disembedded from economics, on the other.

In the nature of systemic analysis and comparison of systems, therefore, I have brought the categories of one system to the data of another, those of the initial system to the ones of the successor system, and the result is to discover only how different are the latter from the former. So concerning the transformed Judaism of the late fourth and fifth centuries we now know everything but the main thing. True, since we compare the given to the new, I have no choice but to proceed as I have. But what I have done thus far is to ask only my questions—that is, the systemic questions of philosophy and political economy or philosophical economics and politics—of a literature that dealt with such questions essentially by dismissing them. For the upshot of the formation of counterpart categories turns out to be the destruction of the received categories, now turned on their heads and emptied of all material and palpable content, refilled then with intangibles of intellect and virtuous attitude alone. Knowing how a system has revalued value and reconstructed the sense of legitimate power by deeming legitimate only the victim and never the actor does not tell us what the system locates at its center.

If I ask myself, then, how am I to identify the systemic foci, the system's sources of the exegetical problematic and its definition of its generative issues, I must propose as the answer not a subjective judgment as to what is dominant and commonplace[1] but, rather, an objective claim as to what is essential and definitive and integrating (which, as a matter of fact, in this context also happens to be commonplace). By objective I mean simply that my results should emerge for anyone else examining the same evidence in accord with the same principles of description and analysis (interpretation is always subjective). Once we concur that a Judaic system by definition responds to the questions deemed compelling with truths regarded as unavoidable and self-evident, then, reading the evidence at hand, anyone should reach the conclusions I present here, if my indicative evidence is correctly identified and accurately described. So the task now is to identify those urgent questions and define the self-evident truths that came about by way of response: the way of life, the worldview, formed by the Israel that the successor system defined for itself. And the issue is joined for us when we can identify the point of differentiation of one system and integration of another: surely an objective fact.

Where to begin? In general, historians of religion concur, the power of religion lies in its capacity to integrate, to hold together discrete components of the social order and explain how they all fit together. And, in general, it seems to me a simple fact that the power of philosophy lies in its capacity to differentiate, discriminate, make distinctions, and clarify the complex by showing its distinct parts. Then a successor system, connected to but autonomous of its antecedent, will prove philosophical if it continues the labor of differentiation—and religious if it undertakes a work of integration. And the Judaism before us addresses the principal, and striking, distinction characteristic of the philosophical system it had inherited. It takes up the separation of economics and politics, (re)integrating what had been kept apart.

Differentiating a Later Religious, from an Earlier Philosophical, System

Let me spell out what I conceive to be the principal success of integration, within a supernatural framework that must be deemed religious and only religion, accomplished by our sages of blessed memory in the Yerushalmi and related writings. The one striking contrast between the social system put forth by Aristotle and that set out by the framers of the Mishnah lay in the superior systematization of politics within the frame of economics accomplished by Aristotle and not achieved at all by the Mishnah's social system.[2] Aristotle's systemic message, delivered through his philosophy, economics, and politics, was carried equally by economics and politics in such a way that the two formed a single statement, one of political economy. To state the matter very simply: the principal economic actor of Aristotle's social system, the householder (in the language of our sources, the landholder or farmer for Aristotle and Xenophon) also constituted the principal political figure, the one who exercised legitimate power, and the joining of the landholder and the civic actor in a single person, moreover, accounted for Aristotle for the formation of society: the polis or lowest whole and indivisible social unit of society.

But for the framers of the Mishnah, the economic actor, the one who controlled the means of production, was the householder, while the householder never played a political role or formed part of the political classes at all. That fact is shown by the simple distinction of usage, in which the subject of most sentences involving the disposition of scarce resources was the householder, while that same social entity ("class") never made an appearance in any of the political tractates and their discourses, which choose, for the subjects of their sentences, such political figures as the king, high priest, (sages') court, and the like. These usages signal the removal of economics from politics, a fact further highlighted by the Mishnah's separation between the economic entity, the village or town made up of householders, and the political entities, royal government, temple authority, sages' court; none of these, as a matter of fact, correspond with the village or town, that is, the polis, in the Mishnah's philosophical system.

What the philosophical Judaism kept apart, the religious Judaism now joined together, and it is just there, at that critical joining, that we identify the key to the system: its reversal of a received point of differentiation,[3] its introduction of new points of differentiation altogether. The source of generative problems for the Mishnah's politics is simply not the same as the source that served the successor system's politics, and, systemic analysis being what it is, it is the union of what was formerly asunder that identifies for us in quite objective terms the critical point of tension, the sources of problems, the centerpiece of systemic concern throughout. And one fundamental point of reversal, uniting what had been divided, is the joining of economics and politics into a political economy, through the conception of *zekhut,* a term that I will define presently.

The other point at which, we find, what the one system treated as distinct the next and connected system chose to address as one and whole is less easily discerned, since to do so we have to ask a question the framers of the Mishnah did not raise in the Mishnah at all. That concerns the character and source of virtue, specifically the effect, upon the individual, of knowledge, specifically knowledge of the Torah or Torah study. To frame the question very simply: If we ask ourselves, what happens to me if I study the Torah? the answer, for the Mishnah, predictably is that my standing and my status change. Torah study and its effects form a principal systemic indicator in matters of hierarchical classification, joining the *mamzer* [illegitimate child] who was also a disciple of sages in a mixture of opposites, for one self-evident example.

But am I changed within? In vain we look in the hundreds of chapters of the Mishnah for an answer to that question. Virtue and learning form distinct categories, a point I shall underline in the pertinent chapter, which follows, and, overall, I am not changed as to my virtue, my character and conscience, by my mastery of the Torah. And still more striking, if we ask whether my Torah study affects my fate in this world and in the life to come, the Mishnah's authorship is strikingly silent about that matter too. Specifically, we find in the pages of that document no claim that studying the Torah either changes me or assures my salvation. But, we shall presently see, the separation of knowledge and the human condition is set aside, and studying the Torah deemed the source of salvation, in the successor system. The philosophical system, with its interest in *homo hierarchicus*, proved remarkably silent about the effect of the Torah upon the inner man.[4] The upshot is at the critical points of bonding, the received system proved flawed, in its separation of learning from virtue and legitimate power from valued resources. So to the simple conclusion:

What philosophy in the Mishnah kept distinct, religion in the Talmud of the Land of Israel joined together: that defines the transformation of Judaism from philosophy to religion.

The reliable rules of sanctification—to invoke theological categories—are joined with the unpredictable event of salvation, and the routine meets the spontaneous. Not to be gainsaid, the social order is made to acknowledge what, if disorderly, also is immediate and therefore necessary. History, that omnipresent but carefully ignored presence in the philosophical Judaism, in the form of not change but crisis, regains its rightful place at the systemic center.

So, it must follow, the comparison between one system and its connected but distinct successor points to quite objective evidence on the basis of which we may characterize the successor in its own terms. For the categories that present themselves now derive from the system subjected to description, not from those of the prior system (let alone from my own theory of the components of a theory of the social order). They emerge at that very point—the joining place of differentiation or its opposite, integration—at which systemic description begins, the exegesis of the system's exegesis. Why virtue joins knowledge, politics links to economics, in the religious system but not in the philosophical one is of course obvious. Philosophy differentiates, seeking the rules that join diverse data; religion integrates, proposing to see the whole all together and all at once, thus (for an anthropology, e.g.) seeing humanity whole: "in our image, after our likeness." Religion by its nature (so it would seem from the case at hand) asks the questions of integration, such as the theory intended to hold together within a single boundary earth and heaven, this world and the other, should lead us to anticipate. So our observations about the broadening of the frontiers of the social order turn out to signal a deeper characteristic of the analysis at hand.

Why should we have taken the route that has led us to this mode of analysis? The reason is that of special interest in the work of systemic description is not so much theology or doctrine or belief as the interplay of religion and society, that is, the relationship between contents and context, conviction and circumstance, each viewed as distinct and autonomous, an independent variable. Religion is a decisive fact of social reality, not merely a set of beliefs on questions viewed in an abstract and ahistorical setting. Our task is now to identify the system that the successor documents' authorships formed, and this we do by proposing to define the questions they pursued, the self-evidently valid answers they set forth, in making a single and coherent statement about their own condition.

Systemic Integration and Theology: The Concept of *Zekhut*

We turn forthwith to the integrating conception of the religious system of Judaism set forth in the Talmud of the Land of Israel and related Midrash compilations, represented by the word *zekhut*. Defining the word in context is best accomplished at M. Avot 2:2, where we find the following:

Tractate Avot 2:2

    C. "And all who work with the community—let them work with them for the sake of Heaven.

    D. "For the [1] *zekhut* of their fathers strengthens them, and their [fathers'] [2] righteousness stands forever.

    E. "And as for you, I credit you with a great reward, as if you had done [all of the work required by the community on your own merit alone]."

Here there is no meaning possible other than that which I have given above: "the heritage of virtue and its consequent entitlements." The reference to an advantage that one gains by reason of inheritance out of one's fathers' righteousness is demanded by the parallel between *zekhut* of clause 1 and *righteousness* of clause 2. Whatever the conceivable ambiguity of the Mishnah, none is sustained by the context at hand, which is explicit in language and pellucid in message. That the sense is exactly the same as the one I have proposed is shown at the following passages, which seem to me to exhibit none of the possible ambiguity that characterized the usage of *zekhut* in the Mishnah:

Tractate Avot 5:18

    A. He who causes *zekhut* to the community never causes sin.

    B. And he who causes the community to sin—they never give him a sufficient chance to attain penitence.

Here the contrast is between causing *zekhut* and causing sin, so *zekhut* is the opposite of sin. The continuation is equally clear that a person attained *zekhut* and endowed the community with *zekhut,* or sinned and made the community sin:

C. Moses attained *zekhut* and bestowed *zekhut* on the community.
D. So the *zekhut* of the community is assigned to his [credit],
E. as it is said, "He executed the justice of the Lord and his judgments with Israel" (Deut. 33:21).
F. Jeroboam sinned and caused the community to sin.
G. So the sin of the community is assigned to his [debit],
H. as it is said, "For the sins of Jeroboam which he committed and wherewith he made Israel to sin" (1 Kings 15:30).

The appropriateness of interpreting the passage in the way I have proposed will now be shown to be self-evident. All that is required is to substitute for *zekhut* the proposed translation:

C. Moses attained the heritage of virtue and bestowed its consequent entitlements on the community.
D. So the heritage of virtue and its entitlements enjoyed by the community are assigned to his [credit],

The sense then is simple. Moses through actions of his own (of an unspecified sort) acquired *zekhut,* which is the credit for such actions that accrued to him and bestowed upon him certain supernatural entitlements; and he for his part passed on as an inheritance that credit, a lien on heaven for the performance of these same supernatural entitlements: *zekhut,* pure and simple.

If we may now define *zekhut* as the initial system explicated in tractate Avot has used the word, we must pay close attention to the antonymic structure before us. The juridical opposites are guilty as against innocent, the religious ones, as we have now seen, sin as against the opposite of sin. That seems to me to require our interpreting *zekhut* as [1] an action, as distinct from a (mere) attitude; that [2] is precisely the opposite of a sinful one; it is, moreover, an action that [3] may be done by an individual or by the community at large, and one that [4] a leader may provoke the community to do (or not do). The contrast of sin to *zekhut* requires further attention. Since, in general, two classes that are compared to begin with, if different, must constitute opposites, the ultimate definition of *zekhut* requires us to ask how *zekhut* is precisely the opposite of sin.

For one thing, as we recall, Scripture is explicit that the burden of sins cannot be passively inherited, willy-nilly, but, to form a heritage of guilt, must be actively accepted and renewed; the children cannot be made to suffer for the sins of the parents, unless they repeat them. Then *zekhut,* being a mirror image, can be passively inherited, not by one's own merit,[5] but by one's good fortune alone. But what constitutes these *actions* that form mirror images of sins? Answers to that critical question must emerge from the systemic documents before us, since they do not occur in those of the initial system.

Because *zekhut* is something one may receive as an inheritance, out of the distant past, *zekhut* imposes upon the definition of the social entity, "Israel," a genealogical meaning. It furthermore imparts a distinctive character to the definitions of way of life. So the task of the political component of a theory of the social order, which is to define the social entity by appeal to empowerment, and of the economic component, which is to identify scarce resources by specification of the rationality of right management, is accomplished in a single word, which stands for a conception, a symbol, and a myth. All three components of this religious theory of the social order turn out to present specific applications, in context, for the general conception of *zekhut.* For the first source of *zekhut* derives from the definition of Israel as family; the entitlements of supernatural power deriving from virtue then are inherited from Abraham, Isaac, and Jacob. The second source is personal: the power one can gain for one's own heirs, moreover, by virtuous deeds. *Zekhut* deriving from either source is to be defined in context: What can you do if you have *zekhut* that you cannot do if you do not have *zekhut* and to whom can you do it? The answer to that question tells you the empowerment of *zekhut.*

Zekhut stands for the empowerment, of a supernatural character, that derives from the virtue of one's ancestry or from one's own virtuous deeds of a very particular order. No single word in English bears the same meaning, nor can I identify a synonym for *zekhut* in the canonical writings in the original either. The difficulty of translating a word of systemic consequence with a single word in some other language (or in the language of the system's documents themselves) tells us we deal with what is unique, beyond comparison and therefore contrast and comprehension. A mark that we have found our way to the systemic center is that we cannot easily translate with a single English equivalent the word that identifies what we conceive to define the system's critical tension and generative concept. What is most particular to, distinctive of, the systemic structure and its functioning requires definition through

circumlocution, such as, "the heritage of virtue and its consequent entitlements."[6] The word *zekhut* for the successor system
forms the systemic counterpart to the mythologoumenon of the
resurrection of Jesus Christ, unique son of God, for important
Christianities.

The Paramount Systemic Position of *Zekhut*

A further mark of the systemic importance accorded to
zekhut is that even though a man was degraded, one action
sufficed to win for him that heavenly glory to which rabbis in
lives of Torah study aspired. The mark of the system's integration around *zekhut* lies in its insistence that all Israelites, not
only sages, could gain *zekhut* for themselves (and their descendants). A single remarkable deed, exemplary for its deep humanity, sufficed to win for an ordinary person the *zekhut* that
elicits supernatural favor enjoyed by some rabbis on account of
their Torah study. The centrality of *zekhut* in the systemic
structure, the critical importance of the heritage of virtue together with its supernatural entitlements, therefore emerges in
a striking claim. Even though a man was degraded, one action
sufficed to win for him that heavenly glory to which rabbis in
general aspired.

The rabbinical storyteller to whom we shall listen identifies
with this lesson. In all three instances that follow, defining what
the individual must do to gain *zekhut,* the point is that the
deeds of the heroes of the story make them worthy of having
their prayers answered, which is a mark of the working of
zekhut. It is deeds beyond the strict requirements of the Torah,
and even the limits of the law altogether, that transform the
hero into a holy man, whose holiness served just like that of a
sage marked as such by knowledge of the Torah. The following
stories should not be understood as expressions of the mere
sentimentality of the clerks concerning the lower orders, for
they deny in favor of a single action of surpassing power the
sages' lifelong devotion to what the sages held to be the highest
value, knowledge of the Torah:

Y. Taanit 1:4.I

>   F. A certain man came before one of the relatives of R. Yan-
>   nai. He said to him, "Rabbi, attain *zekhut* through me [by
>   giving me charity]."
>   G. He said to him, "And didn't your father leave you
>   money?"
>   H. He said to him, "No."

I.   He said to him, "Go and collect what your father left in deposit with others."

J.   He said to him, "I have heard concerning property my father deposited with others that it was gained by violence [so I don't want it]."

K.   He said to him, "You are worthy of praying and having your prayers answered."

The point of K, of course, is self-evidently a reference to the possession of entitlement to supernatural favor, and it is gained, we see, through deeds that the law of the Torah cannot require but must favor: what one does on one's own volition, beyond the measure of the law. Here I see the opposite of sin. A sin is what one has done by one's own volition beyond all limits of the law. So an act that generates *zekhut* for the individual is the counterpart and opposite: what one does by one's own volition that also is beyond all requirements of the law.

L.   A certain ass driver appeared before the rabbis [the context requires: in a dream] and prayed, and rain came. The rabbis sent and brought him and said to him, "What is your trade?"

M.   He said to them, "I am an ass driver."

N.   They said to him, "And how do you conduct your business?"

O.   He said to them, "One time I rented my ass to a certain woman, and she was weeping on the way, and I said to her, 'What's with you?' and she said to me, 'The husband of that woman [me] is in prison [for debt], and I wanted to see what I can do to free him.' So I sold my ass and I gave her the proceeds, and I said to her, 'Here is your money, free your husband, but do not sin [by becoming a prostitute to raise the necessary funds].' "

P.   They said to him, "You are worthy of praying and having your prayers answered."

The ass driver clearly has a powerful lien on heaven, so that his prayers are answered, even while those of others are not. What did he do to get that entitlement? He did what no law could demand: impoverished himself to save the woman from a "fate worse than death."

Q.   In a dream of R. Abbahu, Mr. Pentakaka ["Five sins"] appeared, who prayed that rain would come, and it rained. R. Abbahu sent and summoned him. He said to him, "What is your trade?"

R. He said to him, "Five sins does that man [I] do every day, [for I am a pimp:] hiring whores, cleaning up the theater, bringing home their garments for washing, dancing, and performing before them."

S. He said to him, "And what sort of decent thing have you ever done?"

T. He said to him, "One day that man [I] was cleaning the theater, and a woman came and stood behind a pillar and cried. I said to her, 'What's with you?' And she said to me, 'That woman's [my] husband is in prison, and I wanted to see what I can do to free him,' so I sold my bed and cover, and I gave the proceeds to her. I said to her, 'Here is your money, free your husband, but do not sin.' "

U. He said to him, "You are worthy of praying and having your prayers answered."

Q moves us still further, since the named man has done everything sinful that one can do, and, more to the point, he does it every day. So the singularity of the act of *zekhut*, which suffices if done only one time, encompasses its power to outweigh a life of sin—again, an act of *zekhut* as the mirror image and opposite of sin. Here again, the single act of saving a woman from a "fate worse than death" has sufficed.

V. A pious man from Kefar Imi appeared [in a dream] to the rabbis. He prayed for rain and it rained. The rabbis went up to him. His householders told them that he was sitting on a hill. They went out to him, saying to him, "Greetings," but he did not answer them.

W. He was sitting and eating, and he did not say to them, "You break bread too."

X. When he went back home, he made a bundle of faggots and put his cloak on top of the bundle [instead of on his shoulder].

Y. When he came home, he said to his household [wife], "These rabbis are here [because] they want me to pray for rain. If I pray and it rains, it is a disgrace for them, and if not, it is a profanation of the Name of Heaven. But come, you and I will go up [to the roof] and pray. If it rains, we shall tell them, 'We are not worthy to pray and have our prayers answered.' "

Z. They went up and prayed and it rained.

AA. They came down to them [and asked], "Why have the rabbis troubled themselves to come here today?"

BB. They said to him, "We wanted you to pray so that it would rain."

CC. He said to them, "Now do you really need my prayers? Heaven already has done its miracle."

DD. They said to him, "Why, when you were on the hill, did we say hello to you, and you did not reply?"

EE. He said to them, "I was then doing my job. Should I then interrupt my concentration [on my work]?"

FF. They said to him, "And why, when you sat down to eat, did you not say to us 'You break bread too'?"

GG. He said to them, "Because I had only my small ration of bread. Why would I have invited you to eat by way of mere flattery [when I knew I could not give you anything at all]?"

HH. They said to him, "And why when you came to go down, did you put your cloak on top of the bundle?"

II. He said to them, "Because the cloak was not mine. It was borrowed for use at prayer. I did not want to tear it."

JJ. They said to him, "And why, when you were on the hill, did your wife wear dirty clothes, but when you came down from the mountain, did she put on clean clothes?"

KK. He said to them, "When I was on the hill, she put on dirty clothes, so that no one would gaze at her. But when I came home from the hill, she put on clean clothes, so that I would not gaze on any other woman."

LL. They said to him, "It is well that you pray and have your prayers answered."

The pious man of V, finally, enjoys the recognition of the sages by reason of his lien upon heaven, able as he is to pray and bring rain. What has so endowed him with *zekhut*? Acts of punctiliousness of a moral order: concentrating on his work, avoiding an act of dissimulation, integrity in the disposition of a borrowed object, his wife's concern not to attract other men and her equal concern to make herself attractive to her husband. None of these stories refers explicitly to *zekhut*; all of them tell us about what it means to enjoy not an entitlement by inheritance but a lien accomplished by one's own supererogatory acts of restraint.

In its integrating power, *zekhut* integrates what has been differentiated. That is why I identify the concept as critical to the system at hand. *Zekhut* here serves to hold together learning, virtue, and supernatural standing, by explaining how Torah study transforms the learning man. The Mishnah's focus upon hierarchical classification, with its demonstration of the upward-reaching unity of all being, gives way to a different, and more compelling, proposition: the unity of all being within the heritage of *zekhut,* to be attained equally and without differentiation in all the principal parts of the social order. The definition of *zekhut* therefore carries us to the heart of the integrating and integrated religious system of Judaism.

Precisely what actions generate *zekhut,* and which ones do not? To find answers to those questions, we have to turn to the successor documents, since not a single passage in the Mishnah or in tractate Avot provides information on the matter of what I must do to secure for myself or my descendants a lien upon heaven, that is, an entitlement to supernatural favor and even action of a miraculous order. We turn first to the conception of the *zekhut* that has been accumulated by the patriarchs and been passed on to Israel, their children. The reason is that the single distinctive trait of *zekhut,* as we have seen it to this point, is its transitive quality: one need not earn or merit the supernatural power and resource represented by the things you can do if you have *zekhut* but cannot do if you do not have it. One can inherit that entitlement from others, dead or living. Moses not only attains *zekhut* but also imparts *zekhut* to the community of which he is leader, and the same is so for any Israelite.

That conception is broadened in the successor documents into the deeply historical notion of *zekhut avot,* empowerment of a supernatural character to which Israel is entitled by reason of what the patriarchs and matriarchs in particular did long ago. That conception forms the foundation for the paramount sense of *zekhut* in the successor system: that Israel possesses a lien upon heaven by reason of God's love for the patriarchs and matriarchs, his appreciation for certain things they did, and his response to those actions not only in favoring them but also in entitling their descendants to do or benefit from otherwise unattainable miracles. *Zekhut,* as we noted earlier, explains the present—particularly what is odd and unpredictable in the present—by appeal to the past, hence forms a distinctively historical conception.

Within the historically grounded metaphor of Israel as a family expressed by the conception of *zekhut avot,* Israel was a family, the children of Abraham, Isaac, and Jacob, or children of Israel, in a concrete and genealogical sense. Israel hence fell into the genus, family, as the particular species of family generated by Abraham and Sarah. The distinguishing trait of that species was that it possessed the inheritance, or heritage, of the patriarchs and matriarchs, and that inheritance, consisting of *zekhut,* served the descendants and heirs as protection and support. It follows that the systemic position of the conception of *zekhut* lies in its power to define the social entity, and hence *zekhut* (in the terms of the initial category formation, the philosophical one) forms a fundamentally political conception[7] and only secondarily an economic and philosophical one.

But *zekhut* serves, in particular, that counterpart category which speaks of not legitimate but illegitimate violence, not power but weakness. *Zekhut* is the power of the weak. People who through their own merit and capacity can accomplish nothing, but through what others do for them in leaving a heritage of *zekhut,* or have done for them, can accomplish miracles. And, not to miss the stunning message of the triplet of stories cited above, *zekhut* also is what the weak and excluded and despised can do that outweighs in power what the great masters of the Torah have accomplished. In the context of a system that represents Torah as supernatural, that claim of priority for *zekhut* represents a considerable transvaluation of power, as much as of value. And, by the way, *zekhut* also forms the inheritance of the disinherited: what you receive as a heritage when you have nothing in the present and have gotten nothing in the past, that scarce resource which is free and unearned but much valued. So let us dwell upon the definitive character of the transferability of *zekhut* in its formulation, *zekhut avot,* the *zekhut* handed on by the ancestors, the transitive character of the concept and its standing as a heritage of entitlements.

It is in the successor documents that the concept of *zekhut* is joined with *avot*, referring to the patriarchs (rarely, also the matriarchs), that is, the *zekhut* that has been left as Israel's family inheritance by the patriarchs or ancestors, yielding the very specific notion, defining the systemic politics, its theory of the social entity, of Israel not as a (mere) community (e.g., as in tractate Avot's reference to Moses' bestowing *zekhut* upon the community) but as a family, with a history that takes the form of a genealogy, precisely as Genesis has represented that history.[8] Now *zekhut* was joined to the metaphor of the genealogy of patriarchs and matriarchs and served to form the missing link, explaining how the inheritance and heritage were transmitted from them to their heirs. Consequently, the family, called "Israel," could draw upon the family estate, consisting of the inherited *zekhut* of matriarchs and patriarchs in such a way as to benefit today from the heritage of yesterday. This notion involved very concrete problems. If "Israel, the family" sinned, it could call upon the *"zekhut"* accumulated by Abraham and Isaac at the binding of Isaac (Genesis 22) to win forgiveness for that sin. True, "fathers will not die on account of the sin of the sons," but the children may benefit from the *zekhut* of the forebears. That concrete expression of the larger metaphor imparted to the metaphor a practical consequence, moral and theological, that was not at all neglected.

Let me give one example of how the systemic writings express the concept of *zekhut* as the medium of historical existence, that is, the *zekhut* deriving from the patriarchs or *zekhut avot*. That *zekhut* will enable the accomplishment of the political goals of Israel: its attaining self-rule and avoiding government by Gentiles. This statement appeals to the binding of Isaac as the source of the *zekhut,* deriving from the patriarchs and matriarchs, which will in the end lead to the salvation of Israel. What is important here is that the *zekhut* that is inherited joins together with the *zekhut* of one's own deeds; one inherits the *zekhut* of the past, and, moreover, if one does what the progenitors did, one not only receives an entitlement out of the past, one secures an entitlement on one's own account. So the difference between *zekhut* and sin lies in the sole issue of transmissibility:

Genesis Rabbah LVI:II.5

A. Said R. Isaac, "And all was on account of the *zekhut* attained by the act of prostration.

B. "Abraham returned in peace from Mount Moriah only on account of the *zekhut* owing to the act of prostration: ' . . . and we will worship [through an act of prostration] and come [then, on that account] again to you' (Gen. 22:5).

C. "The Israelites were redeemed only on account of the *zekhut* owing to the act of prostration: 'And the people believed . . . then they bowed their heads and prostrated themselves' (Ex. 4:31).

D. "The Torah was given only on account of the *zekhut* owing to the act of prostration: 'And worship [prostrate themselves] you afar off' (Ex. 24:1).

E. "Hannah was remembered only on account of the *zekhut* owing to the act of prostration: 'And they worshipped before the Lord' (1 Sam. 1:19).

F. "The exiles will be brought back only on account of the *zekhut* owing to the act of prostration: 'And it shall come to pass in that day that a great horn shall be blown and they shall come that were lost . . . and that were dispersed . . . and they shall worship the Lord in the holy mountain at Jerusalem' (Is. 27:13).

G. "The Temple was built only on account of the *zekhut* owing to the act of prostration: 'Exalt you the Lord our God and worship at his holy hill' (Ps. 99:9).

H.   "The dead will live only on account of the *zekhut* owing to the act of prostration: 'Come let us worship and bend the knee, let us kneel before the Lord our maker' (Ps. 95:6)."

The entire history of Israel flows from its acts of worship ("prostration") beginning with that performed by Abraham at the binding of Isaac. Every sort of advantage Israel has ever gained came about through that act of worship done by Abraham and imitated thereafter. Israel constitutes a family and inherits the *zekhut* laid up as a treasure for the descendants by the ancestors. Israel draws upon that *zekhut,* but, by doing the deeds the ancestors did, it also enhances its heritage of *zekhut* and leaves to the descendants greater entitlement than they would enjoy by reason of their own actions. But their own actions—here, prostration in worship—generate *zekhut* as well. Accordingly, *zekhut* may be personal or inherited. The *zekhut* deriving from the prior generations is collective and affects all Israel. But one's own deeds can generate *zekhut* for oneself, with the simple result that *zekhut* is as much personal as it is collective.

Religion and the Social Order

For if we now ask what the sorts of deeds are that generate *zekhut,* we realize that those deeds produce a common result of gaining for their doer, as much as for the heirs of the actor, an entitlement for heavenly favor and support when needed. And that fact concerning gaining and benefiting from *zekhut* brings us to the systemic message to the living generation, its account of what now is to be done. And that message proves acutely contemporary, for its stress is on the power of a single action to create sufficient *zekhut* to outweigh a life of sin. Then the contrast between sin and *zekhut* gains greater depth still. One sin of sufficient weight condemns, one act of *zekhut* of sufficient weight saves; the entire issue of entitlements out of the past gives way, then, when we realize what is actually at stake.

Torah study is one—but only one—means for an individual to gain access to that heritage, to get *zekhut.* There are other equally suitable means, and, not only so, but the merit gained by Torah study is no different from the merit gained by acts of a supererogatory character. If one gets *zekhut* for studying the Torah, then we must suppose there is no holy deed that does not generate its share of *zekhut.* But when it comes to specifying the things one does to get *zekhut,* the documents before us speak of what the Torah does not require but does recommend: not what we are commanded to do in detail, but what the right attitude, formed within the Torah, leads us to do on our own volition:

Y. Taanit 3:11.IV

C. There was a house that was about to collapse over there [in Babylonia], and Rab set one of his disciples in the house, until they had cleared out everything from the house. When the disciple left the house, the house collapsed.

D. And there are those who say that it was R. Adda bar Ahwah.

E. Sages sent and said to him, "What sort of good deeds are to your credit [that you have that much merit]?"

F. He said to them, "In my whole life no man ever got to the synagogue in the morning before I did. I never left anybody there when I went out. I never walked four cubits without speaking words of Torah. Nor did I ever mention teachings of Torah in an inappropriate setting. I never laid out a bed and slept for a regular period of time. I never took great strides among the associates. I never called my fellow by a nickname. I never rejoiced in the embarrassment of my fellow. I never cursed my fellow when I was lying by myself in bed. I never walked over in the marketplace to someone who owed me money.

G. "In my entire life I never lost my temper in my household."

H. This was meant to carry out that which is stated as follows: "I will give heed to the way that is blameless. Oh when wilt thou come to me? I will walk with integrity of heart within my house" (Ps. 101:2).

What I find striking in this story is that mastery of the Torah is only one means of attaining the merit that enabled the sage to keep the house from collapsing. The question at E provides the key, together with its answer at F.

For what the sage did to gain such remarkable merit is not to master such-and-so many tractates of the Mishnah. Nor does the storyteller refer to carrying out the commandments of the Torah as specified. It was, rather, acts of that expressed courtesy, consideration, restraint. These acts, which no specification can encompass in detail, produced the right attitude, one of gentility, that led to gaining merit. Acts rewarded with an entitlement to supernatural power are those of self-abnegation or the avoidance of power over others—not taking great strides among the associates, not using a nickname, not rejoicing in the embarrassment of one's fellow, not singling out one's debtor—and the submission to the will and the requirement of self-esteem of others.

Here, in a moral setting, we find the politics replicated: the form of power that the system promises derives from the rejection of power that the world recognizes—legitimate violence replaced by legitimation of the absence of the power to commit violence or of the failure to commit violence. Not exercising power over others, that is, the counterpart politics, moreover, produced that scarcest of all resources, supernatural favor, by which the holy man could hold up a tottering building. Here then we find politics and economics united in the counterpart category formed of *zekhut*: the absence of power yielding supernatural power, the valuation of the intangible, Torah, yielding supernatural power. It was, then, that entitlement to supernatural favor which formed the systemic center.

The system through *zekhut* speaks to everybody, Jew and Gentile, past and present and future; *zekhut* therefore defines the structure of the cosmic social order and explains how it is supposed to function. It is the encompassing quality of *zekhut,* its pertinence to past and future, high and low, rich and poor, gifted and ordinary, that marks as the systemic statement the message of *zekhut,* now fully revealed as the conception of reciprocal response between heaven and Israel on earth, to acts of devotion beyond the requirements of the Torah but defined all the same by the Torah. Gentiles could secure *zekhut* too. As Scripture had said, God responds to the faith of the ancient generations by supernatural acts to which, on their own account, the moderns are not entitled, hence a heritage of entitlement. But those acts, now fully defined for us, can and ought to be done, also, by the living generation, and, as a matter of fact, there is none today, at the time of the system builders, exempt from the systemic message and its demands: even steadfastness in accomplishing the humble work of the everyday and the here and now.

The systemic statement made by the usages of *zekhut* speaks of relationship, function, the interplay of humanity and God. One's store of *zekhut* derives from a relationship, that is, from one's forebears. That is one dimension of the relationships in which one stands. *Zekhut* also forms a measure of one's own relationship with heaven, as the power of one person, but not another, to pray and so bring rain attests. What sort of relationship does *zekhut*, as the opposite of sin, then posit? It is not one of coercion, for heaven cannot force us to do those types of deeds which yield *zekhut,* and that, story after story suggests, is the definition of a deed that generates *zekhut:* doing what we ought to do but do not have to do. But then, we cannot coerce heaven to do what we want done either, for example, by carrying out the commandments. These are obligatory but do not obligate heaven.

Whence, then, our lien on heaven? It is through deeds of a supererogatory character—to which heaven responds by deeds of a supererogatory character: supernatural favor to this one, who through deeds of ingratiation of the other or self-abnegation or restraint exhibits the attitude that in heaven precipitates a counterpart attitude, hence generating *zekhut,* rather than to that one, who does not. The simple fact that rabbis cannot pray and bring rain but a simple ass driver can tells the whole story. The relationship measured by *zekhut*—heaven's response by an act of uncoerced favor to a person's uncoerced gift, for example, act of gentility, restraint, or self-abnegation—contains an element of unpredictability for which appeal to the *zekhut* inherited from ancestors accounts. So while I cannot coerce heaven, I can through *zekhut* gain acts of favor from heaven, and that is by doing what heaven cannot require of me. Heaven then responds to my attitude in carrying out my duties—and more than my duties. That act of pure disinterest—giving the woman my means of livelihood—is the one that gains for me heaven's deepest interest.

So *zekhut* forms the political economy of the religious system of the social order put forward by the Talmud of the Land of Israel, Genesis Rabbah, Leviticus Rabbah, and related writings. Here we find the power that brought about the transvaluation of value, the reversal of the meaning of power and its legitimacy. *Zekhut* expresses and accounts for the economic valuation of the scarce resource of what we should call moral authority. *Zekhut* stands for the political valorization of weakness, that which endows the weak with a power that is not only their own but their ancestors'. It enables the weak to accomplish goals through, not their own power, but their very incapacity to accomplish acts of violence—a transvaluation as radical as that effected in economics. And *zekhut* holds together both the economics and the politics of this Judaism: it makes the same statement twice.

Zekhut is the power of the powerless, the riches of the disinherited, the valuation and valorization of the will of those who have no right to will. In the context of Christian Palestine, Jews found themselves on the defensive, their ancestry called into question, their supernatural standing thrown into doubt, their future denied, they called themselves "Israel" and the land "the Land of Israel." But what power did they possess, legitimately, if need be through violence, to assert their claim to form "Israel"? And, with the Holy Land passing into the hands of others, what scarce resource did they own and manage, to take the place of that measure of value which now no longer was subjected to their rationality? Asserting a politics in which all violence was illegitimate, an economics in which nothing tangible, even real property in the Holy Land,[9] had value, the system through its counterpart categories made a single, simple, and sufficient statement.

IX

Judaism's City
of God

The Place of God in the Social Order

"Make his wishes yours, so that he will make your wishes
his. . . . Anyone from whom people take pleasure, God takes
pleasure" (Avot 2:4). These statements hold together the two
principal elements of the conception of the relationship to God
that in a single word *zekhut* conveys. (1) Give up, please others,
do not impose your will but give way to the will of the other
and (2) heaven will respond by giving a lien that is not to be
coerced but only evoked. By the rationality of discipline
within, we have the power to form rational relationships beyond ourselves, with heaven; and that is how the system ex-
pands the boundaries of the social order to encompass not only
the natural but also the supernatural world.[1]

For it is the rationality of that relationship to God which
governs the social order, defining the three components
thereof: ethics, ethnos, and ethos. Within that relationship we
discern the model of not merely ethics but economics, not
merely private morality in society but the public policy, the
politics that delineates the limns of the ethnic community, and
not alone the right attitude of the virtuous individual but the
social philosophy of an entire nation—so the system proposes.
And that is the this-worldly social order that joins with heaven,
the society that is a unique and holy family, so transformed by
zekhut inherited and *zekhut* accomplished as to transcend the
world order. That ordering of humanity in society, empowered
and enriched in an enchanted political economy, links private
person to the public polity through the union of a common
attitude: the one of renunciation that tells me how to behave at

home and in the streets and that instructs Israel how to conduct its affairs among the nations and throughout history.

Treating every deed and every gesture as capable of bringing about enchantment, the successor system imparted to the givens of everyday life—at least in their potential—remarkable power. The conviction that, by dint of special effort, I may so conduct myself as to acquire an entitlement of supernatural power turns my commonplace circumstance into an arena encompassing heaven and earth. God responds to my—and holy Israel's—virtue, filling the gap, so to speak, about myself and about my entire family that I and we leave when we forbear, withdraw, and give up what is mine and ours: our space, my self. When I do, then God responds; my sacrifice evokes memories of Abraham's readiness to sacrifice Isaac;[2] my devotion to the other calls up from heaven what by demanding I cannot coerce. What imparts critical mass to the conception of *zekhut,* that gaining of supernatural entitlements through the surrender of what is mine, is the recasting, in the mold and model of that virtue of surrender, of the political economy of Israel in the Land of Israel. That accounts for the definition of legitimate power in politics as only weakness, economics as the rational increase of resources that are, but need not be, scarce, valued things that are capable of infinite increase.

That explains why a quite fresh, deeply religious system has taken the place of a compelling and well-composed philosophical one. The Mishnah's God can scarcely compete with the God of the Yerushalmi and the Midrash compilations.[3] For the God of the philosophers, the apex of the hierarchy of all being as the framers of the Mishnah have positioned God, has made the rules and is shown by them to form the foundation of order. All things reach up to one thing, one thing contains within itself many things: These twin propositions of monotheism, which the philosophical system demonstrates in theory and proposes to realize in the facts of the social order, define a God who in an orderly way governs all the palpable relationships of nature as of supernature—but who finds a place, who comes to puissant expression, in not a single one of them. The God of the philosophers assures, sustains, supports, nourishes, guarantees, governs. But the way that God responds to what we do is all according to the rule. That is, after all, what natural philosophy proposes to uncover and discern, and what more elevated task can God perform than the nomothetic one accomplished in the daily creation of the world.

But God who acts every day and here and now, the God of the successor system, gains what the philosophical God lacks, which is personality, active presence, pathos, and empathy.[4] The working of *zekhut* shows how this is so. The God of the religious system breaks the rules, accords an entitlement to this one, who has done some one remarkable deed, but not to that one, who has done nothing wrong and everything right. So a life in accord with the rules—even a life spent in the study of the Torah—in heaven's view is outweighed by a single moment, a gesture that violates the norm, extending the outer limits of the rule, for instance, of virtue. And who but a God who, like us, feels, not only thinks, responds to impulse and sentiment, can be portrayed in such a way as this?

> "So I sold my ass and I gave her the proceeds, and I said to her, 'Here is your money, free your husband, but do not sin [by becoming a prostitute to raise the necessary funds].' "
>
> They said to him, "You are worthy of praying and having your prayers answered."[5]

No rule exhaustively describes a world such as this. If the God of the philosophers' Judaism makes the rules, the God of the religious Judaism breaks them. The systemic difference, of course, is readily extended outward from the personality of God: the philosophers' God thinks, the God of the religious responds, and we are in God's image, after God's likeness, not only because we through right thinking penetrate the principles of creation, but because we through right attitude replicate the heart of the Creator. Humanity on earth incarnates God on high, the Israelite family in particular, and, in consequence, earth and heaven join—within.

Why Did Philosophy Give Way to Religion in the Formation of a Judaism?

Perhaps the first system contained within itself the flaw that, like a grain of sand in an oyster, so irritated the innards as to form a pearl. And perhaps even the philosophers, with their exquisitely ordered and balanced social world, can have made a place for God to act outside of all rules; but, knowing how they thought, we must imagine that, like philosophers later on, they will have insisted that miracles too follow rules and demonstrate the presence of rules. But now, in the religious Judaism, the world now is no longer what it seems. At stake in what is remarkable is what falls beyond all power of rules either to describe or to prescribe.

What is asked of Israel and of the Israelite individual now is a godly restraint, supernatural generosity of soul that is "in our image, after our likeness": that is what sets aside all rules. And since, as a matter of simple fact, that appeal to transcend the norm defined not personal virtue but the sainthood of all Israel, living all together in the here and in the now, we must conclude that, within Israel's society, within what the Greco-Roman world will have called its *polis*, its political and social order, the bounds of earth have now extended to heaven. In terms of another great system composed in the same time and in response to a world historical catastrophe of the same sort, Israel on earth dwells in the city of God. And, it must follow, God dwells with Israel, in Israel: "today, if you will it."[6]

That insistence upon the systemic centrality of the conception of *zekhut,* with all its promise for the reshaping of value, draws our attention once more to the power of a single, essentially theological, conception to impart shape and structure to the social order. The Judaism set forth in the successor documents portrayed a social order in which, while taking full account of circumstance and historical context, individuals and nation alike controlled their own destiny. The circumstance of genealogy dictated whether or not the moral entity, whether the individual or the nation, would enjoy access to entitlements of supernatural favor without regard to the merit of either one. But, whether favored by a rich heritage of supernatural empowerment as was the nation, or deprived, by reason of one's immediate ancestors, of any lien upon heaven, in the end both the nation and the individual had in hand the power to shape the future. How was this to be done? It was not alone by keeping the Torah, studying the Torah, dressing, eating, making a living, marrying, procreating, raising a family, burying and being buried, all in accord with those rules.

That life in conformity with the rule, obligatory but merely conventional, did not evoke the special interest of heaven. Why should it? The rules describe the ordinary. But (in language used only in a later document) "God wants the heart," and that is not an ordinary thing. Nor was the power to bring rain or hold up a tottering house gained through a life of merely ordinary sanctity. Special favor responded to extraordinary actions. This view drew by analogy on the belief that misfortune punished sin. And just as culpable sin, as distinct from mere error, requires an act of will, specifically arrogance, so an act of extraordinary character requires an act of will. But, as mirror image of sin, the act would reveal in a concrete way an attitude of restraint, forbearance, gentility, and self-abnegation. A sinful act, provoking heaven, was one that one did deliberately to defy heaven. Then an act that would evoke heaven's favor, so imposing upon heaven a lien that heaven freely gave, was one that, equally deliberately and concretely, displayed humility.

But the systemic focus upon the power of a single act of remarkable generosity, the surrender to the other of what is most precious to the self, whether that constituted an opinion or a possession or a feeling, in no way will have surprised the framers of the philosophical Judaism. They had laid heavy emphasis upon the power of human intentionality to settle questions of the status of interstitial persons, objects, or actions, within the larger system of hierarchical classification. So, in the philosophical Judaism, attitude and intentionality classified what was of doubtful status, that is to say, forming the active and motivating component of the structure and transforming the structure, a tableau of fixed and motionless figures, into a system of action and reaction. Then, in the process of transformation, we should hardly find surprising the appeal to the critical power of attitude and intentionality. For what we find in the successor system is a fundamental point of connection. What was specific before, intentionality, is now broadened and made general through extension to all aspects of one's attitude.

Now the powerful forces coalescing in intentionality gained very precise definition, and in their transformation from merely concrete cases of the taxonomic power of intentionality that worked one way here, another way there, into very broad-ranging but quite specific and prescribed attitudes the successor system took its leave from the initial one without a real farewell. Then what is the point of departure? It is marked by the intense interest, in the religious Judaism, upon not the fixed given of normative intentionality[7] but rather changing people, both individually and nationally, from what they were to something else. And if the change is in a single direction, it is nonetheless also always personal and individual.

The change is signaled by the conception that study of the Torah not only illuminated and educated but transformed and, moreover, so changed the disciple that he gained in supernatural standing and authority. This gnostic conception of knowledge, however, proved only a component of a larger conception of national transformation and personal regeneration, since, as we saw, Torah study produced *zekhut,* and all things depended upon the *zekhut* that a person, or the nation as a whole, possessed. Mastery of what we classify as "the system's worldview" changed a person by generating *zekhut,* that is, by so affecting the person as to inculcate attitudes that would produce remarkable actions (often: acts of omission, restraint, and forbearance) to generate *zekhut*. The change was the end, the Torah study was the medium.

But the system's worldview was not the sole, or even the principal, component that showed how the received system was transformed by the new one. The conception of *zekhut* came to the fore to integrate the system's theory of the way of life of the social order, its economics, together with its account of the social entity of the social order, its politics. The remarkable actions—perhaps those of omission more than those of commission—that produced *zekhut* yielded an increase in the scarcest of all resources, supernatural favor, and at the same time endowed a person rich in entitlements to heavenly intervention with that power to evoke which vastly outweighed the this-worldly power to coerce in the accomplishment of one's purpose.

This rapid account of the systemic structure and system, its inversion of the received categories and its formation of anti-categories of its own, draws our attention to the specificity of the definition of right attitude and puissant intentionality by contrast to the generality of those same matters when represented in the philosophical system of the Mishnah. We have, therefore, to ask ourselves whether the definition of those attitudes and correct will and proper intentionality which lead to acts that generate *zekhut* will have surprised framers of documents prior to those which attest the transformed Judaism before us. The answer is negative, and that fact alerts us to yet another fundamental continuity between the two Judaisms.

As a matter of fact, the doctrine defining the appropriate attitude persisted pretty much unchanged from the beginning.[8] The repertoire of approved and disapproved attitude and intentionality remained constant through the half-millennium of the unfolding of the canon of Judaism from the Mishnah onward: humility, forbearance, accommodation, a spirit of conciliation. For one thing, Scripture itself is explicit that God shares and responds to the attitudes and intentionality of human beings. God cares what humanity feels—wanting love, for example—and so the conception that actions that express right attitudes of humility will evoke in heaven a desired response will not have struck as novel the authors of the Pentateuch or the various prophetic writings, for example. The biblical record of God's feelings and God's will concerning the feelings of humanity leaves no room for doubt. What is fresh in the system before us is not the integration of the individual with the nation but the provision, for the individual, of a task and a role analogous to that of the nation.

With its interest in classifying large-scale and collective classes of things, the Mishnah's system treats matters of attitude and emotion in that same taxic context. For instance, while the Mishnah casually refers to emotions, for example, tears of joy, tears of sorrow, where feelings matter, it always is in a public and communal context. Where there is an occasion of rejoicing, one form of joy is not to be confused with some other, or one context of sorrow with another. Accordingly, marriages are not to be held on festivals (M. Mo'ed Qatan 1:7). Likewise, mourning is not to take place then (M. M.Q. 1:5; 3:7–9). Where emotions play a role, it is because of the affairs of the community at large, for example, rejoicing on a festival, mourning on a fast day (M. Suk. 5:1–4). Emotions are to be kept in hand, as in the case of the relatives of the executed felon (M. San. 6:6). If I had to specify the single underlying principle affecting all forms of emotion, for the Mishnah it is the profoundly philosophical attitude that attitudes and feelings must be kept under control, never fully expressed without reasoning about the appropriate context. Emotions must always lay down judgments.

We see in most of those cases in which emotions play a systemic and indicative, not merely an episodic and random, role that the basic principle is the same. We can and must so frame our feelings as to accord with the appropriate rule. In only one case does emotion play a decisive role in settling an issue, and that has to do with whether or not a farmer was happy that water came upon his produce or grain. That case underlines the conclusion just now drawn. If people feel a given sentiment, it is a matter of judgment and therefore invokes the law's penalties. So in this system emotions are not treated as spontaneous but as significant aspects of a person's judgment.

Whence, then, the doctrine, made so concrete and specific in the conception of *zekhut* as made systemically generative in the successor documents, that very specific attitudes, particular to persons, bear the weight of the systemic structure as a whole? It is in tractate Avot, which supplies those phrases cited at the outset to define the theology that sustains the conception of *zekhut*. Tractate Avot, conventionally attached to the Mishnah and serving as the Mishnah's advocate, turns out to form the bridge from the Mishnah to the Yerushalmi and its associated compilations of scriptural exegeses. That tractate presents the single most comprehensive account of religious affections. The reason is that, in that document above all, how we feel defines a critical aspect of virtue. The issue proves central, not peripheral. The very specific and concrete doctrine emerges fully exposed.

A simple catalog of permissible feelings comprises humility, generosity, self-abnegation, love, a spirit of conciliation of the other, and eagerness to please. A list of impermissible emotions is made up of envy, ambition, jealousy, arrogance, sticking to one's opinion, self-centeredness, a grudging spirit, vengefulness, and the like. Nothing in the wonderful stories about remarkable generosity does more than render concrete the abstract doctrine of the heart's virtue that tractate Avot sets forth.

People should aim at eliciting from others acceptance and goodwill and should avoid confrontation, rejection, and humiliation of the other. This they do through conciliation and giving up their own claims and rights. So both catalogs form a harmonious and uniform whole, aiming at the cultivation of the humble and malleable person, one who accepts everything and resents nothing. True, these virtues, in this tractate as in the system as a whole, derive from knowledge of what really counts, which is what God wants. But God favors those who please others. The virtues appreciated by human beings prove identical to the ones to which God responds as well. And what single virtue of the heart encompasses the rest? Restraint, the source of self-abnegation, humility, serves as the anecdote for ambition, for vengefulness, and, above all, for arrogance. It is restraint of our own interest that enables us to deal generously with others, humility about ourselves that generates a liberal spirit toward others. And the correspondence of heavenly and mortal attitudes is to be taken for granted—as is made explicit.

So the emotions prescribed in tractate Avot turn out to provide variations of a single feeling, which is the sentiment of the disciplined heart, whatever affective form it may take. And where does the heart learn its lessons, if not in relationship to God? So: "Make his wishes yours, so that he will make your wishes his" (Avot 2:4). Applied to relationships between human beings, this inner discipline of the emotional life will yield exactly those virtues of conciliation and self-abnegation, humility and generosity of spirit, that the framers of tractate Avot spell out in one example after another. Imputing to heaven exactly those responses felt on earth, for example, "Anyone from whom people take pleasure, God takes pleasure" (Avot 3:10), makes the point at the most general level.

Then what has the successor system contributed? Two things: (1) the conception that acts of omission or commission expressing an attitude of forbearance and self-abnegation generate *zekhut* in particular; and (2) the principle that *zekhut* functions in those very specific ways that the system deems critical: as the power to attest to human transformation and regeneration, affording, in place of philosophical politics and philosophical economics, that power inhering in weakness, that wealth inhering in giving up what one has, that in the end promise the attainment of our goals. Briefly put, the path from one system to the other is in three stages: (1) The philosophical Judaism for its reasons, portrayed by the Mishnah, assigns to intentionality and attitude systemic centrality; (2) tractate Avot, in presenting in general terms the rationale of the Mishnah's system, defines precisely the affective attitude and intentionality that are required; and (3) the religious Judaism of the Yerushalmi and associated writings joins together the systemic centrality of attitude and intentionality with the doctrine of virtue laid out in tractate Avot.

But in joining these received elements the new system emerges as distinct from the old.[9] For when the attitude of affirmation and acceptance, rather than aggression, and the intentionality of self-abnegation and forbearance are deemed to define the means for gaining *zekhut*, what we are saying is contrary and paradoxical: if you want to have, then give up, and if you want to impose your judgment, then make the judgment of the other into your own, and if you want to coerce heaven, then evoke in heaven attitudes of sympathy that will lead to the actions or events that you want, whether rain, whether long life, whether the salvation of Israel and its hegemony over the nations: to rule, be ruled by heaven; to show heaven rules, give up what you want to the other. *Zekhut* results: the lien upon heaven, freely given by heaven in response to one's free surrender to the will and wish of heaven. And by means of *zekhut*, whether one's own or whether one's ancestors', the social order finds its shape and system, and the individual his or her place within its structure.

The correspondence of the individual to the nation, both capable of gaining *zekhut* in the same way, linked the deepest personal emotions to the cosmic fate and transcendent faith of that social group of which each individual formed a part. The individual Israelite's innermost feelings, the inner heart of Israel, the microcosm, correspond to the public and historic condition of the nation, of Israel, the macrocosm. In the innermost chambers of the individual's deepest feelings, the Israelite therefore lives out the public history and destiny of the people, Israel.

The Social Foundations of a Judaic Religious System

What precipitated deep thought upon fundamental questions of social existence was a simple fact. From the time that Christianity attained the status of a licit religion, the Jews of Palestine witnessed the formation of circumstances that had formerly been simply unimaginable: another Israel, in the same place and time, competed with them in their terms, quoting their Scriptures, explaining who they were in their own categories but in very different terms from the ones that they used. We need not explain the profundities of religious doctrine by reducing them to functions and necessities of public policy. But it is a matter of simple fact that the Jews in the fourth century had witnessed a drastic decline in their power to exercise legitimate violence (which is to say, violence you can make stick) as well as in their command of the real estate of Palestine that they knew as the Holy Land and its wealth. The system's stress upon matters of intentionality and attitude, subject to the governance of even the most humble of individuals, even the most insignificant of nations, exactly corresponded to the political and social requirements of the Jews' condition in that time. The transformed Judaism made of necessity a theological virtue and, by the way, the normative condition of the social order.

In the fourth century, from Constantine's great victory and legitimation of Christianity in the beginning to the Theodosian code that subordinated Jewry and limited its rights at nearly the end, Jews confronted a remarkable shift in the character of the Roman Empire. The state first legalized Christianity, then established Christianity as the most favored religion, and—by the end of that century—finally undertook to extirpate paganism and, by the way, to subordinate Judaism. Therein lies the urgency of the critical question addressed by the system as a whole—if not the self-evidence of the truth of its response to that question. Dealing with world-historical change in the character of the Roman Empire consequent on the legalization of Christianity by Constantine and the establishment of Christianity as the state-religion by his heirs and successors, the transformed Judaism made its statement in answer to the fundamental question confronting the social order: Precisely what are we now to do?

That political question—the "do" part of the question—concerning the assessment of the legitimate use of violence in this Judaism called into doubt the legitimacy of any kind of violence at all, Jews' having none. But no less subject to reflection was that "doing" which referred to making a living, the economics of the acquisition and management of scarce resources, and, it goes without saying, the making of a life, the philosophy of rational explanation of all things in some one way. At stake, then, were the very shape and structure of the social order, reconsidered at what was, and was certainly perceived as, the critical turning.

This utter reordering of society framed a question that had to be faced and could not be readily answered.[10] It concerned the meaning and end of history, Israel's history, now that the prophetic promises were claimed by the Christian competition to have been kept in the past, leaving nothing in the future for which to hope. When, for a brief moment, in A.D. 361–363 the emperor Julian disestablished Christianity and restored paganism, proposing also to rebuild the Jews' Temple in Jerusalem, Christianity met the challenge and regained power. The Temple was not rebuilt, and Julian's brief reign brought in its wake a ferocious counterrevolution, with the Christian state now suppressing the institutions of paganism and Christian men in the streets of the towns and villages taking an active role on their own as well. Julian's successors persecuted pagan philosophy. In A.D. 380 the emperor Theodosius (A.D. 379–395) decreed the end of paganism:

> It is our desire that all the various nations which are subject to our clemency and moderation should continue in the profession of that religion which was delivered to the Romans by the divine Apostle Peter.

Paganism found itself subjected to penalties. The state church—a principal indicator of the Christian civilization that the West was to know—now came into being. In A.D. 381 Theodosius forbade sacrifices and closed most temples. In A.D. 391–392 new sets of penalties imposed sanctions on paganism. And, while tolerated, Judaism, together with the Jews, suffered drastic change in their legal standing as well.

In the beginning of the fourth century Rome was pagan, in the end, Christian. In the beginning Jews in the Land of Israel administered their own affairs. In the end their institution of self-administration lost the recognition it had formerly enjoyed. In A.D. 300 Palestine where Jews lived was mainly the Land of Israel, in A.D. 400 the country was populated with Christian shrines.[11] In the beginning Judaism enjoyed entirely licit status, and the Jews, the protection of the state. In the end Judaism suffered abridgment of its former liberties, and the Jews of theirs. In the beginning the Jews lived in the Land of Israel, and in some numbers. In the end they lived in Palestine.

As a matter of fact, each of the important changes in the documents first redacted at the end of the fourth century dealt with a powerful challenge presented by the triumph of Christianity in Constantine's age.[12] The first change revealed in the unfolding of the sages' canon pertains to the use of Scripture. The change at hand specifically is in making books out of the collection of exegeses of Scripture. That represents an innovation because the Mishnah, and the exegetical literature that served the Mishnah, did not take shape around the order of biblical passages, even when relevant, let alone the explanation of verses of Scripture. In the third century, and especially in the later fourth century, other writings, entering the canon, took shape around the explanation of verses of Scripture, not a set of topics. What this meant was that a second mode of organizing ideas, besides the topical mode paramount for the Mishnah, the Tosefta, the Yerushalmi (and the Bavli later on), now made its way.

The second concerned extensive consideration of the topic of the Messiah, formerly not accorded a principal place among the parts of the social system.[13] The philosophers of the Mishnah did not make use of the Messiah myth in the construction of a teleology for their system. They found it possible to present a statement of goals for their projected life of Israel which was entirely separate from appeals to history and eschatology. The appearance in the Talmuds of a messianic eschatology fully consonant with the larger characteristic of the rabbinic system—with its stress on the viewpoints and proof texts of Scripture, its interest in what was happening to Israel, its focus upon the national-historical dimension of the life of the group—indicates that the encompassing rabbinic system stands essentially autonomous of the prior, mishnaic system.

Third, the Mishnah had presented an ahistorical and, in the nature of things, non-eschatology teleology and did not make use of the messiah theme to express its teleology. By contrast, the Talmud provides not only an eschatological and therefore a messiah-centered teleology for their system. Its authorship also formed a theory of history and found it appropriate to compose important narratives, episodic to be sure, concerning events that, in prior systemic writings, were treated as mere taxic indicators. Now what happened counted, not only that something happened, and the details of events were to be narrated and preserved. So far as the definition of an event comprises a cultural indicator, the telling of stories about events tells us that, for the Talmud of the Land of Israel and related writings, the very formation of culture has been transformed.

No wonder, then, that the Mishnah's philosophical (therefore also social-scientific) and ahistorical Judaism, a Judaism of rules, gave way to the religious and historical (therefore also eschatological) Judaism of the Talmud of the Land of Israel, a

Judaism of exceptions to the rules. These important shifts show that the later system set forth a Judaism intersecting with the Mishnah's but essentially asymmetrical with it. Given the political changes of the age, with their implications for the meaning and end of history as Israel would experience it, the foci of the connected but autonomous system now directed attention to the media for salvation in the here and now, for Israel and the individual alike, and in time to come for all Israel. A single word captured the whole: *zekhut* yielded a broad variety of answers to one urgent question. It was a question encompassing society and history, now and the coming age, Israel and the nations, the social order in the here and now and the great society comprised by nature and supernature. To the question posed by the simple statement of the religious system set forth in the documents of the late fourth and fifth centuries is this: The entire social order forms one reality, in the supernatural world and in nature, in time and in eternity: Judaism's city of God.

Epilogue

In the past thirty years I believe I have commenced a completely fresh reading of the formation of Judaism. Let me now spell out what I think has been, and now is, at stake in my work. First, I have insisted that the holy books of Judaism are holy, that is, they are statements about God and what God wants of us. Second, I have underscored that what God wants of us concerns the social order that we construct for ourselves. Third, I have maintained that the revealed works of the Torah, the one whole Torah, oral and written, that God gave to Moses, our rabbi, at Mt. Sinai, properly understood show us how to compose a social order that nurtures the life of humanity in the image and after the likeness of God. Judaism is the religion that asks itself, What does it mean to build a society of human beings "in our image, after our likeness"? and How are we to live together as God's children here on earth? And the holy books of Judaism, the very works that I have surveyed in these pages, answer precisely those questions. My life has been devoted to explaining in this place and to this age what those answers are and how we are to understand them.

If I have to say in a single sentence what it is about religion—Judaism in particular—that I am trying to demonstrate through the case of Judaism, it is this: religion is public and not personal. But religion is not *merely* public, something that we do together. Religion is the single most important force in the shaping of the world as we know it. Ours is an age that has given more compelling evidence for the vitality of religion than any prior age in the history of humanity. So my work has taken as its premise, but also has meant to demonstrate, that religion forms the foundation of the social order. Religion defines an independent variable for the interpretation of politics and culture. For those who, like me, believe that it is God who calls religion into being, so that, when we pray or (in my case) study the Torah or engage in acts of religious sanctification and service it is in response to God who calls, the power of religion in the world today attests to the glory of God. But for those who deem religion a wholly this-worldly fact, a work of humanity alone, the proposition remains the same, though the explanation will certainly diverge. Religion explains the state of politics and culture and accounts for the formation of the social order.

Perhaps in the study of Judaism as I have defined that study over the past three decades I have placed too much emphasis on society and behavior, performance and public action. In my *Enchantments of Judaism,*[1] for example, I described the present practice of Judaism within the theory of a bifurcated world, with religion as private and personal, corporate community as secular and political. In describing, analyzing, and interpreting the formation of Judaism, I may well have asked too intensively about the relationship between the historical, including political, circumstance of a religious system and the statements of that system. In doing so, I may have carried too far the program of Max Weber in his investigation of the role of religion in economic and other modes of social behavior. But it is not common these days for scholarship on religion to emphasize the public and the political. The prevailing prejudice has laid stress upon the private, individual, idiosyncratic, eccentric, and personal.

True, when we study religion we also want to know about its intellectual aspect: the teachings of religion. And the intellectual aspect requires us to read books: individually, privately, idiosyncratically. But those teachings which come to us in the holy books of the Torah of Judaism do not stand for the personal feelings or opinions of this believer or that one. The Torah makes demands upon Israel, the people, and the canon presents the faith we are meant to bring to realization as a kingdom of priests and a holy people—not the heart of the individual believer—except, to be sure, after the fact.

Mine has been a quest for the religious reading of religious books. I see religion as a way in which people work together to solve the most urgent problems, the most acute questions, that confront them. That is why I have proposed that we read the Mishnah as a philosophical statement and system, the Talmud of the Land of Israel as a religious one, and the City of God as the goal for Israel's quest and adventure. When theologians treat religion as personal, they do no less to trivialize religion than when secularists treat it as private. From both sides religion finds itself denied its principal trait: it beats as the heart and the soul of humanity's social life. Religion as arbiter of culture and source of the values of politics and economy alike defines the public life of humanity—public and visible, therefore subject to description, reasoned analysis, and sustained, rigorous interpretation—for the rest of our life on earth, whether that is one year or one million.

Notes

1. In chapter VI, I return to introduce these documents in context.

2. I have set forth the problem in a theological context in Jacob Neusner, *The Myth of a Judeo-Christian Dialogue* (Philadelphia and London: Trinity Press International and SCM Press, 1990). What kind of hermeneutics and consequent exegesis will emerge when we take seriously the simple fact that, in their times, Christianities took their places among Judaisms, we can now only imagine. But once we realize that Judaisms were many and varied and contradictory, then we also recognize that the Jewish writers of the bulk of the New Testament books, people who thought of themselves as "Israel," along with all the rest of holy Israel, have to be read as evidence for Judaisms, not alone Christianities. That does tend to complicate matters, and another generation is going to have to address the complication. Right now, it is all we can do to get New Testament scholarship to abandon its conception of a single Orthodox Judaism; to this time, all we have accomplished in the last half-century is to persuade a fair part of New Testament scholarship that the Orthodox Judaism we know in the twentieth century, in the State of Israel or in Western Europe or in the United States, in no way adumbrates, let alone embodies, the religion of Jesus and his followers. I do think that twentieth-century Orthodox Judaism's anachronistic retrojections to the first century have ceased to be common. But it is still the case that much of New Testament scholarship opens the Mishnah, the Midrash compilations, the Talmud of the

Land of Israel, or the Talmud of Babylonia, and related writings, as mediated in the rather dubious theological prism of Strack-Billerbeck, to find out what people around Jesus and Paul were doing or thinking. See in this connection E. P. Sanders, *Jesus and the Law* (Philadelphia and London: Trinity Press International and SCM Press, 1990).

3. In several works of mine I have related my findings to the study of what was happening in the same time and place in Christianity. Most currently, see Jacob Neusner, *Transformation of Judaism: From Philosophy to Religion* (Champaign, Ill.: University of Illinois Press, 1991), where I compare Augustine's *City of God* with the Judaic sages' social construction of the Torah. The title of chapter IX alludes to that comparison.

4. But the debunking, in the case of the historical study of the sources of Judaism, was joined to an attitude of gullibility in the historical character and usefulness of those same sources. The entire scholarly agenda pursued by the former generation (and by many of its continuators today, with diminishing effect, to be sure) rests upon the conviction that if sources say that something happened, it really happened; if they assign a saying to someone, then he really said it, and we can then write the intellectual history of his day as well, because everybody agreed with him, except, of course, the people who didn't, but they were heretics (and so the argument runs on breathlessly). In chapters III and IV, I review the character of historical thinking that has produced history out of these sources. Its odd combination of gullibility and a program of debunking yields picking and choosing: that obviously did not happen that way but in some other way; this he said not out of a good motive but out of a bad motive. All of this work yields triviality, and that is the weightiest reason I offer for the paradigm shift away from the program of positivist-historicist learning: it really proves rather dull. People have moved in other directions, not because of the subjective judgment that other approaches yield boring or trivial results, but because the new reading of the received writing produces compelling and important ones. Merely rejecting historicism and its program in no way marks a paradigm shift.

5. True, biblical scholarship by Roman Catholic and Judaic scholars followed the lines laid out by Protestant ones (comparing the *Journal of Biblical Literature* with the *Catholic Biblical Quarterly* yields more similarities than differences), but scholarship on religion has undergone radical revision.

6. Mircea Eliade, *The Myth of the Eternal Return,* tr. Willard R. Trask (Princeton, N.J.: Princeton University Press, 1954).

Chapter I: From Judaism to Judaisms

1. The convention of referring to the first seven centuries A.D. is based on the broadly held conviction that with the Muslim conquest of the Near and Middle East in the seventh century, a new era in the history and history of religion of that region commenced. For Judaisms the first century is a convenient starting point, since the destruction of the Temple of Jerusalem in A.D. 70 is universally regarded as a turning point as well, since it marked changes of a political as much as a cultic character for the life of Israel, the Jewish People, and for the Land of Israel (also called "Palestine") as well. Very commonly when people refer to "late antiquity," they mean these centuries, or most of them. But medieval history often commences with the founding of Constantinople in the early fourth century.

2. The dogma that "we have to believe whatever 'the sources' say, unless we can prove they were wrong or uninformed or deliberately concealing facts" defined the critical-historical program and even today is held with perfect faith in Israeli scholarship in this field. The vivid debates in the most recent past in the Israeli historical journal *Zion*—e.g., on whether a certain talmudic rabbi was nice or nasty—show the character of scholarship within that premise.

3. George Foot Moore, *Judaism in the First Centuries of the Christian Era: The Age of the Tannaim,* 3 vols. (Cambridge, Mass.: Harvard University Press, 1927–1930).

4. This is not the place to spell out all of the attitudes that characterize the historical researches of the recent scholars, though, for a beginning, one should study the late Renée Bloch's "Note méthodologique pour l'étude de la littérature rabbinique," *Recherches de Science Religieuse* 43 (1955): 194–225. Helpful, if not original, Géza Vermès paraphrases and summarizes Bloch's methodological proposals in *Scripture and Tradition in Judaism: Haggadic Studies* (Leiden: E. J. Brill, 1961), and compare Brevard S. Childs, "Interpretation in Faith," *Interpretation, A Journal of Bible and Theology,* 18 (1964): 432–449. The issue is not merely a broadening of the focus of interpretation, however. A graver problem is whether we know as much as we think we know. The former generation of historians working with talmudic literature, for example, treated that literature as if descriptions of events were written by a stenographer for the use of a newspaper reporter; as if, in other words, talmudic sources provide an adequate, critical description of events. The great issue was to establish an accurate text. If they had such a text, the former historians thought that

all their problems were solved and that they knew fairly well exactly what had happened, what had been said, what had been done, even though the interpretation of events might still have posed problems. When one realizes that critical history is a modern conception, and that no one in late antiquity, least of all Jewish chroniclers, wrote without a very clear-cut didactic purpose, and that in any case the talmudic accounts we have of events pertaining to the Jews and Judaism are by no means word-for-word transcriptions of what, if anything, observers saw and heard, then matters become much more complicated. An example of the literalism, not to say historiographical fundamentalism, of the greatest of talmudic historians may be seen in G. Alon's discussions of Yohanan ben Zakkai's escape to Yavneh, cited and criticized in Jacob Neusner, *A Life of Rabban Yohanan ben Zakkai: Ca. 1–80 C.E.* (Leiden: E. J. Brill, 1962), pp. 104–128, 147–171. Alon offers an exegesis of what Yohanan said and did not say in his encounter with Vespasian which, to my way of thinking, ignores the nature of the sources available for such exegesis. There are numerous lessons still to be learned by students of this period from New Testament scholarship, the very first of them being the need to take a hard-headed ("higher-critical") view of what in fact we know and how we know it. Other areas of learning, to be sure, are characterized by a critical perspective absent in the study of the rabbinic sources. See, for two fine examples, Y. Liver, *Toledot Bet David* (Jerusalem, 1959), and Y. Heinemann, *HaTefila biTekufat HaTannaim veHaAmoraim* (Jerusalem, 1964). But much new research ignores the most fundamental critical problems and therefore is disappointing, if not completely useless. See Jacob Neusner, *Reading and Believing: Ancient Judaism and Contemporary Gullibility* (Atlanta: Scholars Press for Brown Judaic Studies, 1986). We return to this matter in our consideration of history and biography.

5. Often without acknowledgment!

6. Saul Lieberman, "Pleasures and Fears," in *Greek in Jewish Palestine: Studies in the Life and Manners of Jewish Palestine in the II–IV Centuries C.E.,* by Saul Lieberman (New York: Jewish Theological Seminary of America, 1942), pp. 115–143; passage cited is on pp. 98–99.

7. Gershom Scholem, *Major Trends in Jewish Mysticism,* 3rd rev. ed. (New York: Schocken Books, 1961); idem, *Jewish Gnosticism, Merkabah Mysticism, and Talmudic Tradition* (New York: Ktav Publishing House, 1960); and idem, *On the Kabbalah and Its Symbolism* (New York: Schocken Books, 1970).

8. Erwin R. Goodenough, *Jewish Symbols in the Greco-Roman Period,* 13 vols. (Princeton: Princeton University Press, 1953–1968). Extensively discussed presently.

9. Morton Smith, "Observations on Hekhalot Rabbati," in *Biblical and Other Studies,* ed. Alexander Altmann (Cambridge, Mass.: Harvard University Press, 1963), pp. 142–160; passage cited is on pp. 153–154.

10. Naturally, efforts have continued to retain the old one-dimensional and rationalistic synthesis, to explain new evidence in terms of old hypotheses. One cannot hope to convince the proponents of the old view that we must reconsider matters in a fundamental way. But such efforts to explain away the evidence will produce less and less insight. Among them is the strikingly unconvincing view of E. E. Urbach ("Rabbinic Laws of Idolatry," in J. G. Weiss, ed., *Papers of the Institute of Jewish Studies, London* [reprint 1989, Lanham, Md.: University Press of America, 1989]), who states: "These finds from Beth She'arim [of scenes from pagan mythology in the sarcophagi of the rabbis] put an end to all the theories based on making a clear distinction between the private world of the Sages, as reflected in the talmudic and mishnaic laws about idolatry, and the other world that existed outside theirs." Urbach prefers to "explain" the evidence in a way calculated to rule out any genuine confrontation with Hellenism. Jewish artisans, he says, were employed in making statues and images for pagans. They sometimes sold their products to Jews without making any change in their design of conventional patterns for idol-worshiping Gentile customers. Urbach never says why Jews bought them or why rabbis let Jews do so. In any event, even the pagans, Urbach says, used idols and images for decorative purposes only. He does not tell us just what that means or how he knows. If these paintings and adornments were introduced into private houses for aesthetic reasons, it is not surprising that they should have found their way into synagogues and cemeteries, so Urbach. But I must ask, Why is it not surprising? It seems that, for all his ostentatious erudition, Urbach has not paid serious attention to how surprising such phenomena would have been in an earlier period (before A.D. 70), as the archaeological evidence reveals, and in the period after they were very rigidly excluded (in the fifth and sixth centuries A.D.). If Jewish craftsmen did not, as Urbach says, consider it a sin to make use of pagan motifs in their work, still how liberal must the rabbis of Beth She'arim have been to accept such artifacts into their burial caves! I cannot regard his explanation, in any case, as wholly congruent to the phenomena to be

explained, as relevant to all situations in which they are found and to all issues posed by their form and explanation.

11. Morton Smith, "Image of God," *Bulletin of the John Rylands Library* 40 (1958): 486–487.

Chapter II: From Yeshiva and Seminary to University

1. Erwin R. Goodenough, *Jewish Symbols in the Greco-Roman Period,* 13 vols. (New York: Pantheon Books, 1953–1968).

2. The implications of my argument for the study of the modernization of other fields of learning within the history of ideas in the twentieth century seem to me self-evident. We have to ask how new were the works of the first generation of new learning in a variety of traditional cultures in transition, both academic cultures defined by a textual community, such as is under discussion here, and also popular and political cultures.

3. Samuel Krauss, *Griechische und lateinische Lehnwörter im Talmud, Midrasch und Targum* (Berlin: S. Calvray & Co., 1898–1899).

4. The decisive impact of that termination on Lieberman's life and career cannot be overestimated—he left the country and went to America, he had to learn a new language and to find a place for himself in a rabbinical seminary that was not Orthodox.

5. Saul Lieberman, *On the Palestinian Talmud* (in Hebrew).

6. Saul Lieberman, *Toseftet Rishonim,* 4 vols. (Jerusalem, 1937–1939).

7. In my translation into English and commentary upon the Mishnah and the Tosefta, I consulted every line of *Tosefet Rishonim* and found it lively, critical, and not merely erudite but interesting and focused upon problem solving. The enormous expansion of the same work in Lieberman's *Tosefta Kifshuta,* by contrast, collects and arranges vast quantities of information but lacks the argumentative and witty traits of mind of the original work.

8. Saul Lieberman, *Greek in Jewish Palestine: Studies in the Life and Manners of Jewish Palestine in the II–IV Centuries C.E.* (New York: Jewish Theological Seminary of America, 1942); and idem, *Hellenism in Jewish Palestine: Studies in the Literary Transmission, Beliefs and Manners of Palestine in the I Century B.C.E.–IV Century C.E.* (New York: Jewish Theological Seminary of America, 1950).

9. Saul Lieberman, "Palestine in the Third and Fourth Cen-

turies," *Jewish Quarterly Review* 36 (1946): 329–370 and 37 (1947): 31–54. While I take this article for my case, every other article he wrote exhibits the same qualities. His magnum opus, the massive commentary to the Tosefta, contains no argument and makes no case, offers no encompassing propositions, and does not even introduce the document. It is simply an enormous collection and arrangement and paraphrase of received materials, with episodic comments, some of them quite clever, on this and that.

10. Lieberman, "Palestine in the Third and Fourth Centuries," pp. 344–370.

11. Ibid., pp. 359–362, passim.

Chapter III: What Do We Now Want to Know About Judaism in the First Six Centuries A.D.?

1. Why should an essentially secular spirit have characterized the bulk of scholarship on Judaism produced by Jewish scholars working in institutions paid for by the Jewish community? I think part of the answer lies in the identification of the ideal life pattern of the scholar: a male who grew up in an Orthodox world and then apostasized. The necessity of growing up in the Orthodox world was explained very simply. If you are not drilled in talmudic study from a very early age, you will never understand the text. While none denied that Talmud study from near infancy would indeed produce a very distinctive perspective on the text, few who studied the document only in mature years could identify in the scholarship of those who were brought up within the yeshiva world results of such richness and depth as to dwarf the results of those who grew up in the academic world. But then, to proceed, why was it necessary to leave Orthodoxy? Because, if one did not, then he would not attain the necessary distance (not to mention disdain) that would make possible critical scholarship—that scholarship of debunking to which I referred in earlier pages. In point of fact, the prescription of growing up Orthodox and then leaving Orthodoxy treated as normative the alienation of a couple of generations, from early Reformers, all of them originally Orthodox, onward. Now that the Orthodox world has found its voice, it retains its own. The academic world, for its part, has defined what it wishes to know about, know from, and do with the canonical writings of Judaism, as I explain in this chapter. In between the two, the world of Reform and Conservative Judaisms' seminaries and of their extension in the Hebrew University and some smaller institutions has found

considerable difficulty in defining a scholarly task for itself. That explains the paucity of publication in what they call "the age of the Mishnah and the Talmud," whether of history or philology or critical texts, deriving from that in-between world, by comparison to the publication deriving from the Orthodox yeshiva world in its framework and the academic world in its idiom.

2. That the new program emerged from the debates in the tradition of Marx, Weber, and Durkheim hardly needs to be made explicit. I have already referred to my appreciation for their contemporary continuators, particularly Clifford Geertz and Mary Douglas, and where in my own work I have utilized their ideas, with full documentation, of course.

3. R. Jackson Wilson, *Figures of Speech: American Writers and the Literary Marketplace, from Benjamin Franklin to Emily Dickinson* (New York: Alfred A. Knopf, 1989), p. 122, writing about William Lloyd Garrison.

4. I obviously do not for one minute suggest that that is all religion is, nor do I dismiss the truth claims of religion or reduce them to merely socially useful formulations of ideology. In asking about one of the many things that I think religion is and does, I do not imply anything about the things that religion is not and does not do.

5. Saul Lieberman's intemperate language in posthumously reviewing a volume of my translation of the Talmud of the Land of Israel, "A Tragedy or a Comedy?" *Journal of the American Oriental Society* 104 (1984): 315–319, aimed at not criticizing my translation but discrediting me, and the uses to which that review were put prove that fact. The editors of *JAOS* refused to permit me to reply to Lieberman's review after it was published. That hardly suggests that these statements, which I think many will find self-evident, in their day were received as self-evident or banal. Among critics who proposed not to correct or even argue but only to discredit, Lieberman, of course, stood at the head of a long line. Shaye J. D. Cohen, "Jacob Neusner, Mishnah, and Counter-Rabbinics," *Conservative Judaism* 37 (1983): 48–63; Hyam Maccoby, "Jacob Neusner's Mishnah," *Midstream* 30 (1984): 24–32; not to mention the numerous reviews by Solomon Zeitlin beginning in 1971 in his *Jewish Quarterly Review*—all prove that there was nothing banal or even obvious in the conclusions I set forth and in my reading of the canonical literature. But to the credit of Zeitlin, Lieberman, Cohen, and Maccoby, they did write reviews. The more routine practice was *Todschweigen,* that death by silence which has taken many forms. Until 1981 I

could not publish a scholarly book of any kind in the United States. Until the present day most of my books are simply not reviewed at all in Judaica scholarly journals, and except for the Hebrew translation (1987) of my *Judaism: The Evidence of the Mishnah,* (Chicago: University of Chicago Press, 1981), not a single book of mine was ever reviewed in the scholarly journals of the Israeli universities. People do not boycott ideas they can disprove; they disprove them. They refuse to acknowledge the existence of that with which they simply cannot cope. For a rather sad example of the ostentatious "ignoring" of my work, see most currently Dov Zlotnick, *The Iron Pillar—The Mishnah: Redaction, Form, and Intent* (Jerusalem: Bialik Institute, 1988). Writing on the theme of "Rabbi's Mishnah and the Development of Jewish Law," Zlotnick argues no thesis but covers various topics, such as the editorial activity of Rabbi, memory and the integrity of the Oral Tradition, some aspects of mishnaic repetition, conservatism in the making of law; strengthening the Oral Law, the inoperative halakhah, is the Mishnah a code, and the like. Writing on a variety of topics on which I have published articles and even entire books, Zlotnick refuses to acknowledge the existence of a single piece of my work, and none appears even in his bibliography. He is to be taken as typical of the response of the adherents of Lieberman, on the one side, and the world of Modern Orthodoxy, on the other. But the same exercise of *Todschweigen* has characterized the bulk of scholarship of the Israeli universities and the U.S. and European Reform and Conservative rabbinical seminaries and associations as well. But the ethics of Israeli scholarship is no different from that of American Jewish rabbinical schools. When in 1984 the Israel Historical Society invited me to give a lecture, I offered a simple explanation of why all work on what they call "talmudic history" in their journal, *Zion,* was methodologically obsolete by reason of credulity in reading sources. I was asked to send the lecture "for translation." One month after doing so, I was formally disinvited. The simple reason was that the Society did not wish to give me a platform in which to make such a case. I subsequently published the lecture in Jacob Neusner, *Ancient Judaism: Debates and Disputes* (Chico, Calif.: Scholars Press for Brown Judaic Studies, 1984). My extended discussion of these matters is in Jacob Neusner, *The Public Side of Learning: The Political Consequences of Scholarship in the Context of Judaism,* Studies in Religion series, (Chico, Calif.: Scholars Press for the American Academy of Religion, 1985).

6. See Jacob Neusner, *Ecology of Religion: From Writing to*

Religion in the Study of Judaism (Nashville: Abingdon Press, 1989), pp. 291–312.

7. Jacob Neusner, ed., *The Formation of the Babylonian Talmud: Studies in the Achievements of Late 19th and 20th Century Historical and Literary-Critical Research* (Leiden: E. J. Brill, 1970); and idem, ed., *The Modern Study of the Mishnah* (Leiden: E. J. Brill, 1973).

8. Jacob Neusner, *The Study of Ancient Judaism* (New York: Ktav Publishing House, 1982), vol. 1: *Mishnah, Midrash, Siddur;* vol. 2: *The Palestinian and Babylonian Talmuds.*

9. See Jacob Neusner, *Paradigms in Passage: Patterns of Change in the Contemporary Study of Judaism,* Studies in Judaism series. (Lanham, Md.: University Press of America, 1988).

10. Jacob Neusner, *First Principles of Systemic Analysis: The Case of Judaism Within the History of Religion,* Studies in Judaism series (Lanham, Md.: University Press of America, 1987).

11. I of course do not claim to have invented the conception of religion as a cultural system, and at appropriate points in my career have devoted sustained attention to current work on that conception, e.g., in the work of Clifford Geertz and Mary Douglas. As to the former, see Jacob Neusner, *A History of the Jews in Babylonia,* 5 parts (Leiden: E. J. Brill, 1966–1970), part 3 (1968): *From Shapur I to Shapur II,* where in the preface I point to Geertz as the key to a religious reading of the data on that subject; as to the latter, see Jacob Neusner, *The Idea of Purity in Ancient Judaism: The Haskell Lectures, 1972–1973* (Leiden: E. J. Brill, 1973), for which Mary Douglas kindly wrote a critique, published there.

12. Jacob Neusner, *Judaism in the Matrix of Christianity* (Philadelphia: Fortress Press, 1986; Edinburgh: T. & T. Clark, 1988; idem, *Judaism and Christianity in the Age of Constantine: History, Messiah, Israel, and the Initial Confrontation* (Chicago: University of Chicago Press, 1987); idem, *Death and Birth of Judaism: The Impact of Christianity, Secularism, and the Holocaust on Jewish Faith* (New York: Basic Books, 1987); and idem, *Self-Fulfilling Prophecy: Exile and Return in the History of Judaism* (Boston: Beacon Press, 1987)—all of these form a complete "field theory" of the history of Judaism within the theory of the systemic approach to the study of a religion, in this case, of Judaisms. Not one of these books was reviewed in any journal of Judaic studies.

13. In the case of a Judaism, this will be expressed in the theory of the social entity "Israel": what it is, who it is. See

Jacob Neusner, *Judaism and Its Social Metaphors: Israel in the History of Jewish Thought* (Cambridge: Cambridge University Press, 1989).

14. Jacob Neusner, E. S. Frerichs, and A. J. Levine, eds., *Religious Writings and Religious Systems: Systemic Analysis of Holy Books in Christianity, Islam, Buddhism, Greco-Roman Religions, Ancient Israel, and Judaism*, 2 vols. (Atlanta: Scholars Press for Brown Studies in Religion, 1989), vol. 1: *Islam, Buddhism, Greco-Roman Religions, Ancient Israel, and Judaism;* vol. 2: *Christianity.*

15. I identify as my masters in the history of religion George F. Moore, Arthur D. Nock, Harry A. Wolfson, and Erwin R. Goodenough. Among the living there is only Jonathan Z. Smith. History of religion is otherwise another name for Buddhist or Hindu studies, on the one side, or totally vacuous generalization, on the other.

Chapter IV: Historical-Critical Method in the Study of Formative Judaism

1. All the more so the scholars who simply dismiss without argument studies they do not approve or positions they do not share. For an example, see Adin Steinsaltz, trans., *The Talmud* (New York: Random House; vol. 1, 1989), who casually refers to and dismisses without argument or even reference ideas and positions of which he has heard but does not approve.

2. One of the components of the new paradigm has been an interest in making public and widely accessible documents formerly deemed incomprehensible except by the initiated. My translations of such documents as the Tosefta and the Talmud of the Land of Israel and Sifra, formerly not presented in any Western language, formed part of the paradigm shift as much as the matters discussed in this chapter concerning critical-historical method. The myth of a tradition on the reading of these documents, deemed so incomprehensible that only insiders, with long years in yeshivas, can grasp them, has fallen by the way. No one suggests that the new translations will never be replaced, and I have labeled some of them preliminary and provisional, absent critical texts, reliable dictionaries, and well-crafted commentaries. But we now have access to most of documents which, formerly, only adepts claimed to understand. And no document of the canon of the Judaism treated here is now not in the English language; many of them are in their second and third translations. Competition among translations is routine in all studies of foreign cultures and religions and

now, also, in studies in Western languages of ancient Judaisms. Those within the received paradigm never translated the documents they utilized in their studies, except, at best, episodically; and they wrote no introductions to them either.

3. I refrain from commenting on the esoteric and self-referential character of the scholarly prose I shall cite. My comments on the esoteric claims laid in behalf of the sources pertain here as well. The scholars we shall read in the main assume that all their readers are Jews, with yeshiva education; technical terms are never translated, and no effort is made to communicate beyond the walls of the schools. The closed circle of discourse, the assumption of privacy and parochiality—these will strike the reader as givens. But, I claim, so too is the entire program of inquiry: what people want to know about the sources and how they propose to find it out. And that underlines my claim in the Prologue that the paradigm shift has been brought about by changes in the institutional setting of learning about Judaism: new people asking new questions and reading the documents in the company of formerly excluded persons (women, Gentiles, e.g.) and for new purposes.

4. Lawrence H. Schiffman, *Who Was a Jew? Rabbinic and Halakhic Perspectives on the Jewish Christian Schism* (Hoboken, N.J.: Ktav Publishing House, 1985), pp. 19–20; cited language on pp. 19–20.

5. Helmut Koester, *Introduction to the New Testament,* vol. 1: *History, Culture, and Religion of the Hellenistic Age* (Philadelphia: Fortress Press, 1982; Berlin and New York: Walter de Gruyter, 1982), p. 406. Translated from the German *Einführung in das Neue Testament* (Berlin: Walter de Gruyter, 1980).

6. Shaye J. D. Cohen, "The Significance of Yavneh: Pharisees, Rabbis, and the End of Jewish Sectarianism," *Hebrew Union College Annual* 55 (1984): 27–53.

7. Ibid., pp. 32–33.

8. Ibid., p. 42.

9. Ibid., p. 48.

10. Ibid., pp. 48–49.

11. Rosalie Gershenzon and Elieser Slomovic, "A Second Century Jewish-Gnostic Debate: Rabbi Jose ben Halafta and the Matrona," *Journal for the Study of Judaism* 16 (1984): 1–41.

Chapter V: From History to Religion

1. William Scott Green, "What's in a Name? The Problematic of Rabbinic 'Biography,' " in *Approaches to Ancient Judaism:*

Theory and Practice, ed. William Scott Green (Missoula, Mont.: Scholars Press for Brown Judaic Studies, 1978), pp. 77–96.

2. Green, "What's in a Name?" p. 77.

3. Ibid., p. 79.

4. Ibid., p. 80.

5. But of course we know the answer. It served because people use history to confirm and validate what they already believe to be true: knowledge in the service of faith.

6. No wonder, then, that in the American State of Texas, once an independent nation, all schoolchildren must study Texas history in three sequences but American history in only one. No wonder, too, that Zionism precipitated the massive rewriting of the histories of Jews as a single, unitary Jewish history, with a beginning, a middle, and an end, with the self-evident message of Zionism as its ubiquitous proposition. The State of Texas and the State of Israel exemplify the uses that for so long guaranteed for history a principal place in the academy, for both appeal to facts to validate the claims of social ideology.

7. Marshall Sahlins, *Islands of History* (Chicago: University of Chicago Press, 1985). I consider this his landmark work.

8. Sahlins, *Islands of History,* p. vii.

9. Sahlins, "Anthropology of History," in ibid., p. 34.

10. Cf. Sahlins, *Islands of History,* p. 72.

11. I estimate that approximately 80 percent of the document in bulk is comprised of "another matter" compositions. The list in this form defines the paramount rhetorical medium and logical structure of the document.

12. William Scott Green, in *Writing with Scripture: The Authority and Uses of the Hebrew Bible in the Torah of Formative Judaism,* Jacob Neusner and William Scott Green (Minneapolis: Augsburg Fortress Press, 1989), p. 19.

13. To make this point concrete, here is a survey of sequences of components of such lists

> Joseph, righteous men, Moses, and Solomon;
>
> patriarchs as against princes, offerings as against merit, and Israel as against the nations; those who love the king, proselytes, martyrs, penitents;
>
> first, Israel at Sinai; then Israel's loss of God's presence on account of the golden calf; then God's favoring Israel by treating Israel not in accord with the requirements of justice but with mercy;
>
> Dathan and Abiram, the spies, Jeroboam, Solomon's marriage to Pharaoh's daughter, Ahab, Jezebel, Zedekiah;

Israel is feminine, the enemy (Egypt) masculine, but God the father saves Israel the daughter;

Moses and Aaron, the Sanhedrin, the teachers of Scripture and Mishnah, the rabbis;

the disciples; the relationship among disciples, public recitation of teachings of the Torah in the right order; lections of the Torah;

the spoil at the sea = the exodus, the Torah, the tabernacle, the ark;

the patriarchs, Abraham, Isaac, Jacob, then Israel in Egypt, Israel's atonement and God's forgiveness;

the Temple where God and Israel are joined, the Temple is God's resting place, the Temple is the source of Israel's fecundity;

Israel in Egypt, at the sea, at Sinai, and subjugated by the Gentile kingdoms, and how the redemption will come;

Rebecca, those who came forth from Egypt, Israel at Sinai, acts of loving-kindness, the kingdoms that now rule Israel, the coming redemption;

fire above, fire below, meaning heavenly and altar fires; Torah in writing, Torah in memory; fire of Abraham, Moriah, bush, Elijah, Hananiah, Mishael, and Azariah;

the Ten Commandments, show fringes and phylacteries, recitation of the Shema and the Prayer, the tabernacle and the cloud of the Presence of God, and the mezuzah;

the timing of redemption, the moral condition of those to be redeemed, and the past religious misdeeds of those to be redeemed;

Israel at the sea, Sinai, the Ten Commandments; then the synagogues and school houses; then the redeemer;

the exodus, the conquest of the Land, the redemption and restoration of Israel to Zion after the destruction of the first Temple, and the final and ultimate salvation;

the Egyptians, Esau and his generals, and, finally, the four kingdoms;

Moses' redemption, the first, to the second redemption in the time of the Babylonians and Daniel;

the litter of Solomon: the priestly blessing, the priestly watches, the Sanhedrin, and the Israelites coming out of Egypt;

Israel at the sea and forgiveness for sins effected through their passing through the sea; Israel at Sinai; the war with Midian; the crossing of the Jordan and entry into the Land; the house of the sanctuary; the priestly watches; the offerings in the Temple; the Sanhedrin; the Day of Atonement;

God redeemed Israel without preparation; the nations of the world will be punished, after Israel is punished; the nations of the world will present Israel as gifts to the royal messiah, and here the base verse refers to Abraham, Isaac, Jacob, Sihon, Og, Canaanites;

the return to Zion in the time of Ezra, the exodus from Egypt in the time of Moses;

the patriarchs and with Israel in Egypt, at the sea, and then before Sinai;

Abraham, Jacob, Moses;

Isaac, Jacob, Esau, Jacob, Joseph, the brothers, Jonathan, David, Saul, man, wife, paramour;

Abraham in the fiery furnace and Shadrach, Meshach and Abednego, the exile in Babylonia, now with reference to the return to Zion.

14. I find myself at a loss for a better word choice and must at this stage resort to the hopelessly inelegant " 'theological' things" to avoid having to repeat the formula that seems to me to fit the data, namely, "names, places, events, actions deemed to bear theological weight and to affect attitude and action." Still, better a simple Anglo-Saxon formulation than a fancy German or Greek or Latin one. And Hebrew, whether mishnaic or modern, simply does not serve for analytical work except when thought conceived in some other language is translated back into that language, should anyone be interested.

15. Jonathan Z. Smith, "Sacred Persistence: Towards a Redescription of Canon," in Green, *Approaches to Ancient Judaism,* pp. 11–28; passage cited is on p. 15.

16. Ibid., p. 18.

17. Ibid., p. 25.

18. Ibid.

Chapter VI: Philosophy and Religion

1. In time to come, I shall show a Judaism as a theological system, but I have not yet reached the point at which, through literary analysis, I can spell out how that system makes its statements—let alone what I conceive those statements to be. My initial probings are in Jacob Neusner, *Symbol and Theology in Early Judaism* (Minneapolis: Fortress Press, 1991).

2. That the same procedure applies to the study of any Judaism, e.g., that adumbrated by the library found at the Dead Sea and commonly attributed to Essene authorship or selection, is obvious. To date, I cannot point to a single study of the Judaism of the Essenes of Qumran that is both systematic and also methodologically well crafted. A good start is made by Philip

R. Davies, *Behind the Essenes: History of and Ideology of the Dead Sea Scrolls* (Atlanta: Scholars Press for Brown Judaic Studies, 1987). That the equivalent methods serve in the study of other religions as well is the hypothesis of the papers collected in Jacob Neusner, E. S. Frerichs, and A. J. Levine, eds., *Religious Writings and Religious Systems: Systemic Analysis of Holy Books in Christianity, Islam, Buddhism, Greco-Roman Religions, Ancient Israel, and Judaism,* 2 vols. (Atlanta: Scholars Press for Brown Judaic Studies, 1989).

3. That is the thesis of Jacob Neusner, *The Canonical History of Ideas: The Place of the So-called Tannaite Midrashim: Mekhilta Attributed to R. Ishmael, Sifra, Sifré to Numbers, and Sifré to Deuteronomy* (Atlanta: Scholars Press for Brown Judaic Studies, 1990).

4. My estimate for the Talmud of the Land of Israel, in the tractates I probed, is that, in volume, as much as 90 percent of the Talmud serves to amplify passages of the Mishnah, and not much more than 10 percent contains intellectual initiatives that are fundamentally fresh and unrelated to anything in the Mishnah passage under discussion; see Jacob Neusner, *The Talmud of the Land of Israel,* vol. 35: *Introduction: Taxonomy* (Chicago: The University of Chicago Press, 1983). Then Jacob Neusner, *Judaism in Society: The Evidence of the Yerushalmi, Toward the Natural History of a Religion* (Chicago: University of Chicago Press, 1983), aims to show that even the passages that (merely) clarify words or phrases of the Mishnah in fact set forth a considerable, autonomous program of their own; see esp. pp. 73–112. But what is clearly distinct from the Mishnah is set forth on pp. 113–254.

5. The term "authorships" is meant to take account of the collective and social character of much of the literary enterprise. I have already underlined the anonymous character of the canonical evidence. Not a single authoritative book of Judaism in late antiquity bears the name of an identified author, and the literary traits of not a single piece of writing may securely be imputed to a private person. The means for gaining acceptance was anonymity, and the medium of authority lay in recapitulating collective conventions of rhetoric and logic, not to mention proposition. To speak of "authors" in this context is confusing, and hence the resort to the word at hand.

6. These statements summarize the results of the following books of mine: *The Mishnah as Philosophy* (Columbia, S.C.: University of South Carolina Press, 1991); *The Economics of the Mishnah: Chicago Studies in the History of Judaism* (Chicago: University of Chicago Press, 1990); and *Rabbinic Politi-*

cal Theory: Religion and Politics in the Mishnah (Chicago: University of Chicago Press, 1991).

7. I have spelled out these matters in great detail in Neusner, *Ecology of Religion*, and do not review the results here.

Chapter VII: The Formation of Judaism: The Mishnah and Philosophy

1. The suspicious attitude toward miracles, expressed at M. Ta. 3:8 in the famous story about Honi the Circle-drawer, forms a very minor footnote. Silences testify far more eloquently than occasional observations or pointed stories.

2. But here I restrict my presentation to the issue of the method of hierarchical classification. Elsewhere I treat the message, to which I merely allude in the present context.

3. That proposition, on the essential unity of the hierarchical nature of all being, falls into the classification of philosophy, since it forms one important, generative premise of Neoplatonism. But here I concentrate on the issue of method and on the theological implications of the choices made by the Mishnah's philosophers.

4. I leave for Philonic scholarship the comparison of the Mishnah's Neoplatonism with that of Philo. Philo's mode of writing, his presentation of his ideas, seems to me so different from the mode and method of the Mishnah that I am not sure how we can classify as Aristotelian (in the taxonomic framework of natural philosophy, which seems to me the correct framework for the Mishnah's philosophical method) the principal methodological traits of Philo's thought. But others are most welcome to correct what is only a superficial impression. I think the selection for comparison and contrast of Aristotle and Neoplatonism, first method, then proposition, is a preferable strategy of analysis (and exposition, as a matter of fact), and I willingly accept the onus of criticism for not comparing and contrasting the method and message of Philo with those of the Mishnah. I mean only to suggest that the questions that Wolfson's *Philo* raised may well be reopened, but within an entirely fresh set of premises and in accord with what I conceive to be a more properly differentiated and therefore critical reading of the data (Harry A. Wolfson, *Philo: Foundations of Religious Philosophy in Judaism, Christianity and Islam,* 2 vols., rev. ed. [Cambridge, Mass.: Harvard University Press, 1962]).

5. I need hardly add that the very eclecticism of the philosophy of Judaism places it squarely within the philosophical

mode of its time. See J. M. Dillon and A. A. Long, eds., *The Question of "Eclecticism": Studies in Later Greek Philosophy* (Berkeley and Los Angeles: University of California Press, 1988).

6. But I hasten to add that further studies of the Mishnah's philosophical context are bound to make much more precise any judgment about the philosophical context of the document and its system. For this initial account, it seems unnecessary to do more than argue, as I do, that the Mishnah's fundamental intellectual structure in its method and message fall into the classification, defined by circumstance and context, of philosophy. The method, I shall show, is standard for natural philosophy, exemplified by Aristotle, and the proposition proves entirely congruent to one principal conception of Middle Platonism, exemplified by Plotinus. At the same time, I point out, the components of congruence, method and message alike, yield far more specific results. If we ask whether the Mishnah's theory of mixtures coincides with that of a specific philosophy of the larger tradition, the answer is, indeed so: the Stoic. But do other components of the Mishnah's metaphysics fit together with the rest of Stoic physics, e.g., theories of space and time? So too, if Middle Platonism will have found entirely familiar the Mishnah's keen interest in showing how one thing yields many things, in demonstrating a hierarchical unity of being through the ordering of all classes of things (that is to say, the ontological unity of things proven on the basis of the natural world), does that make the Mishnah's philosophy in general a form of Middle Platonism? If we ask about the concept of space or place, we look in vain for a familiar conception; cf. S. Sambursky, *The Concept of Place in Late Neoplatonism* (Jerusalem: The Israel Academy of Sciences and Humanities, 1982). My general impression is that when all is said and done, the philosophy of Judaism is far less abstract, even at its most abstract level, than other philosophy of the same tradition and temporal setting; as to the issue of space or place, my sense is that the Judaic philosophers were deeply concerned with *what* things are, not where they are; Jerusalem, for instance, is a profoundly abstract, taxic indicator. That conforms to the larger Aristotelianism of the system. Here, as I stress, I prove only that by the synchronic and even diachronic standards of philosophy, Judaism—method, message, if not medium—in this system is philosophical. These preliminary remarks are meant only to point the way toward a further range of inquiry into the philosophy of Judaism: the comparison and contrast in detail of that philosophy with other philosophies of the Greco-Roman tradition.

7. And no less than Philo's philosophy was a philosophy. My sense is that these results when properly digested and refined as already noted must reopen the questions addressed by the great Harry A. Wolfson in his *Philo.*

8. I consulted Jonathan Barnes, *Aristotle's Posterior Analytics* (Oxford: Clarendon Press, 1975).

9. And, as to proposition about the hierarchical ordering of all things in a single way, the unity of all being in right order, while we cannot show and surely do not know that the Mishnah's philosophers knew anything about Plato, let alone Plotinus's Neoplatonism (which came to expression only in the century after the closure of the Mishnah!), we can compare our philosophers' proposition with that of Neoplatonism. For that philosophy, as we shall see, did seek to give full and rich expression to the proposition that all things emerge from one thing, and one thing encompasses all things, and that constitutes the single proposition that animates the system as a whole.

10. For this section I consulted the following:

A. W. H. Adkins, *From the Many to the One: A Study of Personality and Views of Human Nature in the Context of Ancient Greek Society, Values, and Beliefs* (Ithaca, N.Y.: Cornell University Press, 1970).

D. J. Allan, *The Philosophy of Aristotle* (London and New York: Oxford University Press, 1952).

A. Hilary Armstrong, "Platonism and Neoplatonism," *Encyclopaedia Britannica* (1975), 14: 539–545.

————, "Plotinus," *Encyclopaedia Britannica* (1975), 14: 573–574.

Émile Bréhier, *The History of Philosophy: The Hellenistic and Roman Age,* trans. Wade Baskin (Chicago and London: University of Chicago Press, 1965).

Harold Cherniss, *Selected Papers,* ed. Leonardo Tarán (Leiden: E. J. Brill, 1977).

Louis H. Feldman, "Philo," *Encyclopaedia Britannica* (1975), 14: 245–247.

Erwin R. Goodenough, *An Introduction to Philo Judaeus,* 2nd ed., (Lanham, Md.: University Press of America Brown Classics in Judaica, 1986).

P. Merlan, "Greek Philosophy from Plato to Plotinus," in *The Cambridge History of Later Greek and Early Medieval Philosophy,* ed. A. Hilary Armstrong (Cambridge: Cambridge University Press, 1967), pp. 14–136.

Lorenzo Minio-Paluello, "Aristotelianism," *Encyclopaedia Britannica* (1975), 1:1155–1161.

Joseph Owens, *A History of Ancient Western Philosophy* (New York: Appleton Century Crofts, 1959).

G. F. Parker, *A Short History of Greek Philosophy from Thales to Epicurus* (London: Edward Arnold, 1967).

Giovanni Reale, *A History of Ancient Philosophy,* vol. 3: *The Systems of the Hellenistic Age,* trans. and ed. John R. Catan (Albany, N.Y.: State University of New York Press, 1985).

11. Adkins, *From the Many to the One,* pp. 170–171.

12. But only Aristotle and the Mishnah carry into the material details of economics that conviction about the true character or essence of definition of things. The economics of the Mishnah and the economics of Aristotle begin in the conception of "true value," and the distributive economics proposed by each philosophy then develops that fundamental notion. The principle is so fundamental to each system that comparison of one system to the other in those terms alone is justified.

13. Minio-Paluello, "Aristotelianism," *Encyclopaedia Britannica,* 1:1155–1161, p. 1155.

14. Allan, *The Philosophy of Aristotle,* p. 60.

15. Ibid., pp. 126ff.

16. Owens, *A History of Ancient Western Philosophy,* pp. 309ff.

17. And for that decision they are criticized by all their successors, chief among them the authorship of Sifra. See Jacob Neusner, *Uniting the Dual Torah: Sifra and the Problem of the Mishnah* (Cambridge: Cambridge University Press, 1990).

18. "Man in the Cosmos," in *Plotinian and Christian Studies,* by A. Hilary Armstrong (London: Variorum Reprints, 1979), no. 17, p. 11.

19. Which is Plato's and Plotinus's.

20. That judgment does not contradict the argument of Neusner, *Uniting the Dual Torah,* concerning the Sifra's authorship's critique of the Mishnah's philosophers' stress upon classification through intrinsic traits of things as against classification through classes set forth solely by the Torah. I mean only to stress the contrast between appeal to Scripture and to nature, which I find in the philosophy of Judaism, and appeal to the ecclesial cosmos. This point registers immediately.

Chapter VIII: The Formation of Judaism: The First Talmud and Religion

1. Let alone a word count or concordance work! I can think of nothing so unlikely to produce insight.

2. I refer to Jacob Neusner, *Rabbinic Political Theory: Reli-*

gion and Politics in the Mishnah (Chicago: University of Chicago Press, 1991).

3. For, after all, the problematic of the Mishnah's politics is the principle of differentiation among legitimate political agencies, first between heaven's and humanity's, and second, among the three political institutions of the Mishnah's "Israel."

4. That the system neglected woman altogether, except as a subordinated outcaste, achieving caste status only through the father at first, and then the husband, served the systemic purpose. By the theory proposed here, however, woman (nearly) as much as man should form a systemic actor, since while for hierarchical purposes, woman can be treated as collective and abnormal, for the work of integration, woman, as much as man, will exhibit the besought unities. In stories cited in chapters 7 and 8 of Jacob Neusner, *Transformation of Judaism: From Philosophy to Religion* (Champaign, Ill.: University of Illinois Press, 1991), I note a number of points at which a woman is a principal figure, either counseling the right response to a dilemma or forming a major actor in a tale. But these are only preliminary observations, and a study of the comparison between the role and the representation of woman in the various documents of the unfolding canon will show whether my guess on the systemic difference and my implicit explanation of that difference make sense when tested against evidence. In Jacob Neusner, *The Canonical History of Ideas: The Place of the So-called Tannaitic Midrashim* (see note 3 of chapter VI), I have carried out part of this inquiry.

5. Indeed, the conception of "merit" is so alien to the concept of *zekhut,* which one enjoys whether or not one personally has done something to merit it, that I am puzzled on how "merit" ever seemed to anyone to serve as a translation of the word *zekhut.* If I can inherit the entitlements accrued by my ancestors, then these entitlements not only cannot be classed as merit(ed by me), they must be classed as a heritage bestowed by others and not merited by me at all. And, along these same lines, the *zekhut* that I gain for myself may entitle me to certain benefits, but it may also accrue to the advantage of the community in which I live (as is made explicit by Avot for Moses' *zekhut*) and also of my descendants. The transitive character of *zekhut,* the power we have of receiving it from others and handing it on to others, serves as the distinctive trait of this particular entitlement, and, it must follow from that definitive characteristic, *zekhut* is the opposite of merit, as I said, and its character is obscured by the confusion created through that long-standing and conventional but wrong translation of the word.

6. The commonly used single word "merit" does not apply, but "merit" bears the sense of reward for carrying out an obligation, e.g., by doing such and such, he merited so and so. *Zekhut,* by contrast, commonly refers to acts of supererogatory free will, and therefore while such acts are meritorious in the sense of being virtuous (by definition), they are not acts that one owes but that one gives. And the rewards that accumulate in response to such actions are always miraculous or supernatural or signs of divine grace, e.g., an unusually long life or the power to prevent a delapidated building from collapsing.

7. And that political definition of the systemic role and function of *zekhut* is strengthened by the polemical power of the concept vis-à-vis the Christian critique of Israel after the flesh. The doctrine of the *zekhut* of the ancestors served as a component of the powerful polemic concerning Israel. Specifically, that concrete, historical Israel, meaning for Christian theologians "Israel after the flesh," in the literature before us manifestly and explicitly claimed fleshly origin in Abraham and Sarah. The extended family indeed constituted precisely what the Christian theologians said: an Israel after the flesh, a family linked by genealogy. The heritage then became an inheritance, and what was inherited from the ancestors was a heavenly store, a treasure of *zekhut,* which protected the descendants when their own *zekhut* proved insufficient. The conflict is a political one, involving the legitimacy of the power of the now-Christian empire, denied by this "Israel," affirmed by the other one.

8. And it is by no means an accident, therefore, that Genesis was one of the two pentateuchal books selected by the system builders for their Midrash exegesis. The systemic centrality of *zekhut* accounts for their selection. In Jacob Neusner, *Judaism and Scripture: The Evidence of Leviticus Rabbah* (Chicago: University of Chicago Press, 1986), I have accounted for the selection of the book of Leviticus, an explanation that accords in a striking way with the one pertaining to Genesis. That means that any system analysis must explain why one scriptural book, and not some other, has been chosen for the Midrash compilation(s) that that system sets forth alongside its Mishnah amplification.

9. A test of this interpretation is whether or not in the provenance of Babylonia stories are told about the equivalence of owning land and studying the Torah. That is to say, if studying the Torah is represented as outweighing owning real estate in Babylonia as much as in the Land of Israel, then something is awry with my results here. But if a survey, e.g., of the Talmud of Babylonia, shows that, in the context of Babylonia and not

the Land of Israel, stories of the superiority of Torah study over land ownership do not occur, then that would form a fair confirmation of my point of insistence here. This test of falsification will be carried on in the context of the next phase of my *oeuvre*, which will bring me deep into the Babylonian part of the canon of the dual Torah.

Chapter IX: Judaism's City of God

1. I use the word "rationality" in the sense in which it is used in the thought of Max Weber: the systemic sense of what is appropriate and proper. The comparison of the rationalities of the initial and the successor systems is undertaken in the closing paragraphs of this chapter.

2. Note the fine perception of S. Levy, *Original Virtue and Other Studies* (London, 1907), pp. 2–3: "Some act of obedience, constituting the Ascent of man, is the origin of virtue and the cause of reward for virtue. . . . What is the conspicuous act of obedience which, in Judaism, forms the striking contrast to Adam's act of disobedience, in Christianity? The submission of Isaac in being bound on the altar . . . is regarded in Jewish theology as the historic cause of the imputation of virtue to his descendants." It is not an accident, then, as we shall see, that Augustine selected as his paradigmatic historical exemplum the conflict of Cain and Abel, the city of God being inhabited by Abel and his descendants; he required a virtue pertinent to all of humanity, not to Israel alone, for his argument, so it seems to me as an outsider to the subject.

3. My initial comments on that matter are in Jacob Neusner, *The Incarnation of God: The Character of Divinity in Formative Judaism* (Philadelphia: Fortress Press, 1988).

4. See Neusner, *The Incarnation of God.*

5. The full source is given above, pp. 149–151.

6. *Bab. Sanhedrin* 97a.

7. That is, an assessment of what people will ordinarily think or propose or wish to have happen. The rule is set by that norm, not by exceptions, and on that basis, in the initial system, we are able to determine what (an ordinary person's) intentionality will dictate in a given interstitial case.

8. I have demonstrated that fact in Jacob Neusner, *Vanquished Nation, Broken Spirit: The Virtues of the Heart in Formative Judaism* (Cambridge: Cambridge University Press, 1987).

9. This is not to suggest that the substance of the doctrine of virtue was richly revised in the successor writings. That is not

so. The transformation was systemic, not doctrinal. Emotions not taken up earlier in the pages of the Yerushalmi did not come under discussion. Principles introduced earlier enjoyed mere restatement and extensive exemplification. Some principles of proper feelings might even generate secondary developments of one kind or another. But nothing not present at the outset—in tractate Avot—drew sustained attention later on. The system proved essentially complete in the earliest statement of its main points. What then do the authors or compilers of the Yerushalmi contribute? Temper marks the ignorant person; restraint and serenity, the learned one. These are mere details.

10. And certainly had not been answered by the Mishnah's system, which treated history—composed of events in particular—as mere occasions for taxonomic inquiry: classifying this event in one way, according to one overriding rule, that event in some other, according to another rule; and neither rule bore any relationship to history. The regularization and ordering of disorderly events—counterpart to what we know as social science today—denied to history all status as the source of category formation. I have spelled all this out in Jacob Neusner, *Messiah in Context: Israel's History and Destiny in Formative Judaism,* vol. 2 of Foundations of Judaism series (Philadelphia: Fortress Press, 1984).

11. Constantine and his mother had built churches and shrines all over the country, but especially in Jerusalem, so the Land of Israel received yet another name, for another important group, now becoming the Holy Land.

12. I have spelled out these matters in Jacob Neusner, *Judaism and Christianity in the Age of Constantine: History, Messiah, Israel, and the Initial Confrontation* (Chicago: University of Chicago Press, 1987); idem, *Midrash in Context: Exegesis in Formative Judaism,* vol. 1 of Foundations of Judaism series (Philadelphia: Fortress Press, 1983); and, in summary, in idem, *Judaism in the Matrix of Christianity* (Philadelphia: Fortress Press, 1986; Edinburgh: T. & T. Clark, 1988).

13. This is worked out in Neusner, *Messiah in Context.*

Epilogue

1. Jacob Neusner, *The Enchantments of Judaism: Rites of Transformation from Birth Through Death* (New York: Basic Books, 1987).

General Index

Abbahu, *zekhut* and Judaism, 150–151
Adkins, A. W. H., 132
Allan, J. D., 133–134
Aqiba, Judaism of, 28
archaeological discoveries and diverse Judaisms, 30–32
Aristotle, philosophy and formative Judaism, 130–134
Armstrong, A. Hilary, 136–138
art, synagogue art in archaeological findings, 30–36
astrology, divisions within Judaism, 33

canonical writings
  evaluation of facts, 66–92
  Judaism as a historical religious system and society, 55–65
Christianity
  in formative age of Judaism, 11, 17–25
  Jewish background for, 27–29
  reshaping of studies in, 17–25
Civilization, Judaism as a historical religion, 97–112
Cohen, Shaye J. D., 76–85

cultural heritage of Judaism, 97–112
  and social order, 176–177

ecumenism in religious dialogue, 24–25
Eliade, Mircea, *The Myth of the Eternal Return,* 23
Essene writings in studies of ancient religions, 20, 30
Ezra, Judaism of, 28

formative Judaism, 11
  and Christianity, 17–25
  history in study of, 66–92
  philosophy and religion, 113–160
  scholarship in, 25
fundamentalism, critical study of historic facts, 66–92

Garrison, William Lloyd, 54
Geertz, Clifford, 99, 103
Gershenzon, Rosalie, and Eleiser Slomovic, "A Second Century Jewish-Gnostic Debate: Rabbi Jose ben Halafta and the Matrona," 85
Goodenough, Erwin R., archaeology and

203

Goodenough cont.
  Hellenistic literature,
    34–35
  *Jewish Symbols in the Greco-
    Roman Period,* 37
Green, William Scott, 15
  "What's in a Name? The
    Problematic of Rabbinic
    Biography," 94, 104

Hanania b. Hakhinai,
  transgressions and
  penalties, 122
Hillel, House of, interpretation
  in Babylonian Talmud,
  75–76, 82–84
history
  facts and Judaism, 27–36
  interpretations of worldview
    in ancient religions,
    21–25, 46–50
  Judaism as a historical
    religion, 97–112
  Song of Songs Rabbah as
    listing persons, events and
    places, 101–112
  in study of formative
    Judaism, 66–92
  uses in religions, 107–112

Idel, Moshe, 34
Isaac, *zekhut* and Judaism, 155

Jesus, Judaism of, 28
Judaism
  changes in, 13
  conversion, 71–74
  credulity of fact and history,
    66–92
  as a historical religion,
    97–112
  history and development of,
    53–65
  philosophy and formative
    Judaism, 113–160
  rabbinic literature, diversity
    within Judaism, 27–36
  rabbinic sources in
    normative Judaism, 28–29

  religion of, 53–65
  religious system and social
    order, 55
  reshaping of studies in,
    17–25
  zekhut and Judaism,
    146–168

Karaism, 14
knowledge, Judaism as a
  historical religion, 97–112
Koester, Helmut, 75–76, 79
Krauss, Samuel, 32
  Griechische und lateinische
    Lehnworter im Talmud,
    Midrasch, und Targum, 41

Lieberman, Saul, 32–33,
    35–36, 63, 81
  Greek in Jewish Palestine, 42
  *Hellenism in Jewish
    Palestine,* 42
  interpretation of history,
    46–50
  "On the Palestinian
    Talmud," 41
  "Pleasures and Fears," 33
  Toseftet Rishonim, 42
  and tradition-changing
    models of study, 40–43,
    45–52
literature
  diversity of rabbinic Judaism
    in, 27–36
  history, biography, and
    rabbinic Judaism, 93–97
  holy books and Jewish
    scholarship, 38–39
  Judaism as a historical
    religion, 97–112
  literary evidence in Judaism,
    30–32
  Song of Songs Rabbah as
    history, biography, events,
    and places, 102–112

Meir, transgressions and
  penalties, 123–124
Moore, George Foote, *Judaism*

Moore, cont.
   in the First Centuries of
   the Christian Era: The Age
   of the Tannaim, 31

Nag Hammadi, 20, 30
normative Judaism
   rabbinic canon, 32
   unitary nature of, 28, 32–36

Orthodox Judaism, Modern
      Orthodoxy and the State
      of Israel, 24
Owens, Joseph, 134

personages
   history, biography, and
      rabbinic Judaism, 93–97
   Judaism as a historical
      religion, 97–112
   Song of Songs Rabbah as
      history, biography events,
      and personages, 101–112
philosophy
   Judaism's City of God,
      161–173
   religion and formative
      Judaism, 113–160

Qabbalah, 14
   mystic mythology, 34–35

rabbinic literature, diversity
      within Judaism, 27–36
religions
   history and social order, 54
   individual conscience and
      social order, 23
   Judaism as a historical
      religion, 97–112
   knowledge of successes in,
      13
   philosophy and formative
      Judaism, 113–160
   positivist historical studies,
      23
   as public force in social
      order, 175–177

   role in social order, 23,
      175–177

Sahlins, Marshall, 100
   "Anthropology of History,"
      99
Schiffman, Lawrence H., *Who
      Was a Jew? Rabbinic and
      Halakhic Perspectives on
      the Jewish-Christian
      Schism,* 71
scholarship
   broadening the academic
      world, 37–52
   classical study and changing
      models, 39–43
   explanations and analysis,
      50–52
   philological approach to
      Judaic study, 41–42
Scholem, Gershom, 33–35
secular Judaism, University
      scholarship and Judaism,
      37–52
Shammai, House of,
      interpretation in
      Babylonian Talmud,
      75–76, 82–84
Simeon b. Gamaliel,
      transgressions and
      penalties, 124
Slomovic, Elieser, 85
Smith, Jonathan Z.,
      109–111
social order
   history and religion, 53–61
   Judaism's City of God,
      161–173
   and new studies, 21–25
   role of religion, 175–177
   zekhut and Judaism,
      146–168
Song of Songs Rabbah as
      history of events,
      biography, and places,
      101–112
Spinoza, Baruch, 20, 66
State of Israel and Modern
      Orthodoxy, 24

symbolism, synagogue art in
archaeological findings,
30–36

Talmudic study and intellectual
discourse, 43–46
Traditions of learning and
changing models of study,
39–43
transgressions and penalties,
121–129

Weber, Max, 59, 64–65, 84
Wilson, R. Jackson, 54
worldview, 32
defining dimensions of
religion, 12

Judaism as a historical
religion, 97–112
religious system and society,
55–65
scholarship and
understanding ancient
religions, 17–25

Yannai, *zekhut* and Judaism,
149–150
Yohanan ben Zakkai, credulity
of Judaism, 79, 90
Yosi, credulity of Judaism,
77–79, 85–92

zekhut and Judaism, 146–168

Index of Biblical
and Talmudic References

Acts
5:34–39   75

Amos
9:7   105

Deuteronomy
22:9   122
22:10   122
22:11   122
23:21   147

Exodus
4:31   155
15:2   105
15:15   105
15:17   105
15:24   105
15:25   105
24:1   155
24:7   105

Ezekiel
16:6   105
20:8   105

Isaiah
27:13   155

Joshua
7:1   106
7:19   106

1 Kings
15:30   147

Leviticus
5:6–7   123
5:11   123
5:7   123
5:17–19   123
19:19   122
21:1   122
23:7   122
25:4   122

Numbers
6:6   122
13:32   106
15:29   123
25:1   106
32:12   106

Psalms
78:30   106
78:40   105
95:6   156
99:9   156
101:2   157
106:7   105
106:19   105

1 Samuel
1:19   155

Song of Songs
1:5   104

MISHNAH
Avot
2:2   146
2:4   161, 168
3:10   168
5:18   146–147

Eduyyot
4:80   . 82, 84

Keritot
1:1   123
1:2   123–124
1:7   123, 125
2:3–6   125
3:1   125
3:1–3   125
3:2   123, 125
3:2–3   125
3:3   125
3:4   123–125
3:4–6   125
3:9   122–123

Mo'ed Qatan
1:5   167
1:7   167
3:7–9   167

Sanhedrin
6:6   167

Shabbat
1:1   126–127

Shabuot
1:1   127
1:2   128
2:1   128
2:1–5   128
3:1–8   129

Sukkot
5:1–4   167

Yebamot
1:80–82   84

TOSEFTA

Hagigah
2:9   80, 82

Niddah
5:3   78

Sanhedrin
7:1   82

Yevamot
1:10–12   82

PALESTINIAN
TALMUD

Hagigah
2:20   80, 82–83

Taanit
1:4   149
3:2   157

Yevamot
1:6   82

BABYLONIAN
TALMUD

Niddah
33b   77

Rosh Hashanah
2b   79–80

Yevamot
47a–b   71

Genesis Rabbah
LVI:II   155

Song of Songs Rabbah
V:II.1   104–105
VII:5   106